5000
DECORATIVE MONOGRAMS
FOR ARTISTS AND CRAFTSPEOPLE

5000 DECORATIVE MONOGRAMS FOR ARTISTS AND CRAFTSPEOPLE

Edited by
J. O'Kane

DOVER PUBLICATIONS, INC.
Mineola, New York

Bibliographical Note

This Dover edition, first published in 2003, is an unabridged republication of *An Encyclopædia of Monograms,* published by J. O'Kane, New York, in 1884.

Library of Congress Cataloging-in-Publication Data

Encyclopædia of monograms.
5000 Decorative monograms for artists and craftspeople / edited by J. O'Kane.—Dover ed.
p. cm.
Originally published: Encyclopædia of monograms. New York : J. O'Kane, 1884.
ISBN-13: 978-0-486-42979-3
ISBN-10: 0-486-42979-2
1. Monograms—Pictorial works. I. Title: Five thousand decorative monograms for artsists and craftspeople. II. O'Kane, James. III. Title.

NK3640.E6 2003
702'.78—dc22

2003055507

www.doverpublications.com

ENCYCLOPÆDIA OF MONOGRAMS.

Preface.

MONOGRAMMIC ART has not heretofore enjoyed its full share of assistance from illustrated works. Although a number of excellent publications on this subject have appeared from time to time, their usefulness has been much circumscribed by their limited range of illustration and their lack of variety. Some of them contain but a single specimen of each two-letter combination, and these all the work of a single artist; while others, somewhat more copious in examples, still labor under a certain monotonous uniformity of style that impairs their value for practical use. There is no lack of good design in the aggregate, but it is so much scattered that if a designer or a manufacturer wishes to avail himself of the ideas of a number of experts on the often very perplexing question of a monogram, he will require quite a collection of expensive books.

These were the considerations that suggested the plan and scope of the present enterprise. It seemed feasible to collect together and merge into a single volume the best results of what had heretofore been achieved by the genius and industry of monogrammic artists, and to re-arrange the whole in a compact form, more convenient for study and reference. This plan has been here carried out with considerable difficulty, but with gratifying success. The material has been diligently gathered from various sources, and carefully compiled; and, as a result, the **ENCYCLOPÆDIA OF MONOGRAMS** contains a voluminous and diversified collection of letter combinations, comprising altogether more than five thousand examples, and illustrating in great profusion the various forms of treatment characteristic of the best schools of design, past and present.

These examples have all been arranged alphabetically in columns, with each series grouped under an appropriate head, plainly designated in Roman letters. This method is believed to be entirely new, and the arrangement will be found exceedingly well adapted for quick reference. Under many of these headings are grouped over a dozen separate devices for constructing the same monogram, varying in style from the severely simple to the more involved and ornate, and exhibiting the work of different artists contrasted side by side—a feature in a work of design that every designer knows so well how to appreciate. A collection of crowns and coronets, and a number of ancient and modern alphabets, are given in the final plates; and throughout the work will be found numerous quaint and beautiful specimens of ornamental lettering.

The function of a work of monogrammic art is twofold: either to supply a design suitable for a given purpose and available for use as it stands, or to supply a good suggestion and starting-point for a new design. With these facts in view, the publisher has aimed to render the **ENCYCLOPÆDIA** as valuable as possible in the first-mentioned capacity, by giving an abundance of good designs that may be turned to account without need of modification. Nevertheless, a new design is sometimes indispensable, or an old one must be modified to adapt it to some special purpose; and, in such an emergency, it is scarcely necessary to point out how much more rapidly a tasteful and elegant result can be reached with the aid of a profusion of good ideas at hand for suggestion. Whether the combination is to be of two or of several letters, it is equally important to have a starting-point; and with such a help a good monogram of three or more letters is often more easily executed than one of two, on account of the greater variety of feature and greater facility for balancing the design. No attempt has been made in this work to give a complete series of three and four letter combinations, for such a series of even one example of each would exceed all reasonable limits—would fill a volume itself; still, the **ENCYCLOPÆDIA** will be found much more copious in this respect than any previous publication. Several hundred examples are given, embracing a great number of ingenious and interesting schemes for combining three or more letters, which will be found equally available for other and different combinations. The framework, or *motif*, of one design can often be made to do duty for a dozen or more of separate monograms. Sometimes it may be preferable to choose a two-letter monogram for a foundation, and encircle it with a third, or append or superimpose one letter or more, as the case may be. A surprising improvement in the general effect will often ensue from this kind of manipulation, the additional letter or letters imparting to the design a certain requisite symmetry and balance so often lacking, of necessity, in bi-literal combinations.

The monogram offers facilities for so many different methods of combining the same letters, that no two of any given ten or twenty individuals need have the same device. It is capable of great diversity of treatment, and almost endless variations may be evolved by a creative imagination. And as its purposes and uses are exceedingly varied and multiform, so the design itself should vary in character. For some uses the intention of the device should be conspicuous and obvious, and its component letters readily distinguishable at first sight. In other cases it is more tasteful and appropriate, by superimposing or interlacing the letters, or other means, to slightly veil, as it were, the meaning of the composition, and to aim at a certain ornamental construction whose component parts shall be less distinct and obvious to the eye. Many of the examples given in the **ENCYCLOPÆDIA** are purposely so constructed as to admit of two or more readings. There is a piquancy derived from this feature, and an enigmatical character that has its peculiar merits. Due discrimination should be exercised in determining just how readily a monogram for a given purpose should be decipherable without a previous knowledge of its purport.

But, however constructed, and for whatever purpose, the composition should be framed with due regard to unity and harmony of effect. A simple idea charms, even in the most elaborately constructed monogram. Whether the device be set forth in interlacing foliage or geometric forms, united with mazy, flowing lines; in delicate idealism or bold simplicity; with lettering caught up in flowery toils or convoluted scrolls, or half revealed, as it were, amid a profusion of ornamental accessories,—all pleasing effects obtained are referable to some expression of the laws of harmony and contrast.

The labor of collecting and compiling such a multitude of examples has been serious and protracted; but the result is unquestionably the most complete and comprehensive work on this branch of design ever offered to the public; and the publisher indulges the hope that it will prove successful in facilitating the labors of many others over the constantly recurring problem of the MONOGRAM.

☞ *It will be observed by an inspection of the plates that throughout the two-letter series there are two groups of examples for each pair of letters,—one for the direct arrangement, and another for the reverse. For instance, one for A-B, and another for B-A. In each group some examples are likely to be found that would serve equally well for a monogram of the same letters reversed, especially where these are interlaced or superimposed, and susceptible of two readings. Therefore, reference to both groups is recommended for examples of any required monogram.*

5000
Decorative Monograms
for Artists and Craftspeople

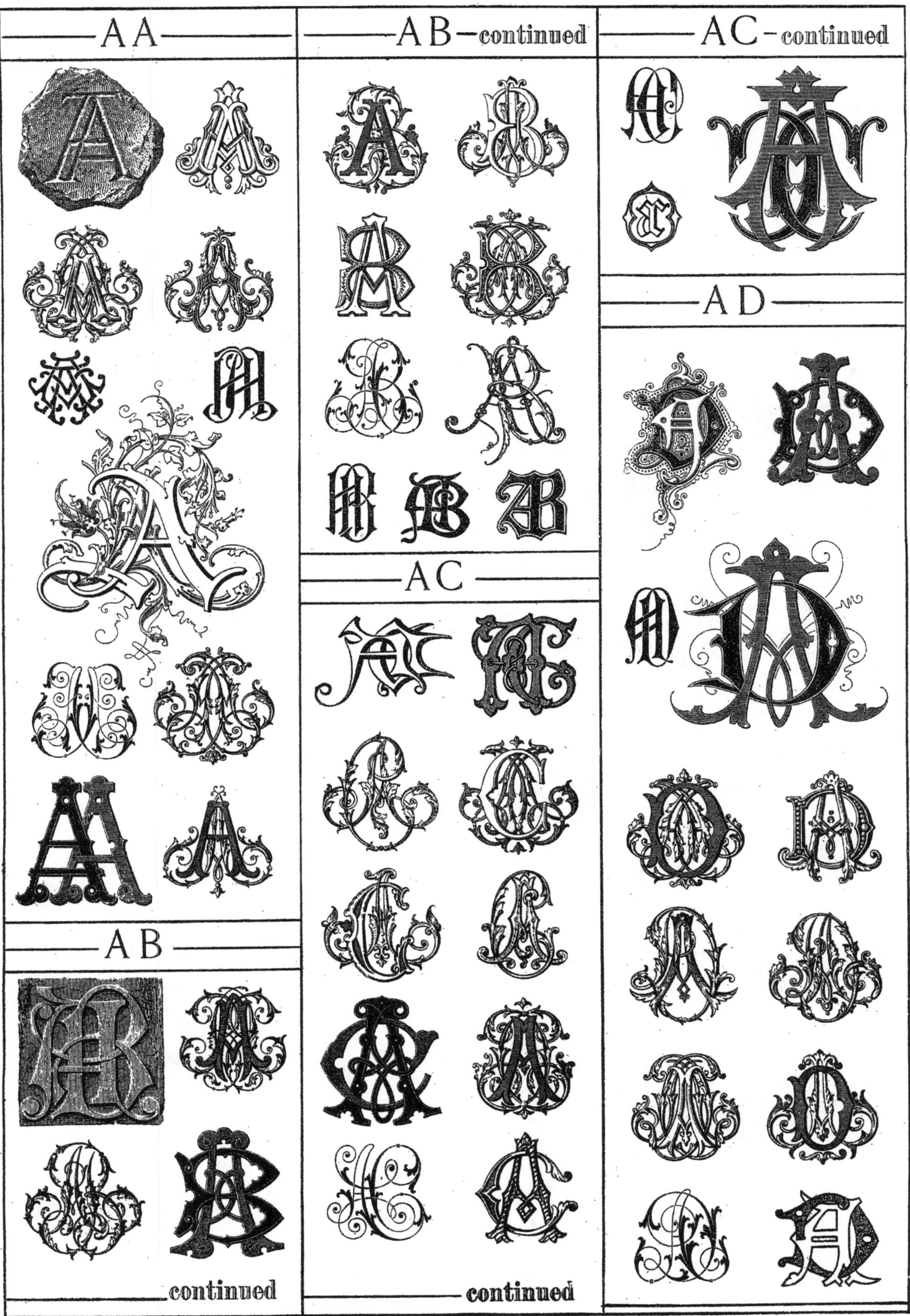
AA
AB—continued
AC—continued
AD
AC
AB
continued
continued

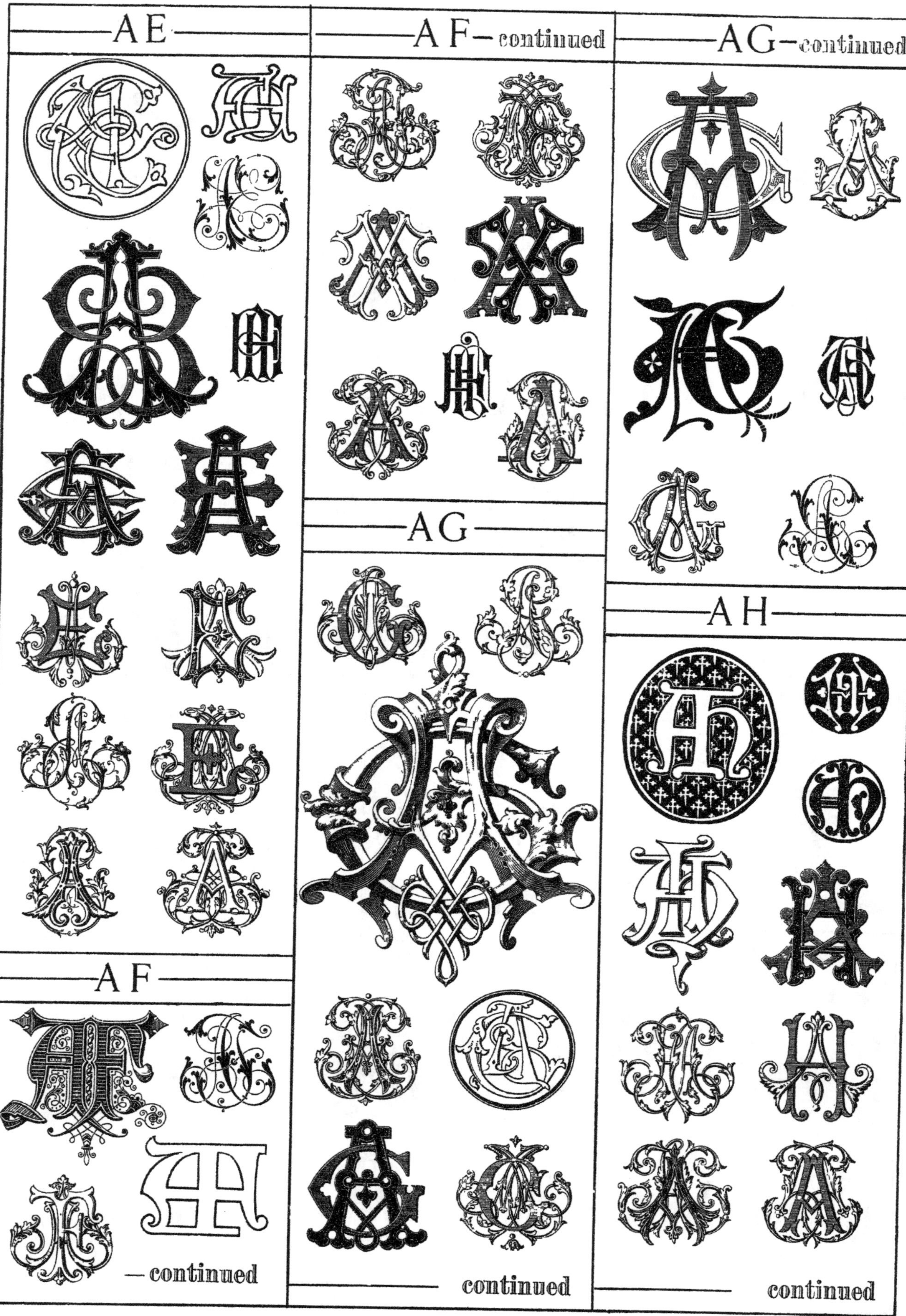
AE
AF—continued
AG—continued
AG
AH
AF
—continued
continued
continued

PLATE 2

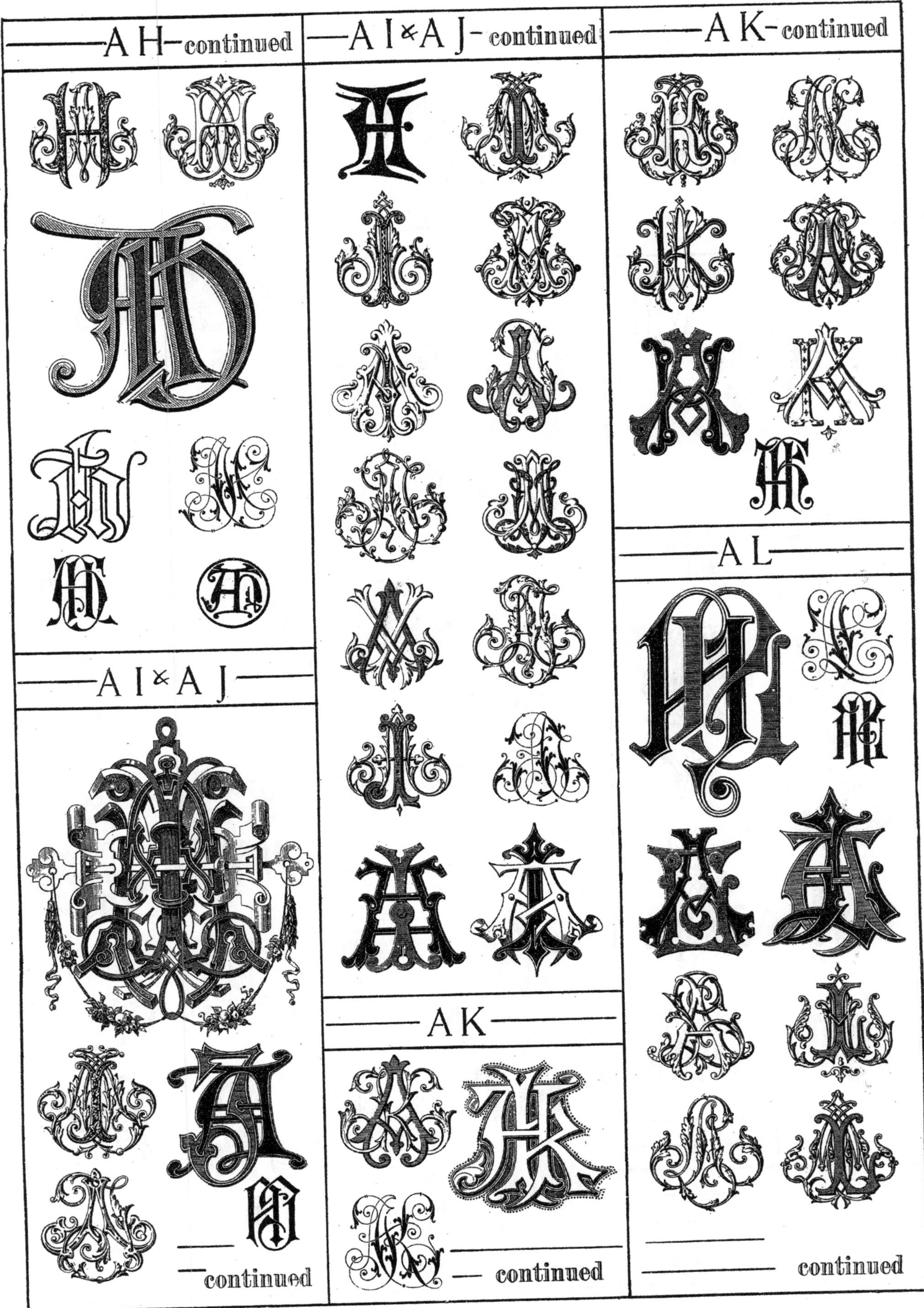
A H—continued
A I & A J—continued
A K—continued
A I & A J
continued
A K
continued
A L
continued

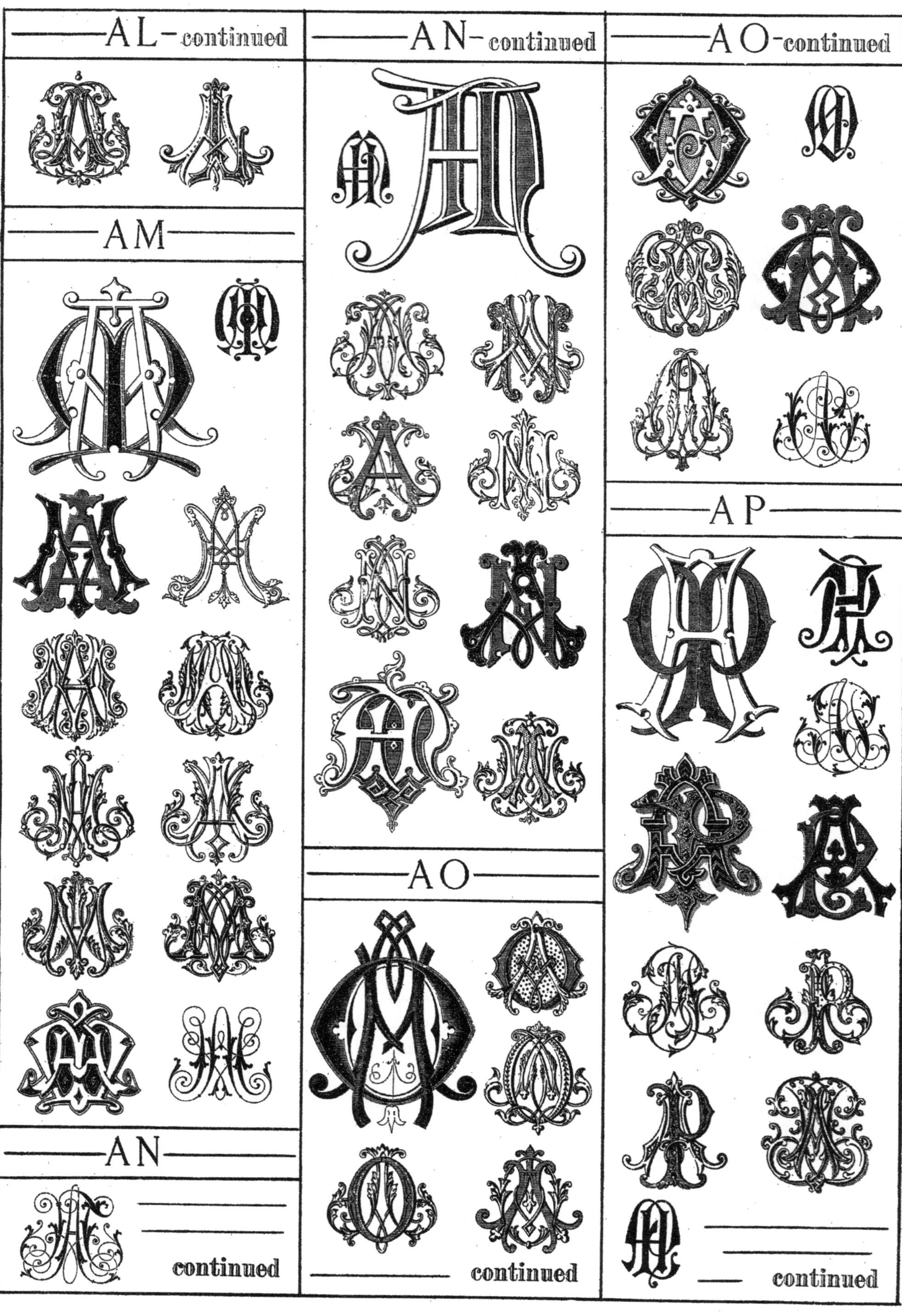
AL-continued
AM
AN
continued
AN-continued
AO
continued
AO-continued
AP
continued

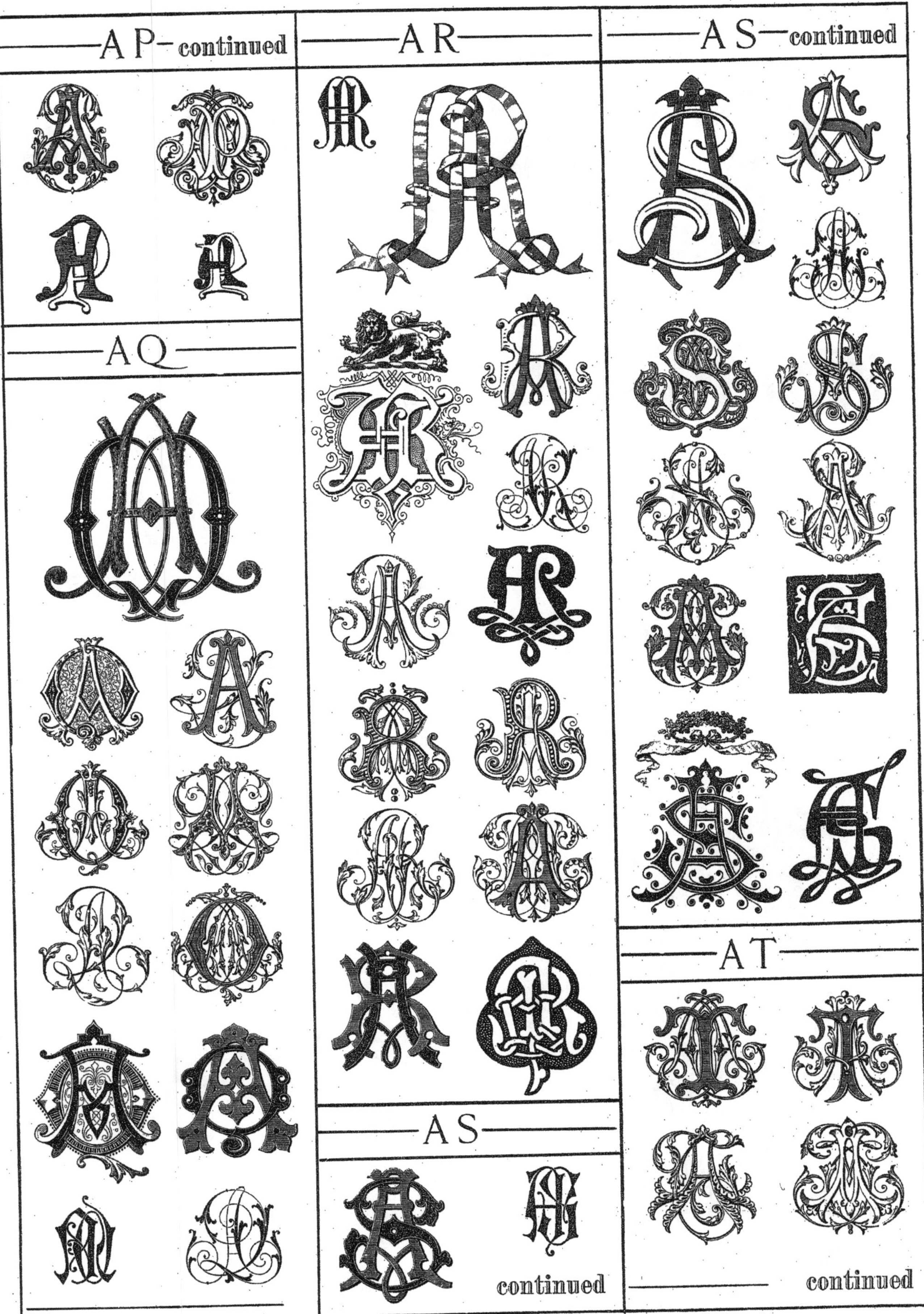

PLATE 5

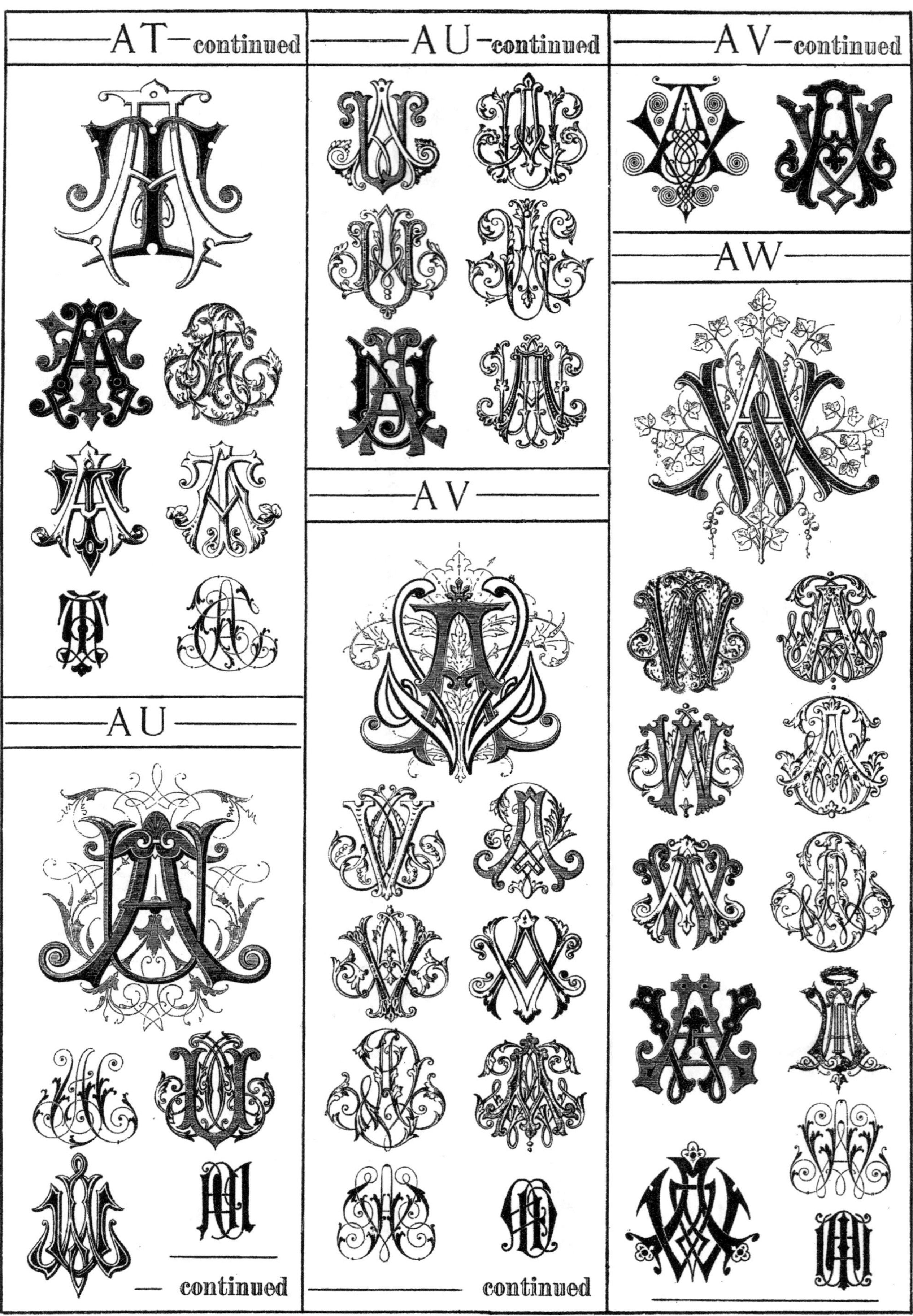
AT—continued
AU—continued
AV—continued
AU
AV
AW
— continued
continued

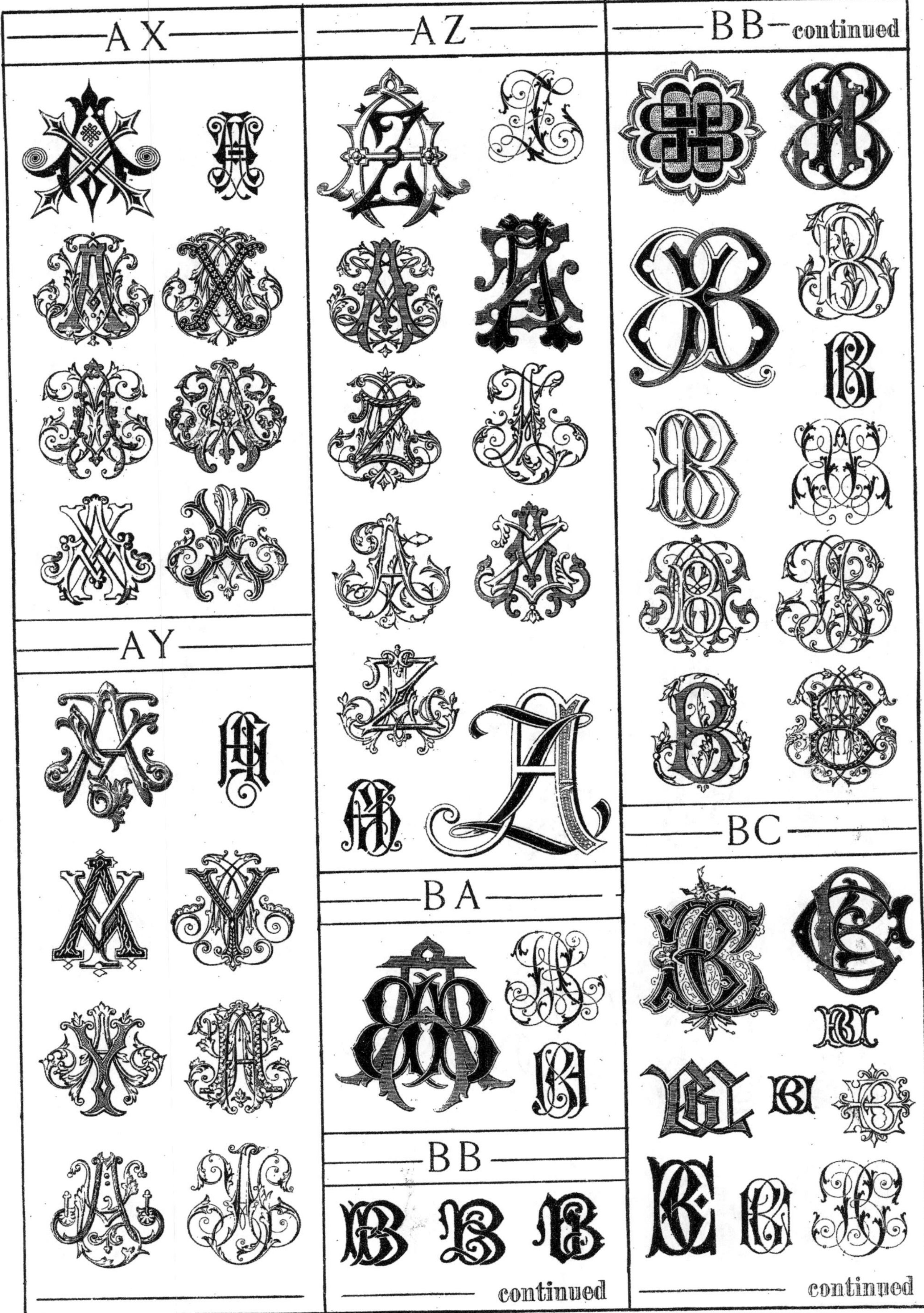
AX
AZ
BB continued
AY
BA
BB
continued
BC
continued
continued

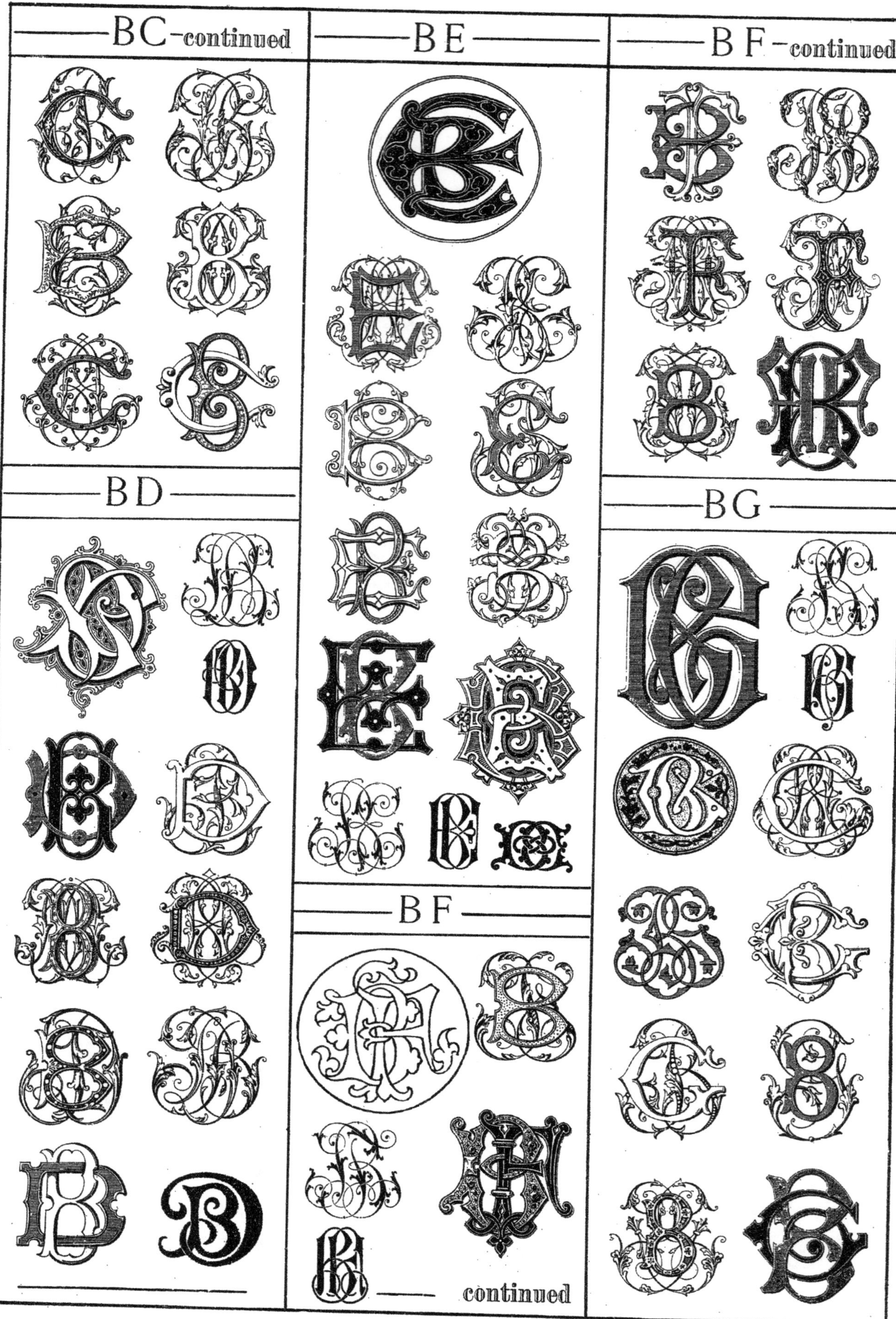
BC-continued
BE
BF-continued
BD
BG
BF
continued

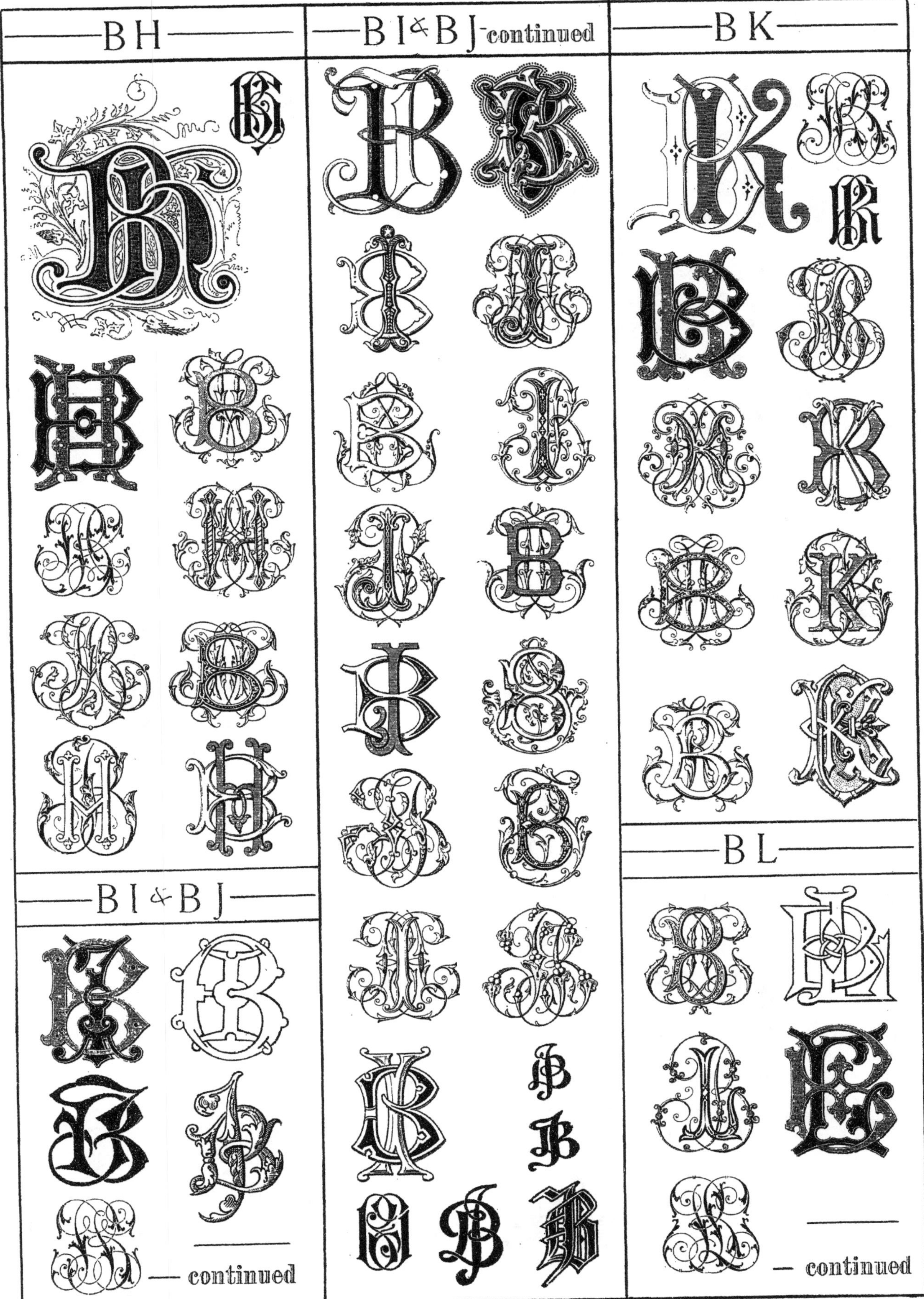
BH
BI & BJ-continued
BK
BI & BJ
BL
continued
continued

B L-continued
B M-continued
B O
B M
B N
B P
continued
continued

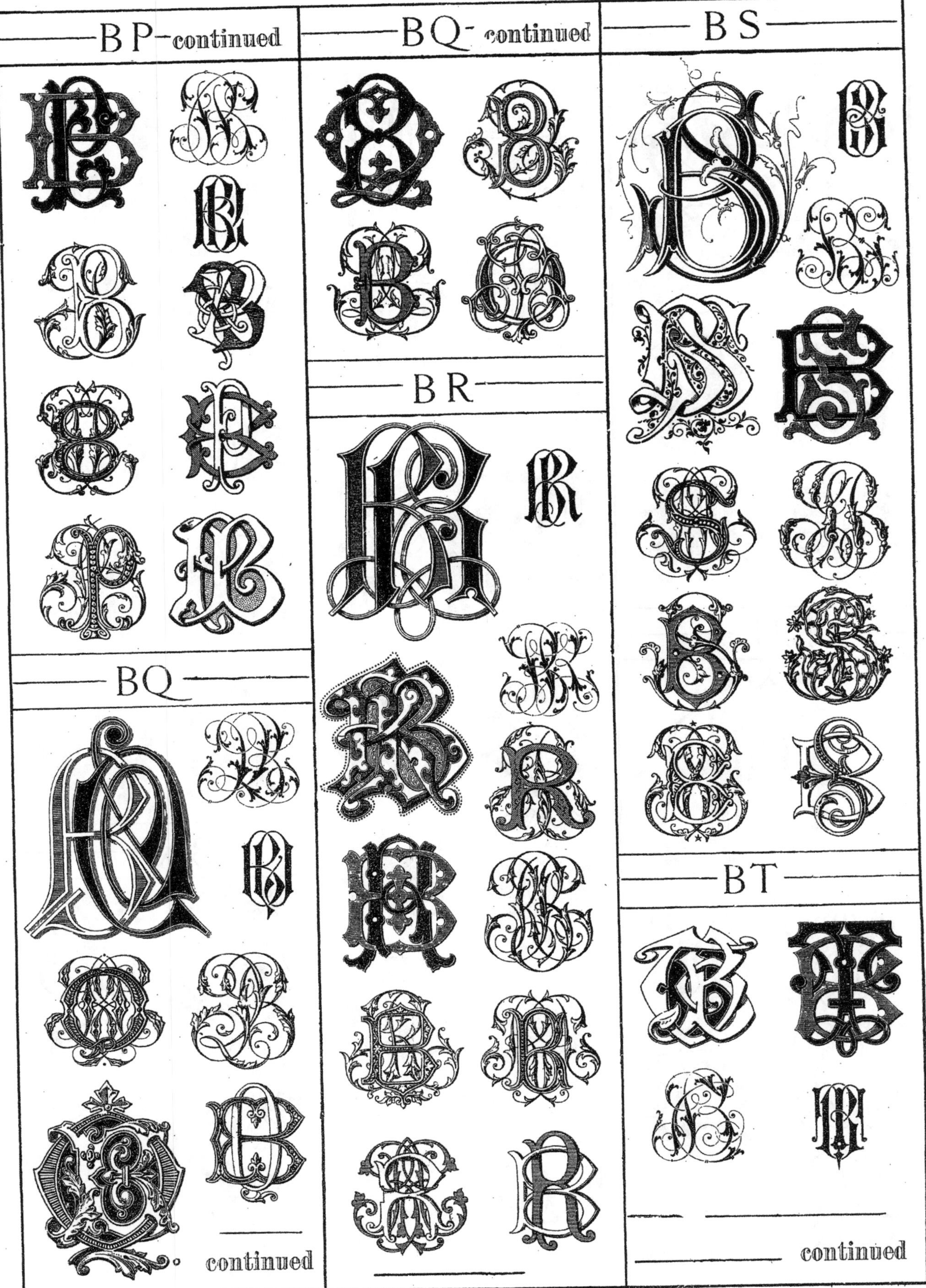
BP—continued
BQ—continued
BS
BR
BQ
BT
continued
continued

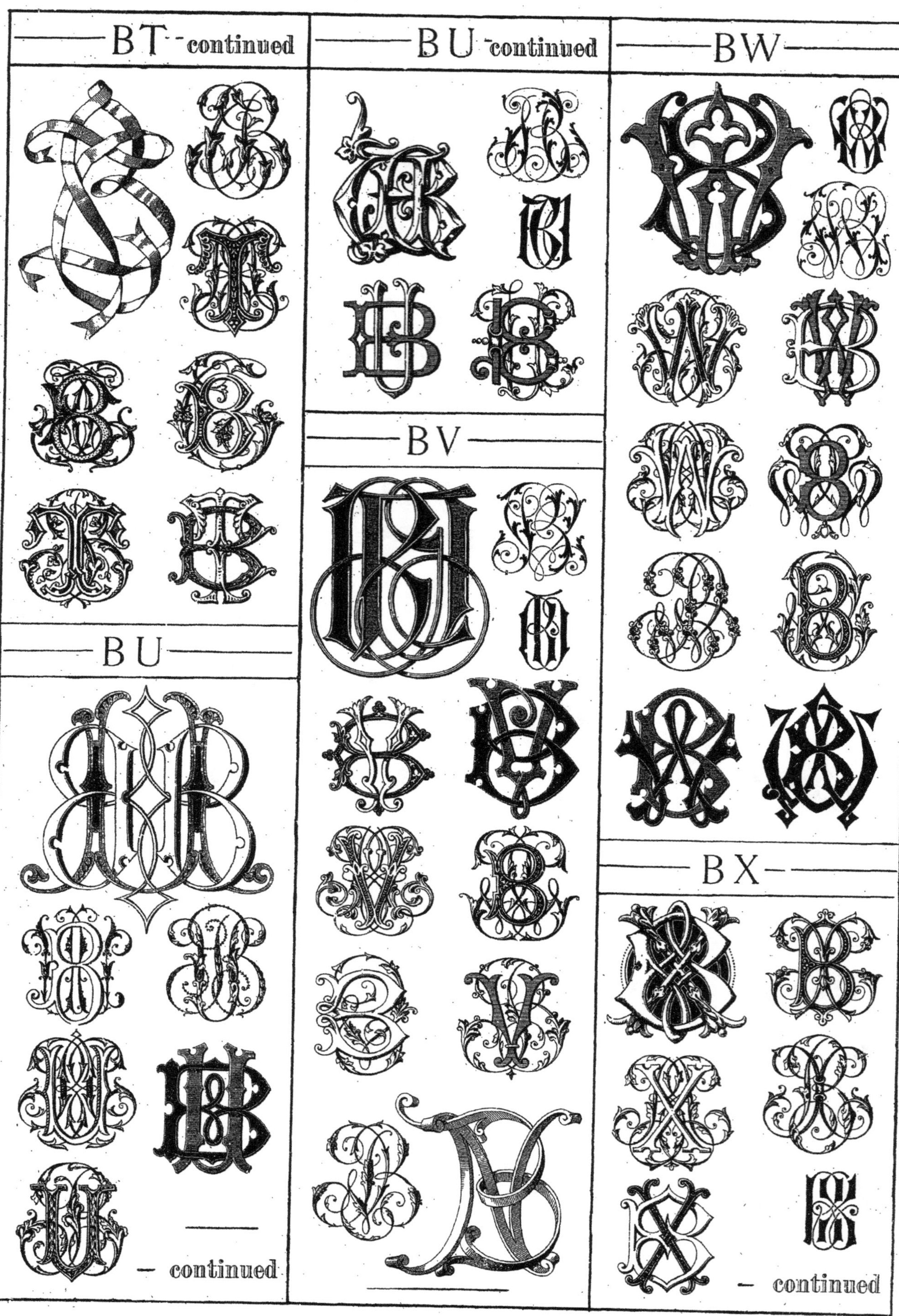
BT - continued
BU - continued
BW
BV
BU
- continued
BX
- continued

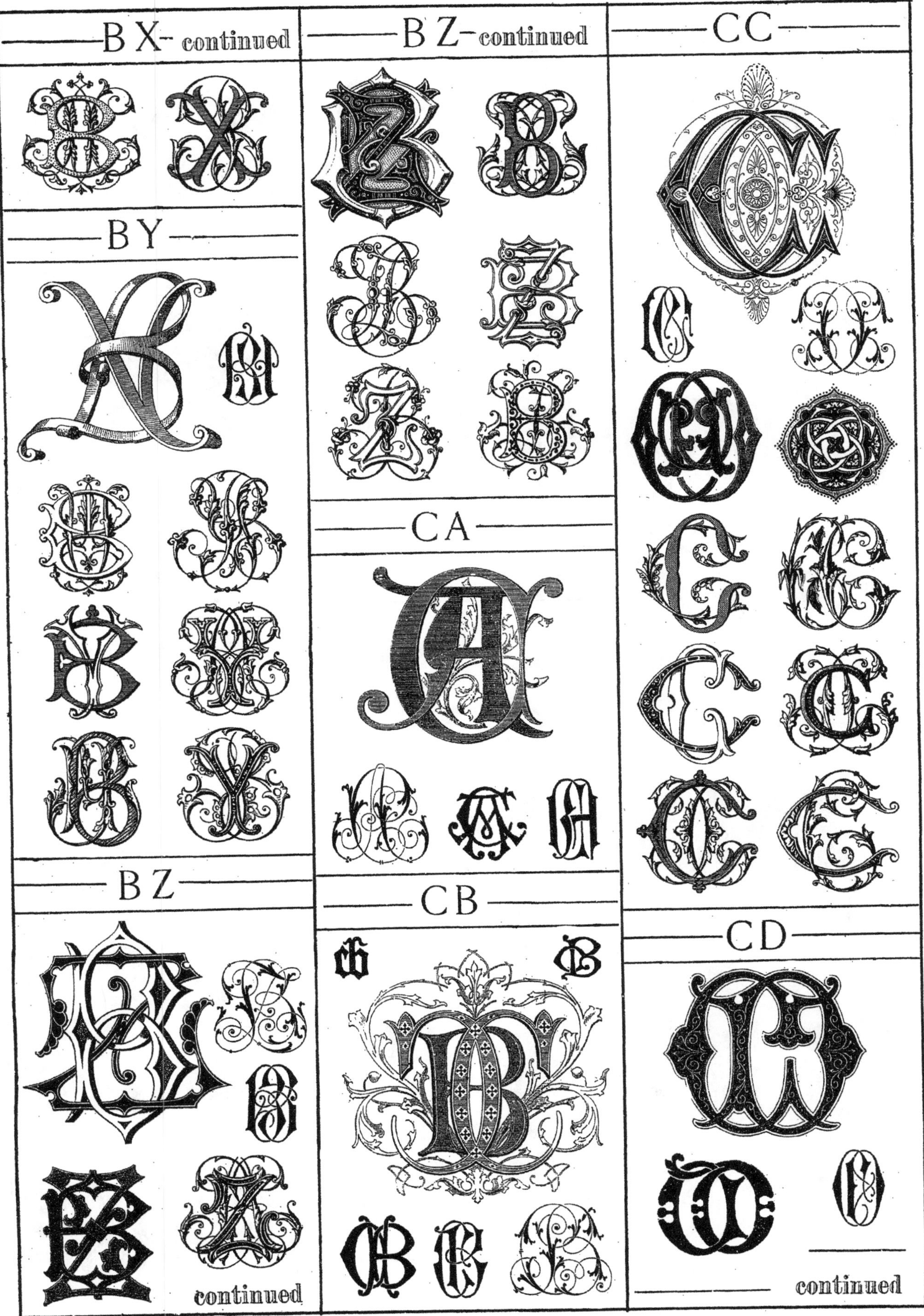
B X– continued
B Z– continued
C C
B Y
C A
B Z
C B
C D
continued
continued

CD continued
CE continued
CF continued
CG
CE
CF
continued
continued

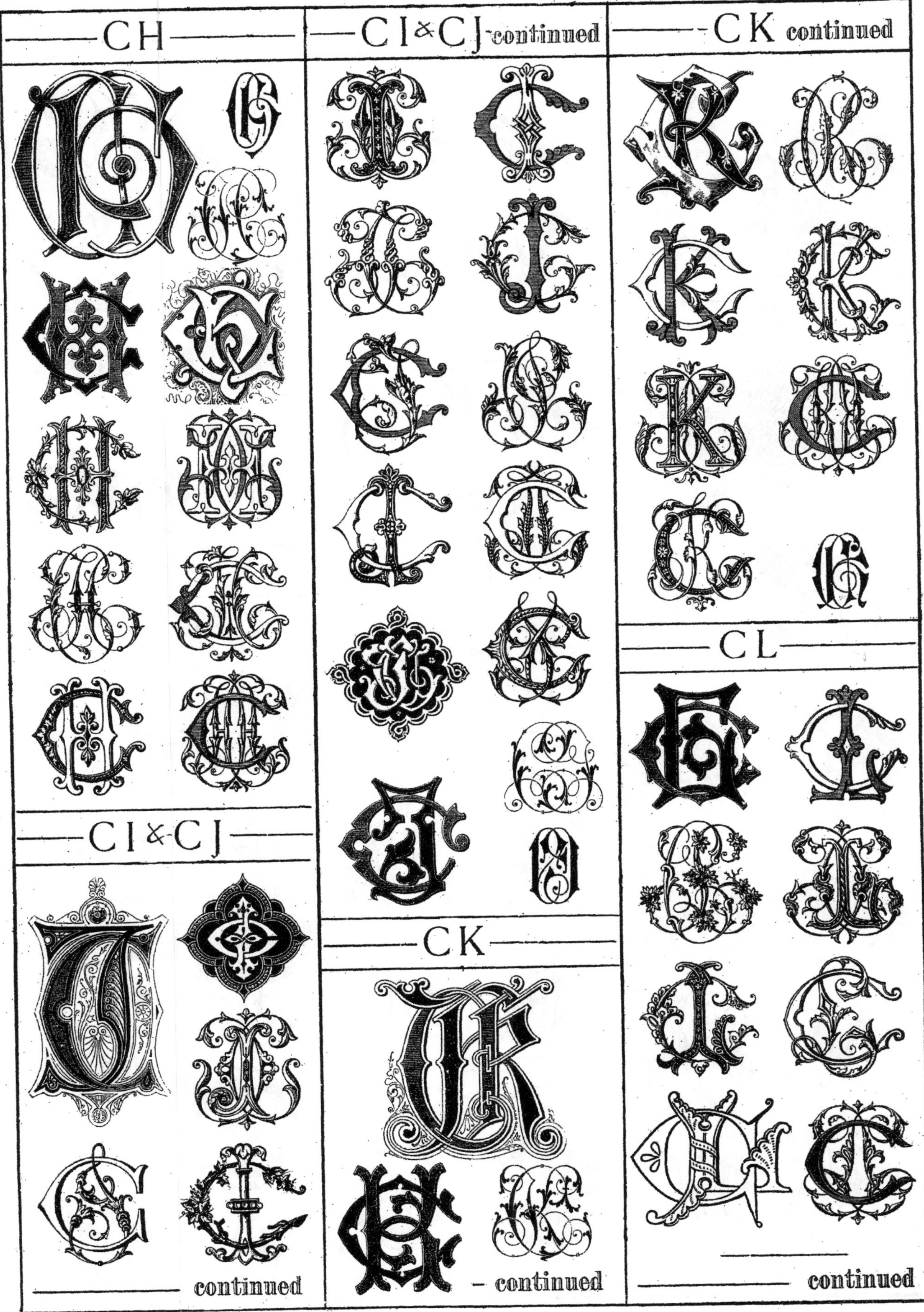
CH
CI & CJ continued
CK continued
CL
CI & CJ
CK
continued
continued
continued

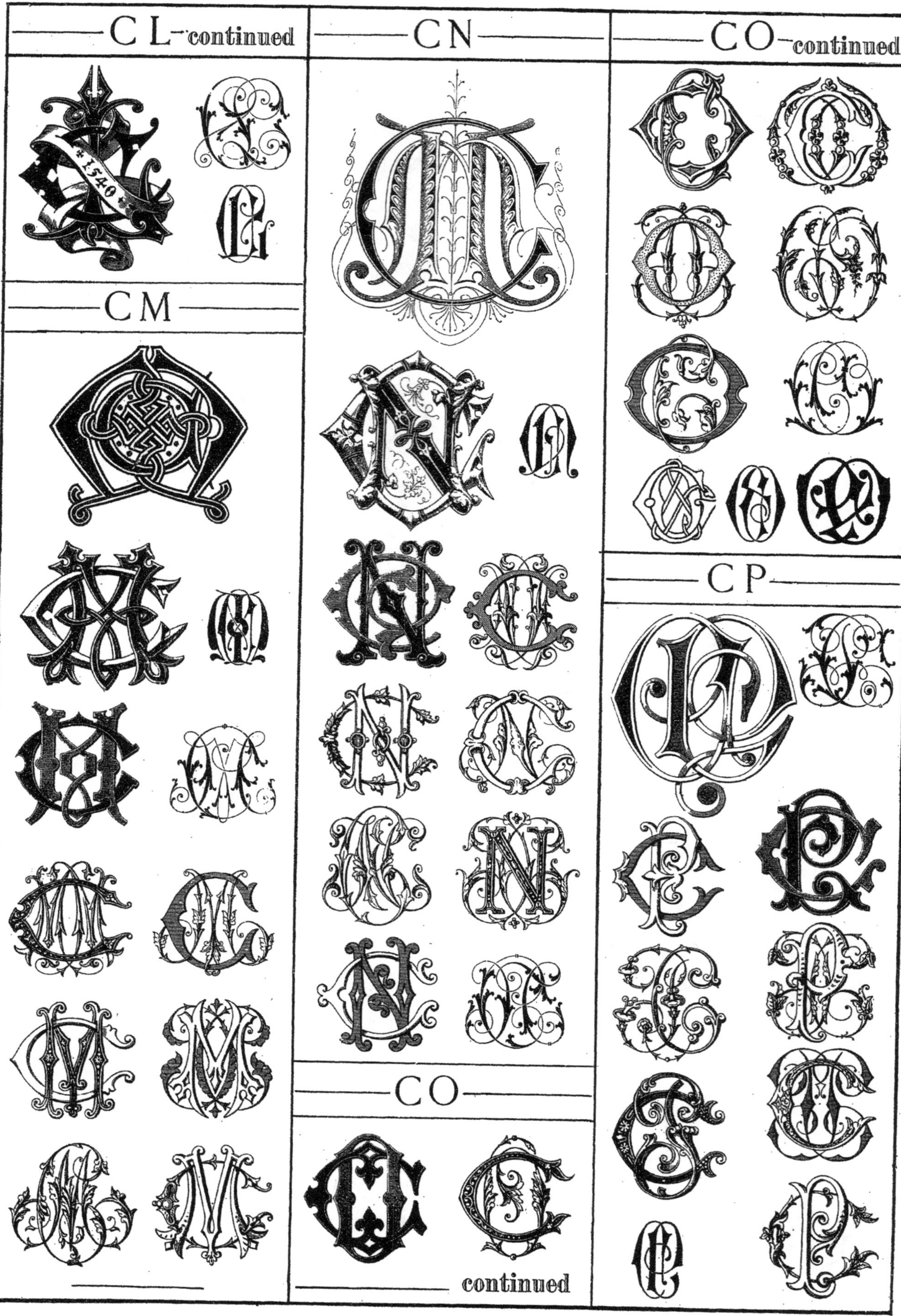
C L–continued
C N
C O–continued
C M
C P
C O
continued

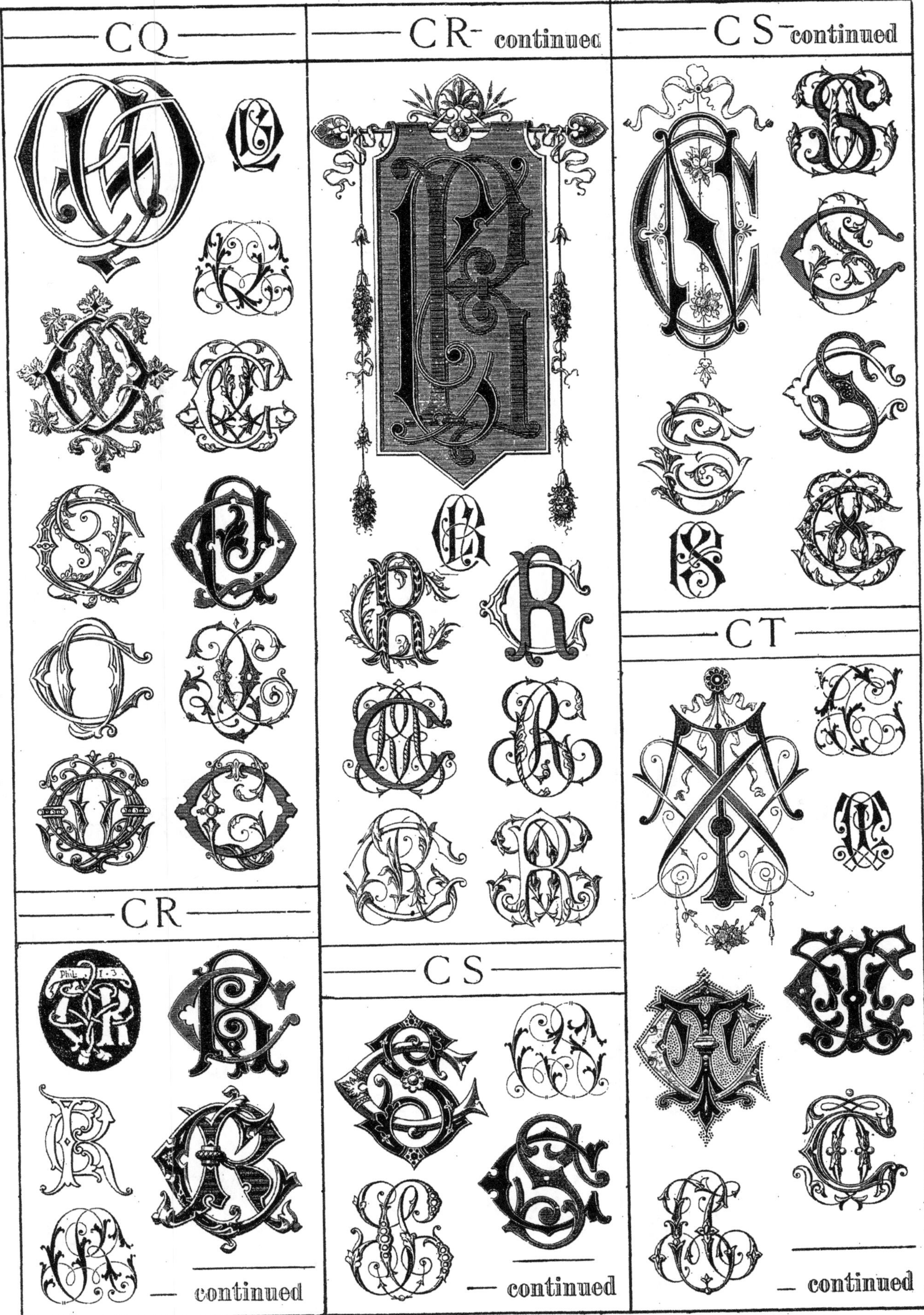
CQ
CR- continued
CS- continued
CR
CS
CT
continued
continued
continued

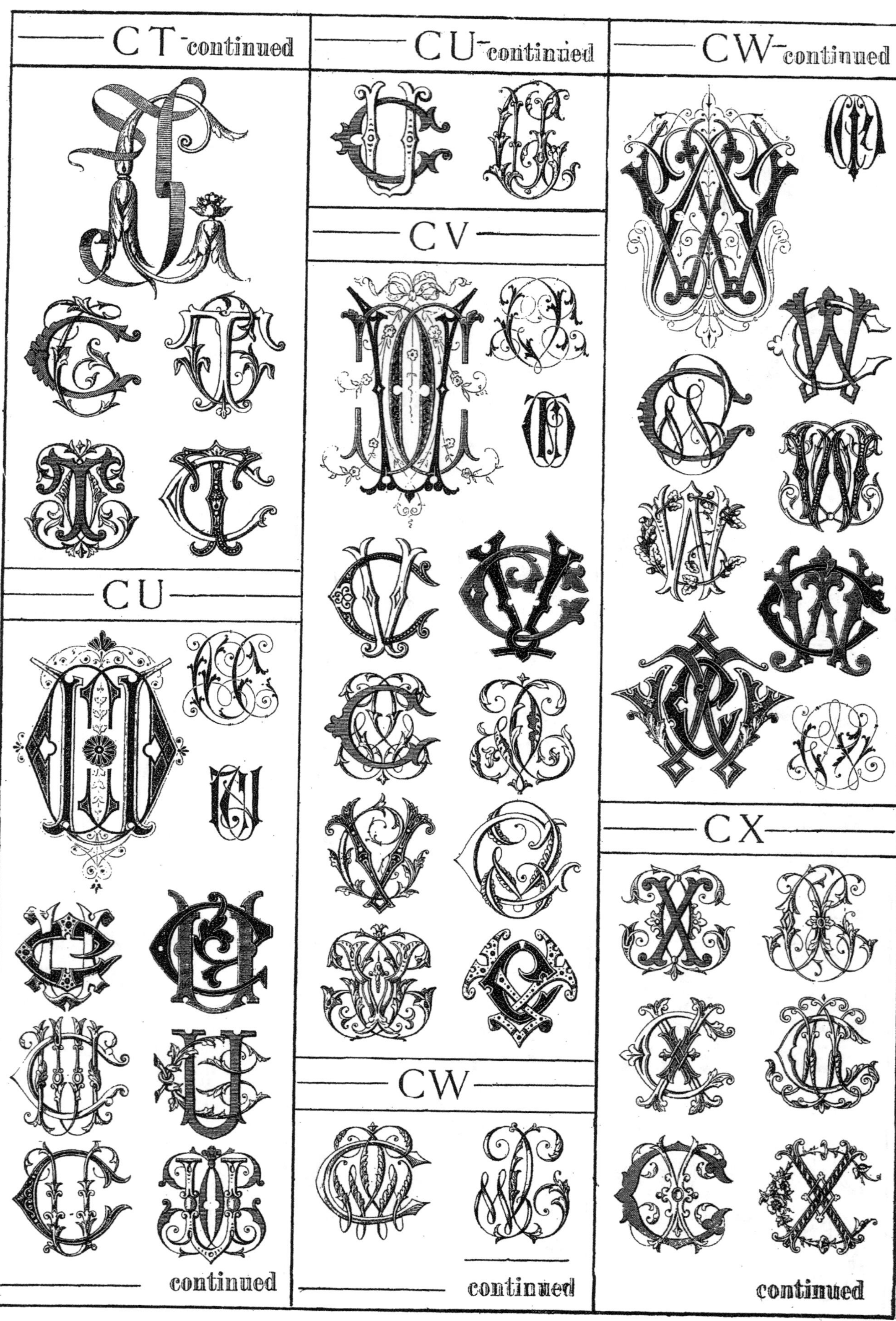

CT-continued
CU-continued
CW-continued
CV
CU
CW
CX
continued
continued
continued

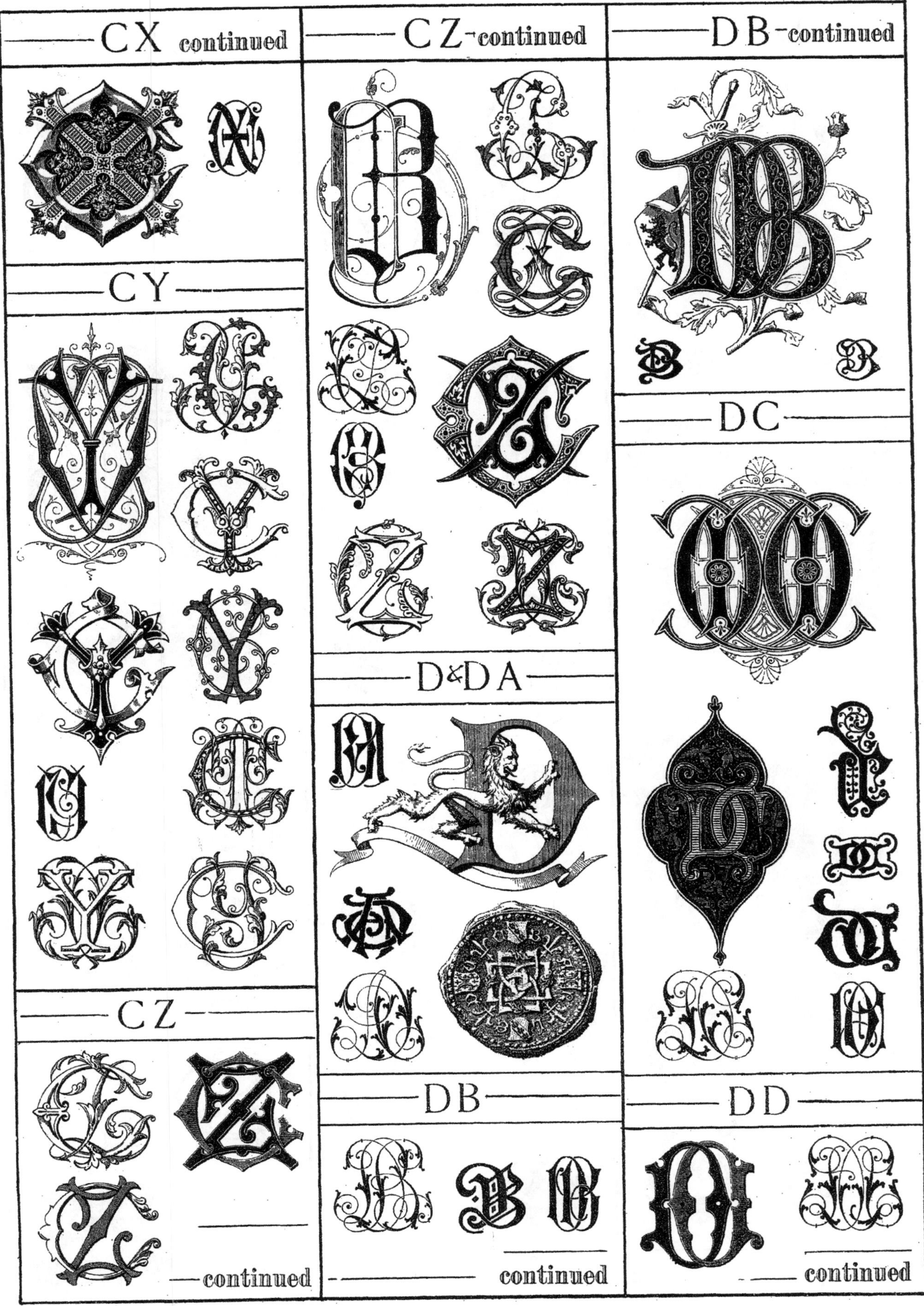
CX continued
CY
CZ
continued
CZ-continued
D&DA
DB
continued
DB-continued
DC
DD
continued

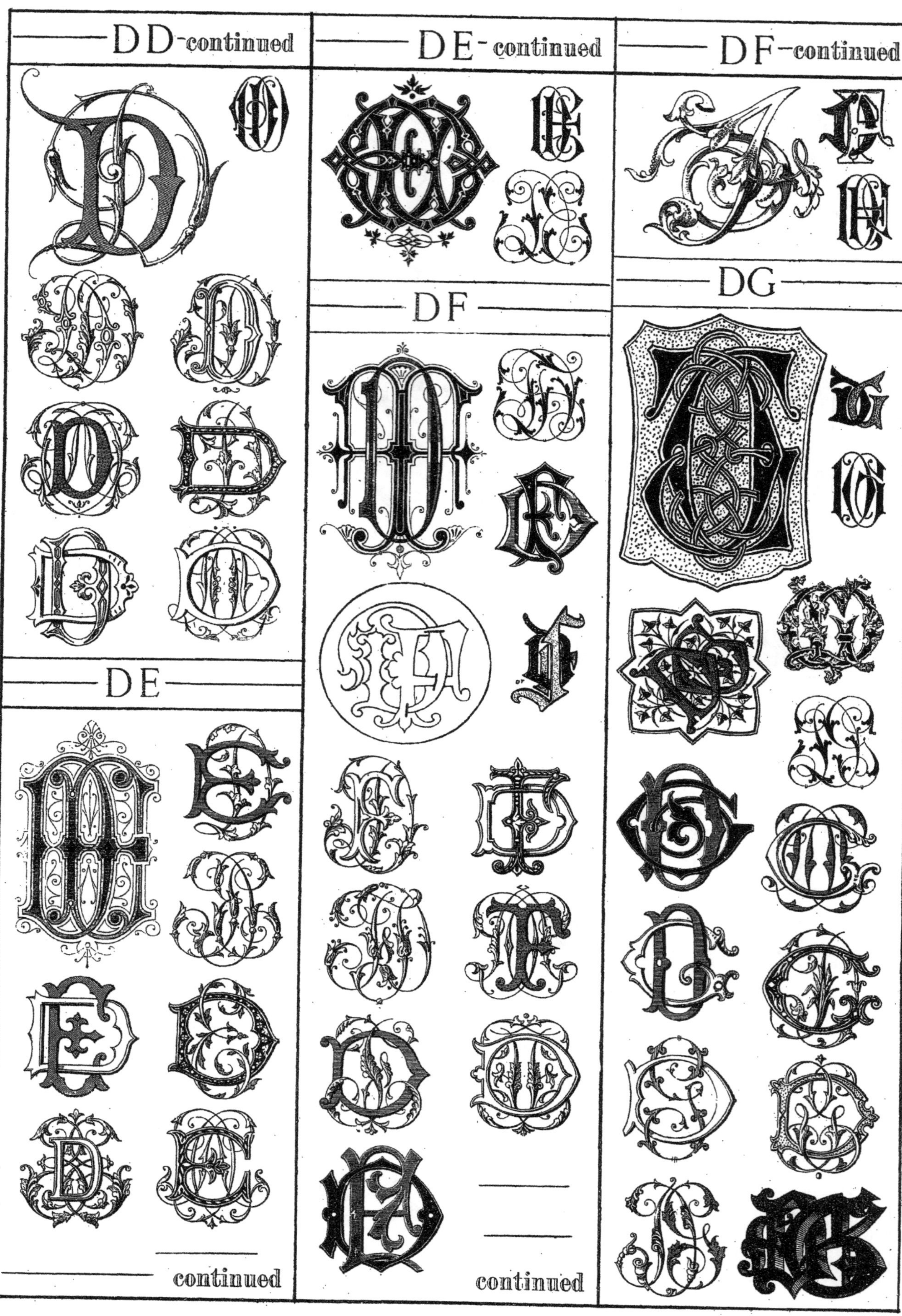

DD-continued
DE-continued
DF-continued
DF
DG
DE
continued
continued

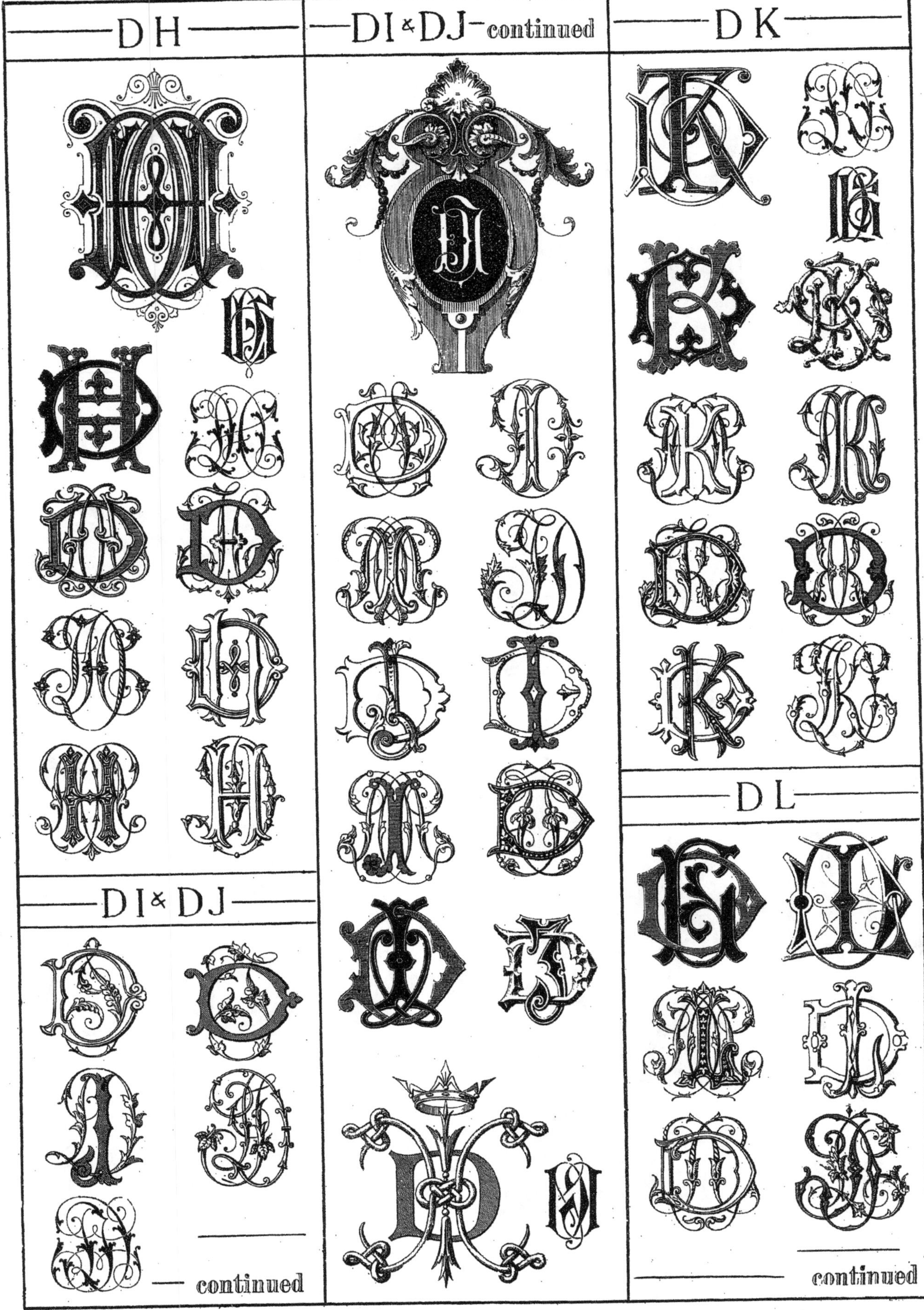
DH
DI & DJ – continued
DK
DL
DI & DJ
continued
continued

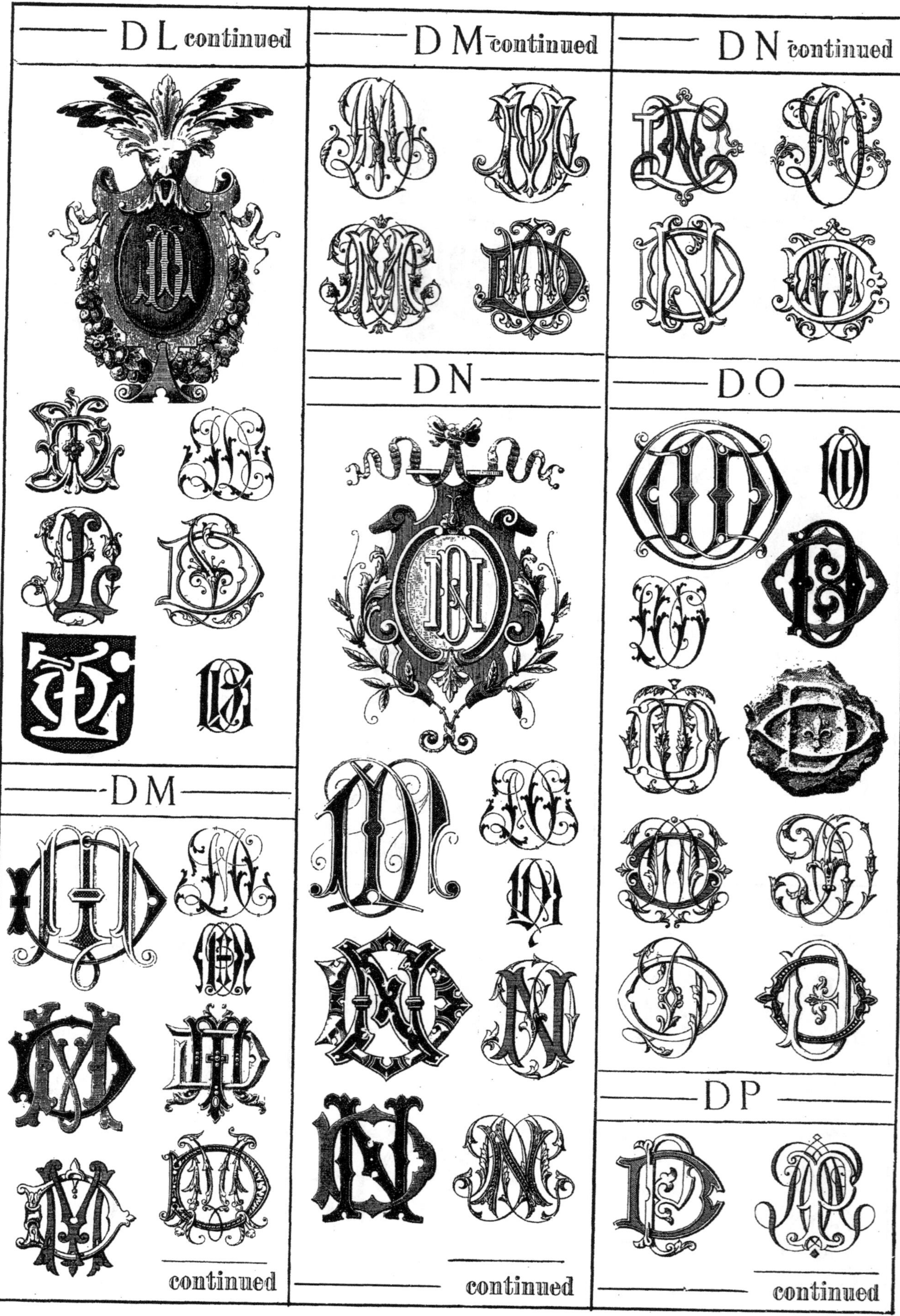

D L continued
D M continued
D N continued
D N
D O
D M
D P
continued
continued
continued

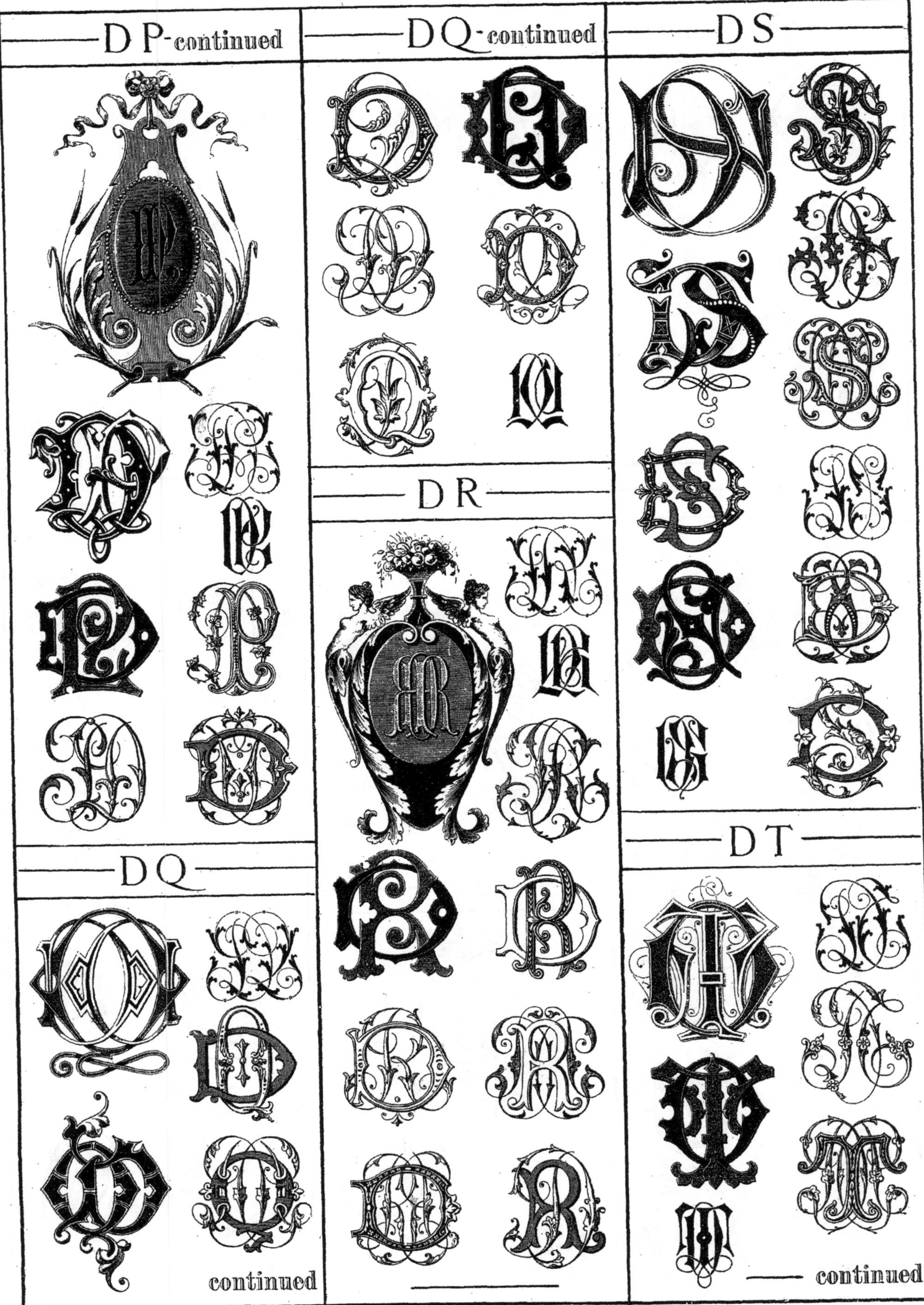
D P-continued
D Q-continued
D S
D R
D Q
D T
continued
continued

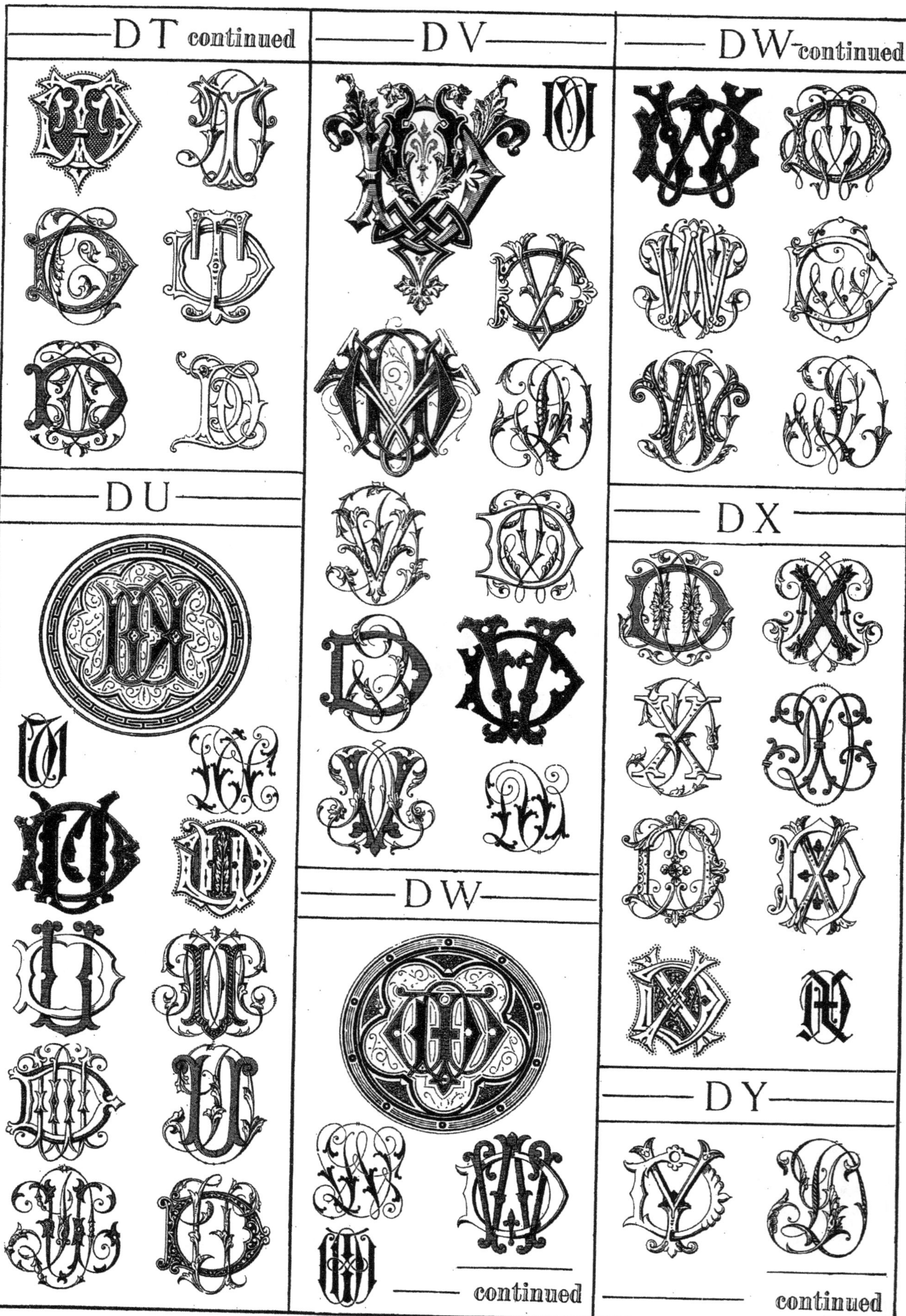

DT continued
DV
DW continued
DU
DX
DW
DY
continued
continued

DY-continued
EA
ED-continued
DZ
EB
EE
EC
ED
continued

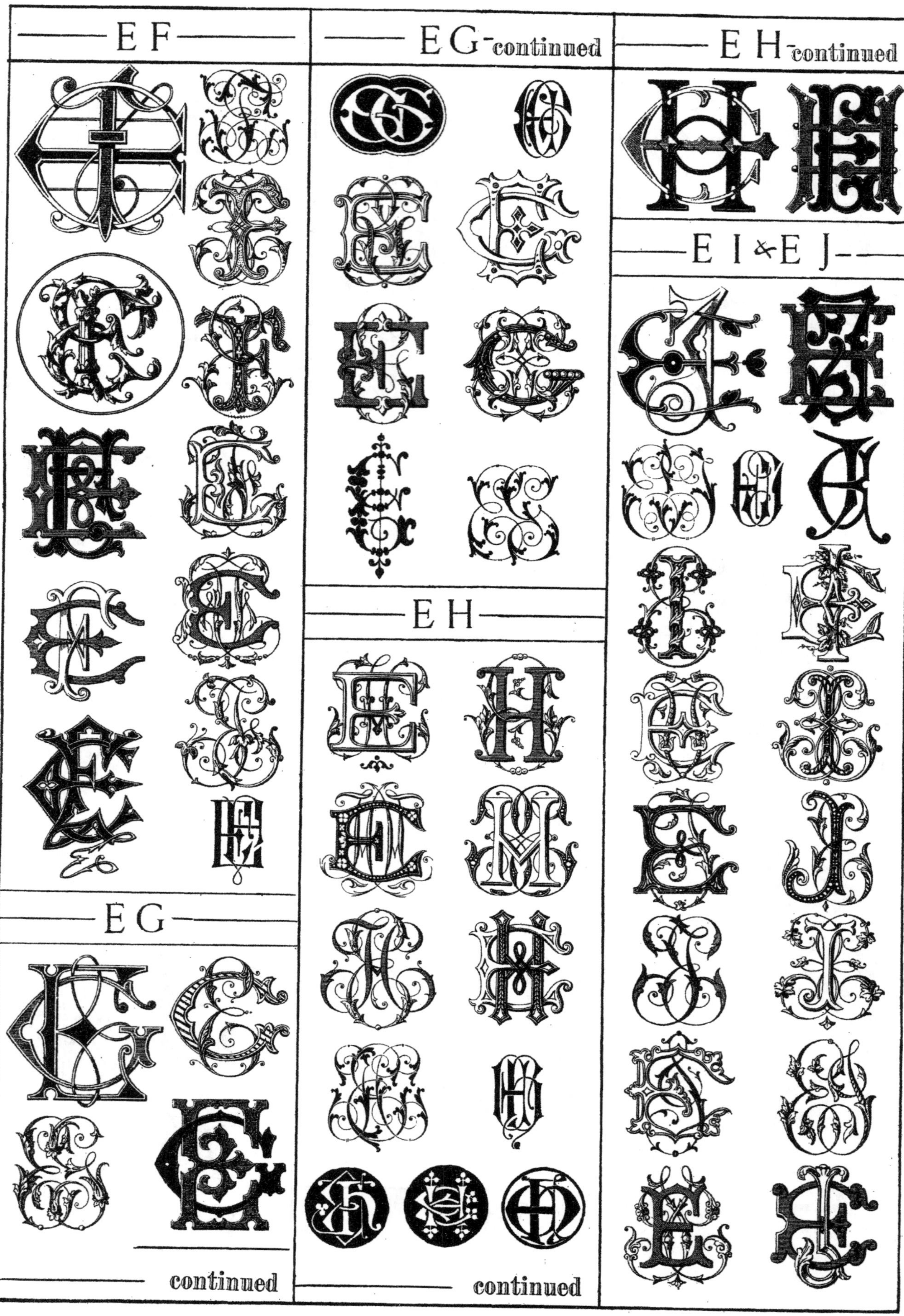
E F
E G–continued
E H–continued
E I & E J
E H
E G
continued
continued

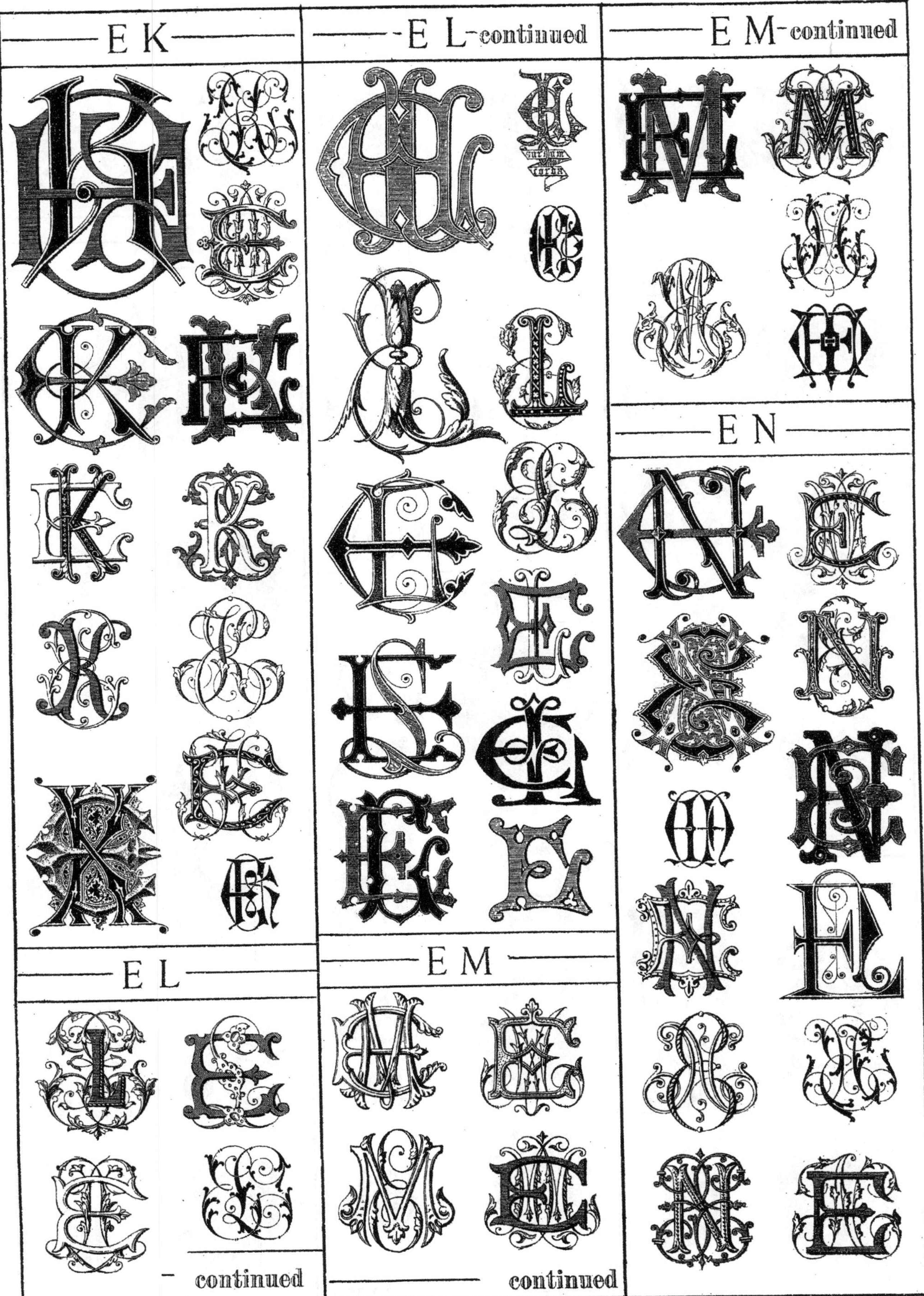
E K
E L-continued
E M-continued
E N
E L
E M
continued
continued
turdum
torba

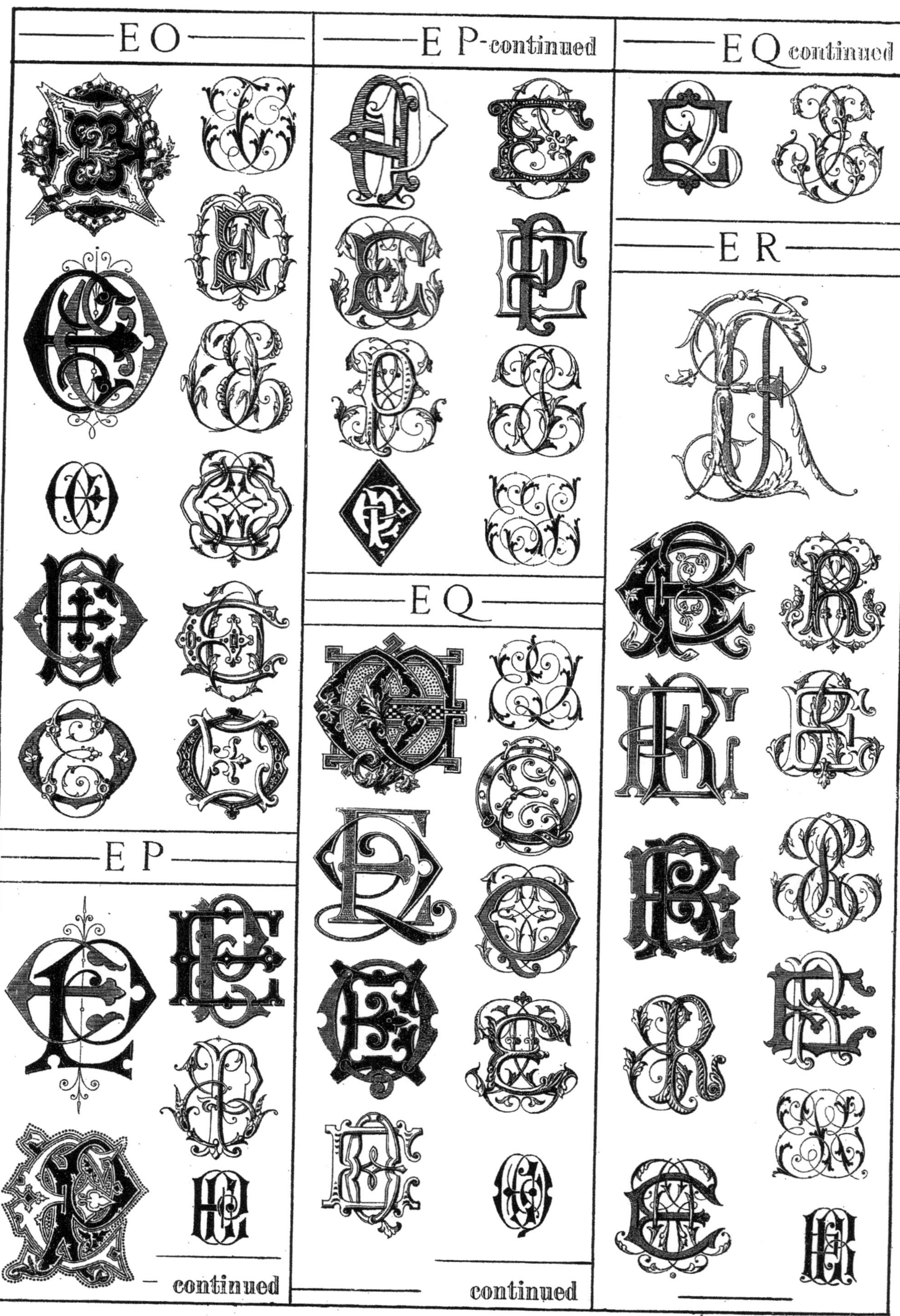
E O
E P
continued
E P-continued
E Q
continued
E Q continued
E R

E S
E T-continued
E U-continued
E T
E U
E V
— continued
— continued
— continued

E V continued
E X
E Z
E W
E Y
F & F A

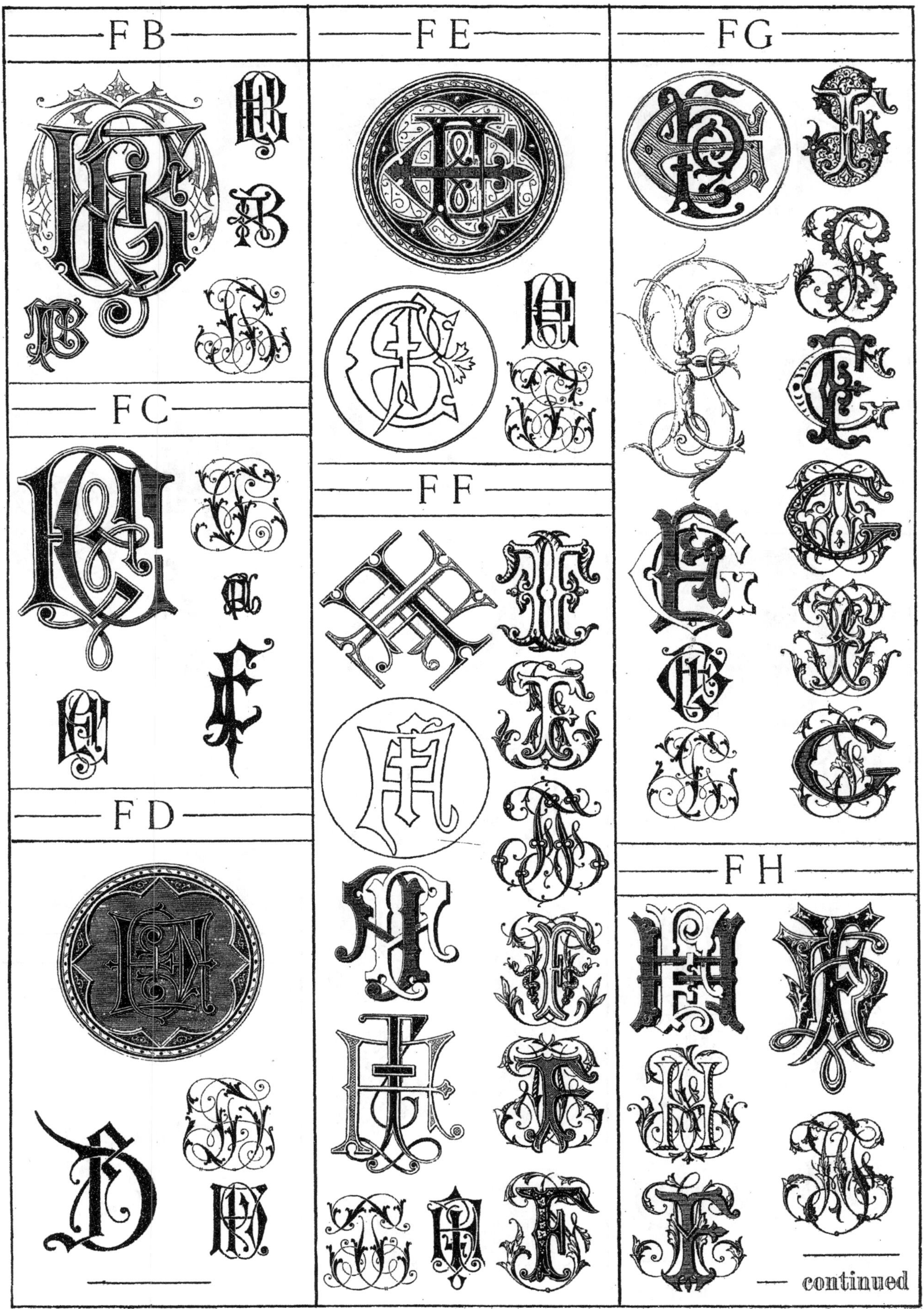
FB
FE
FG
FC
FF
FD
FH
continued

FH continued
FI & FJ continued
FL
FI & FJ
FK
FM
Love
Love
continued
continued

FM continued
FN continued
FP
FN
continued
FO
FQ
continued
continued

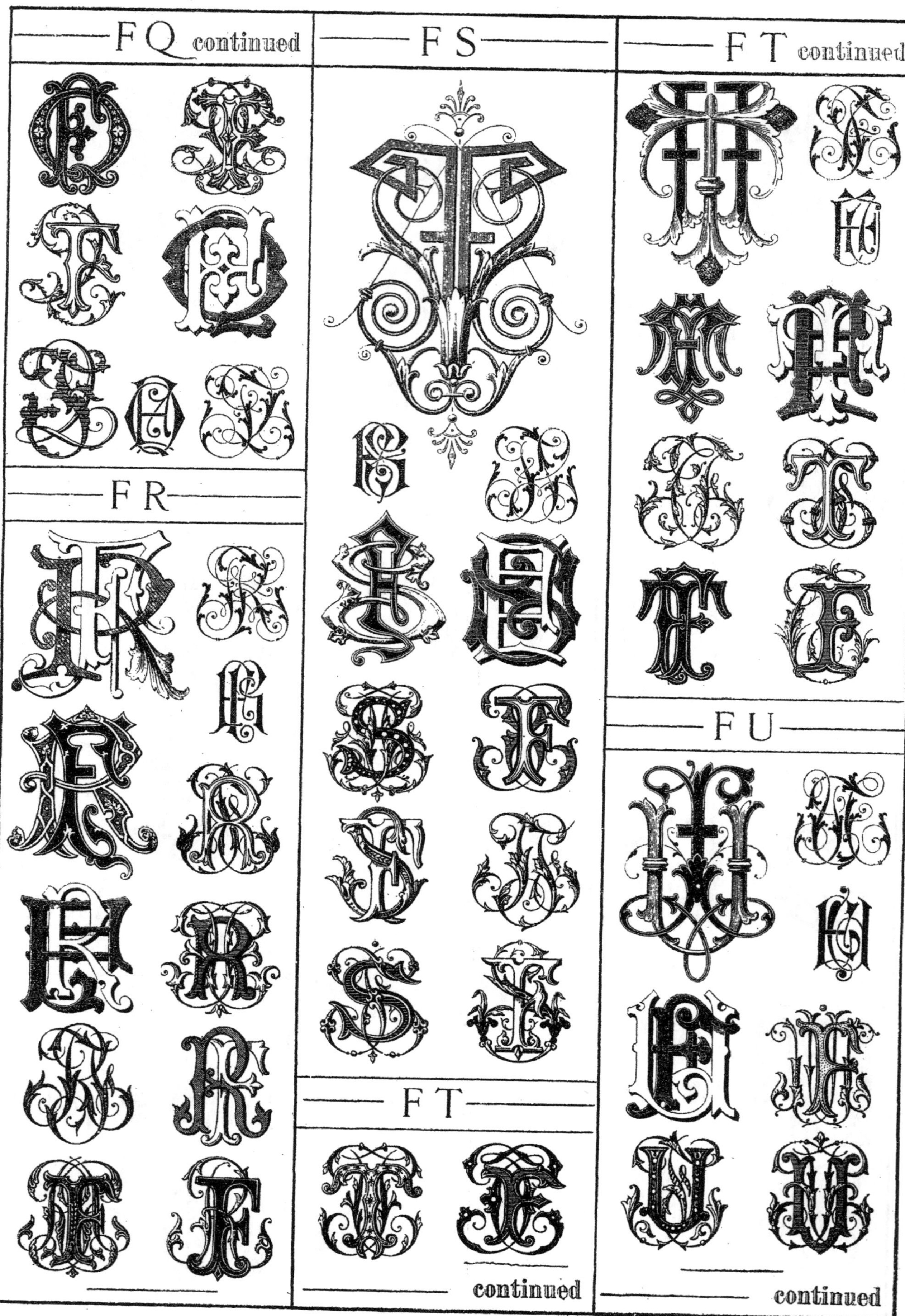
FQ continued
FS
FT continued
FR
FT
continued
FU
continued
continued

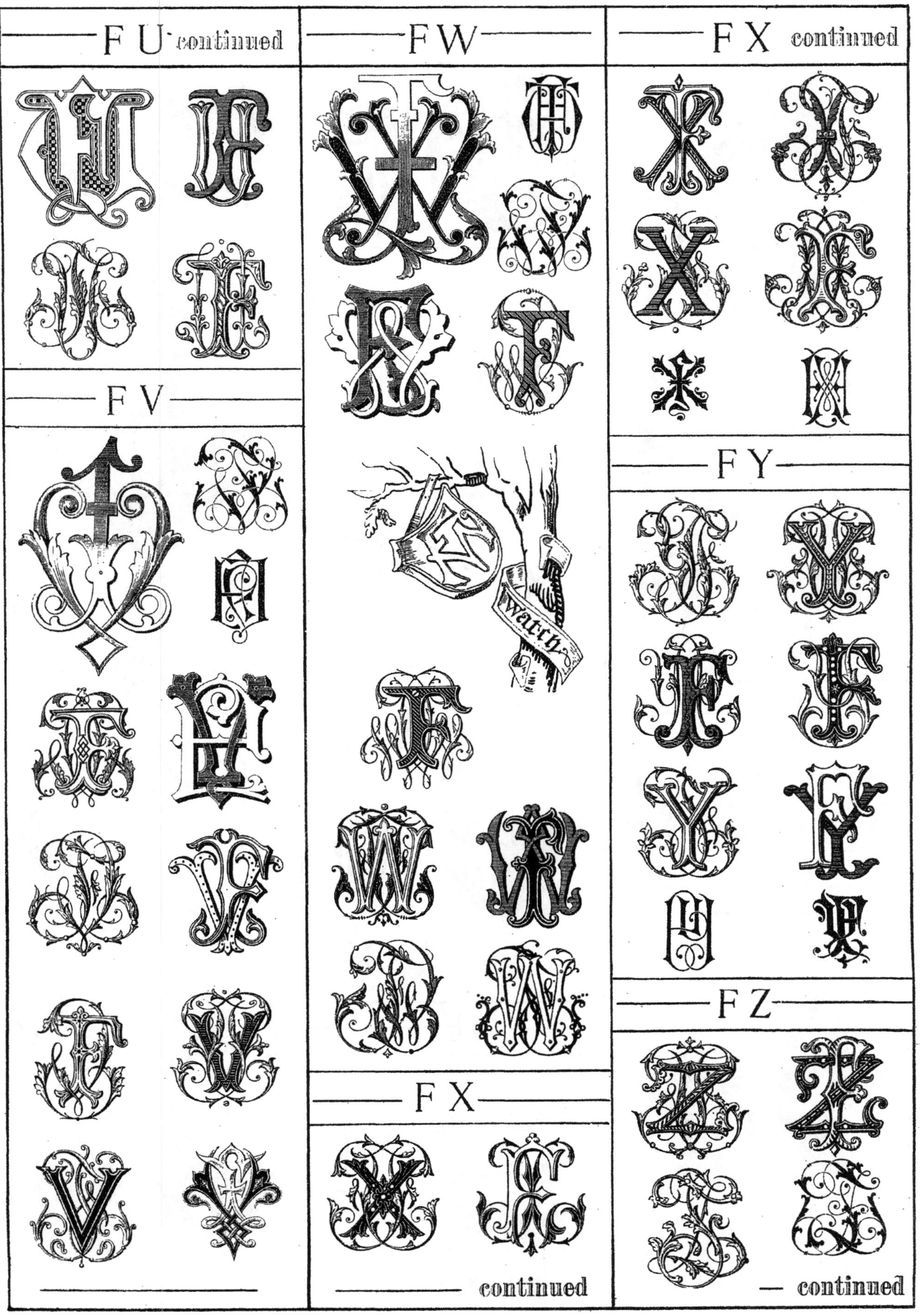
F U continued
F W
F X continued
F V
watch
F Y
F Z
F X
continued
continued

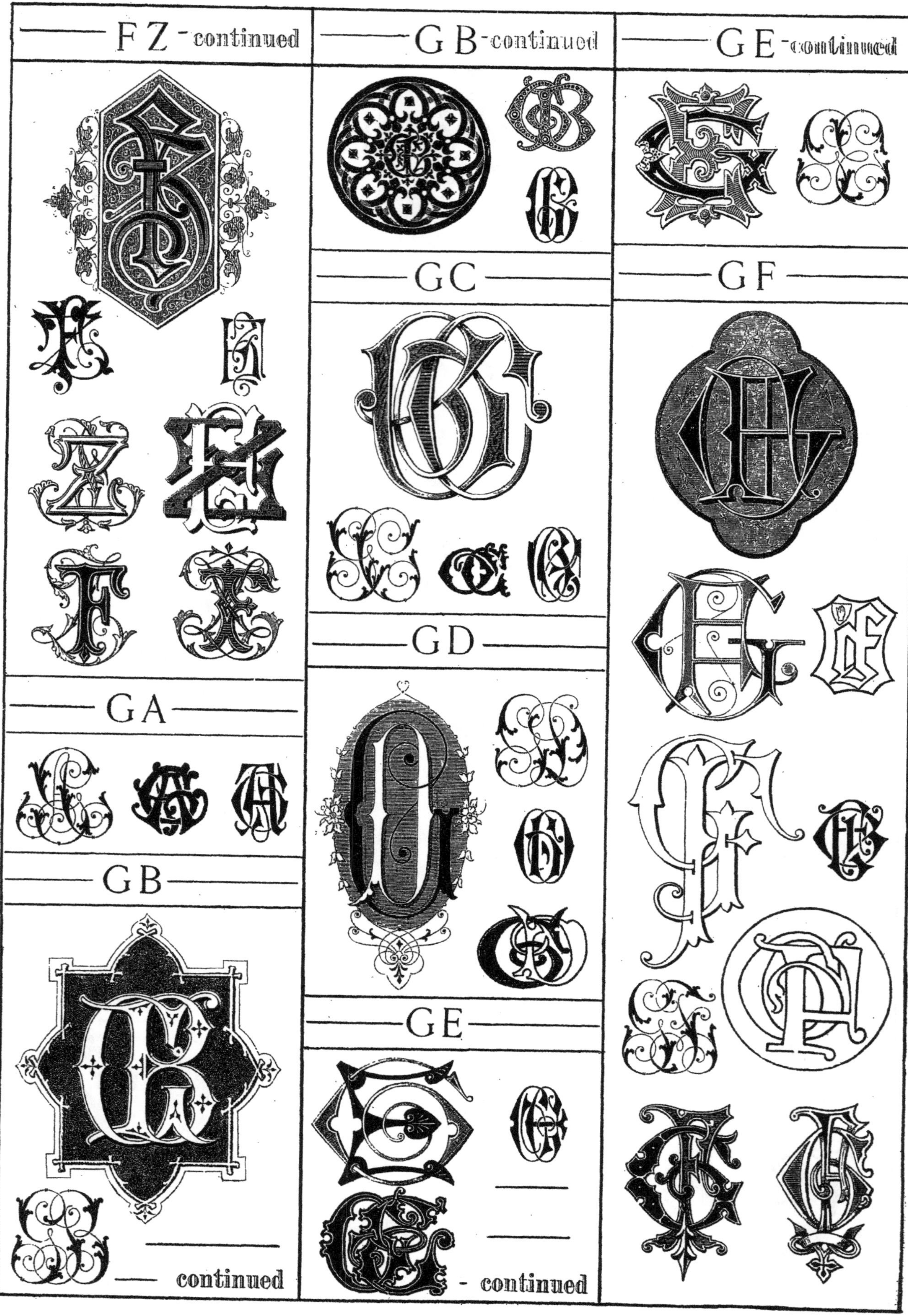

FZ-continued
GB-continued
GE-continued
GC
GF
GD
GA
GB
GE
continued
- continued

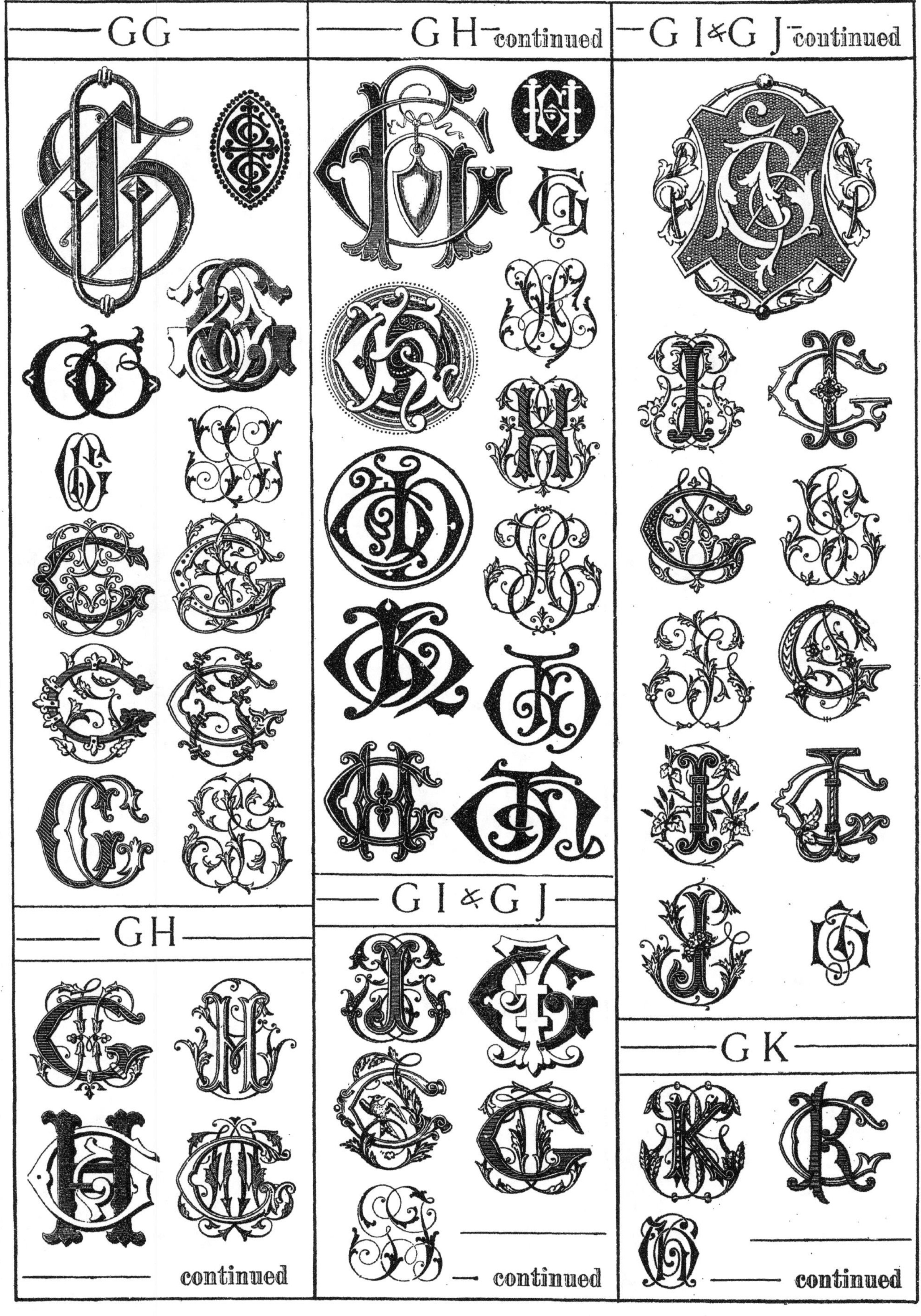
GG
GH continued
GI & GJ continued
GH
continued
GI & GJ
continued
GK
continued

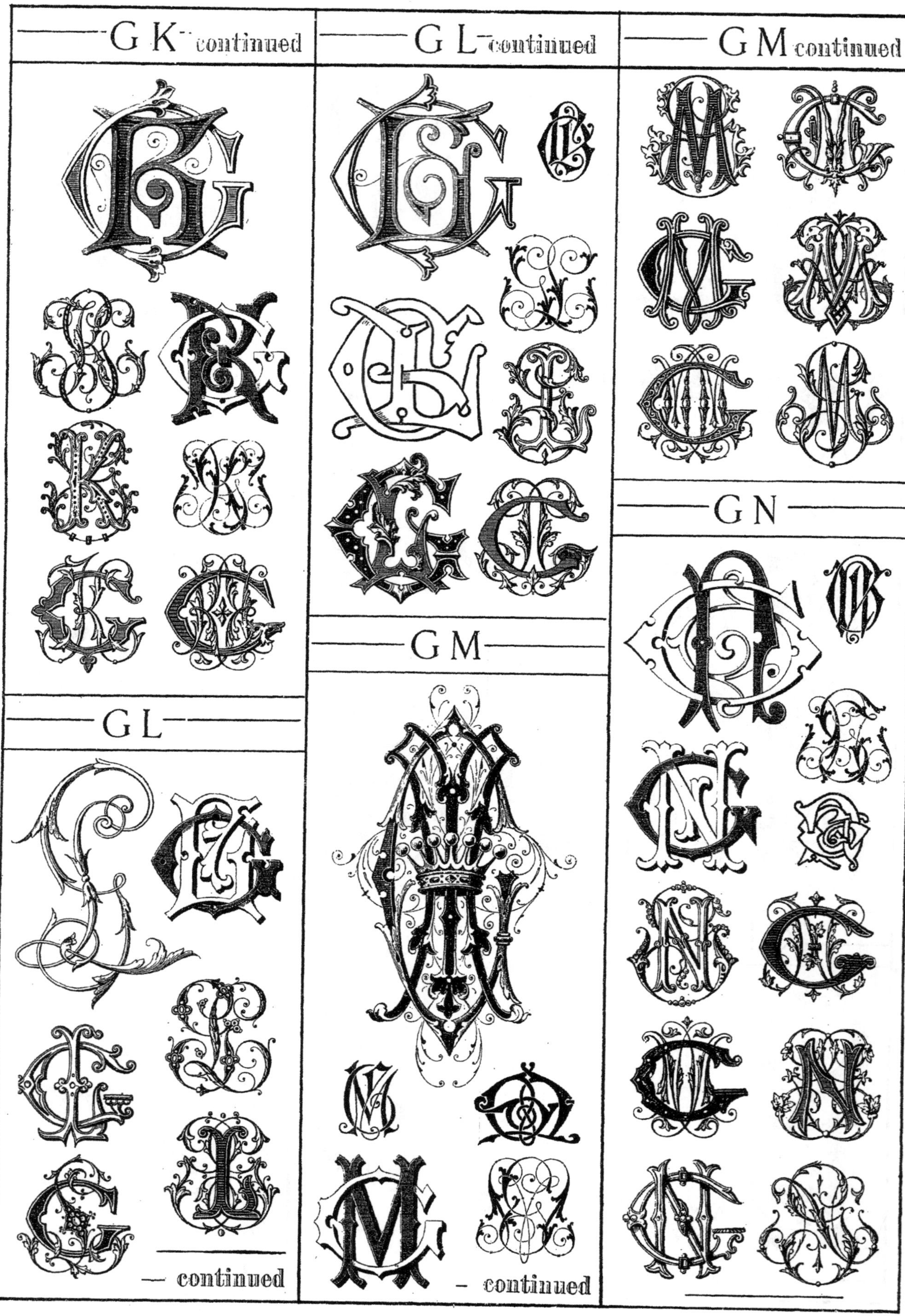
G K continued
G L continued
G M continued
G L
G M
G N
— continued
- continued

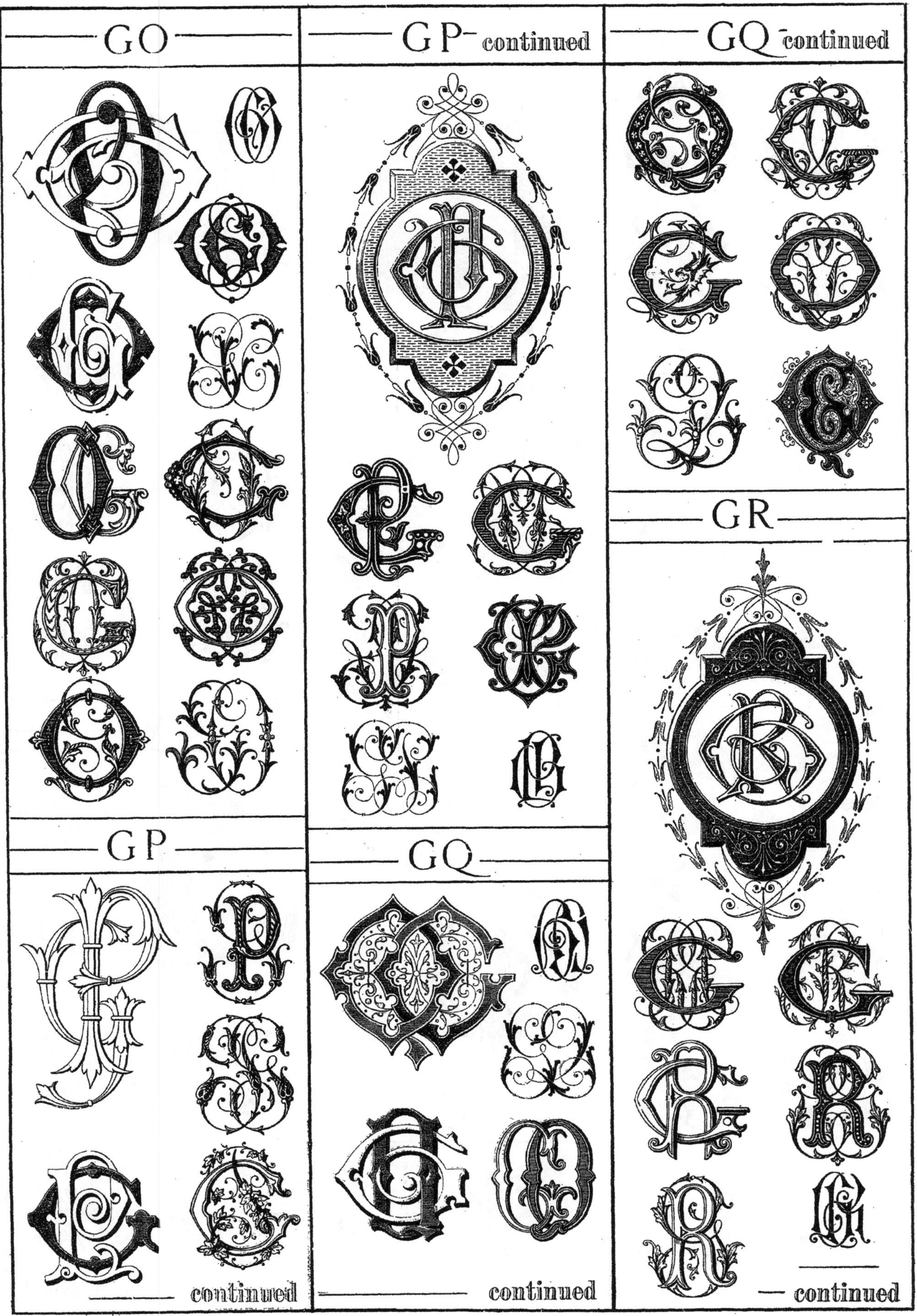
GO
GP
continued
GP–continued
GQ
continued
GQ–continued
GR
continued

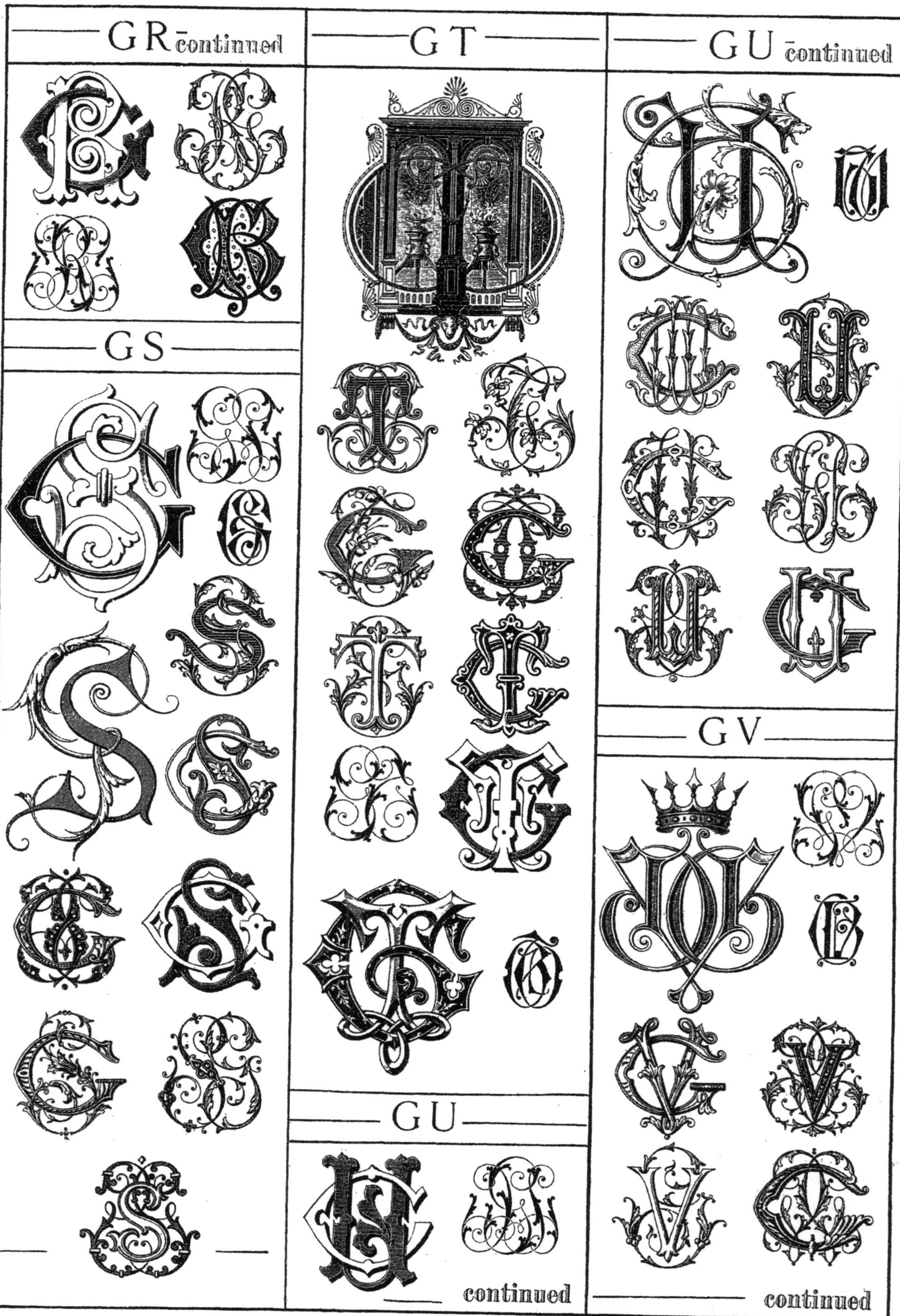
GR–continued
GT
GU–continued
GS
GU
GV
continued
continued

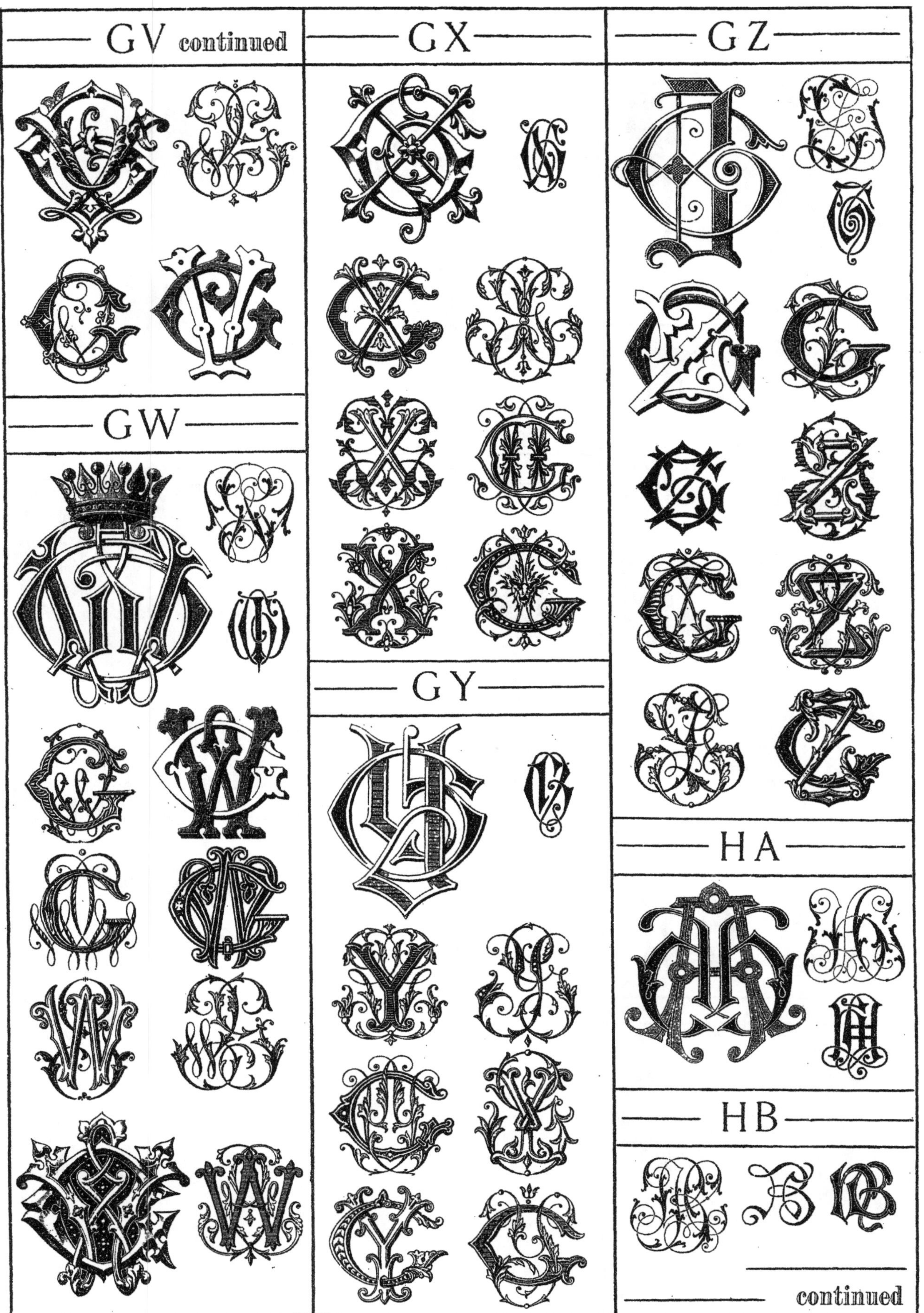
GV continued
GX
GZ
GW
GY
HA
HB
continued

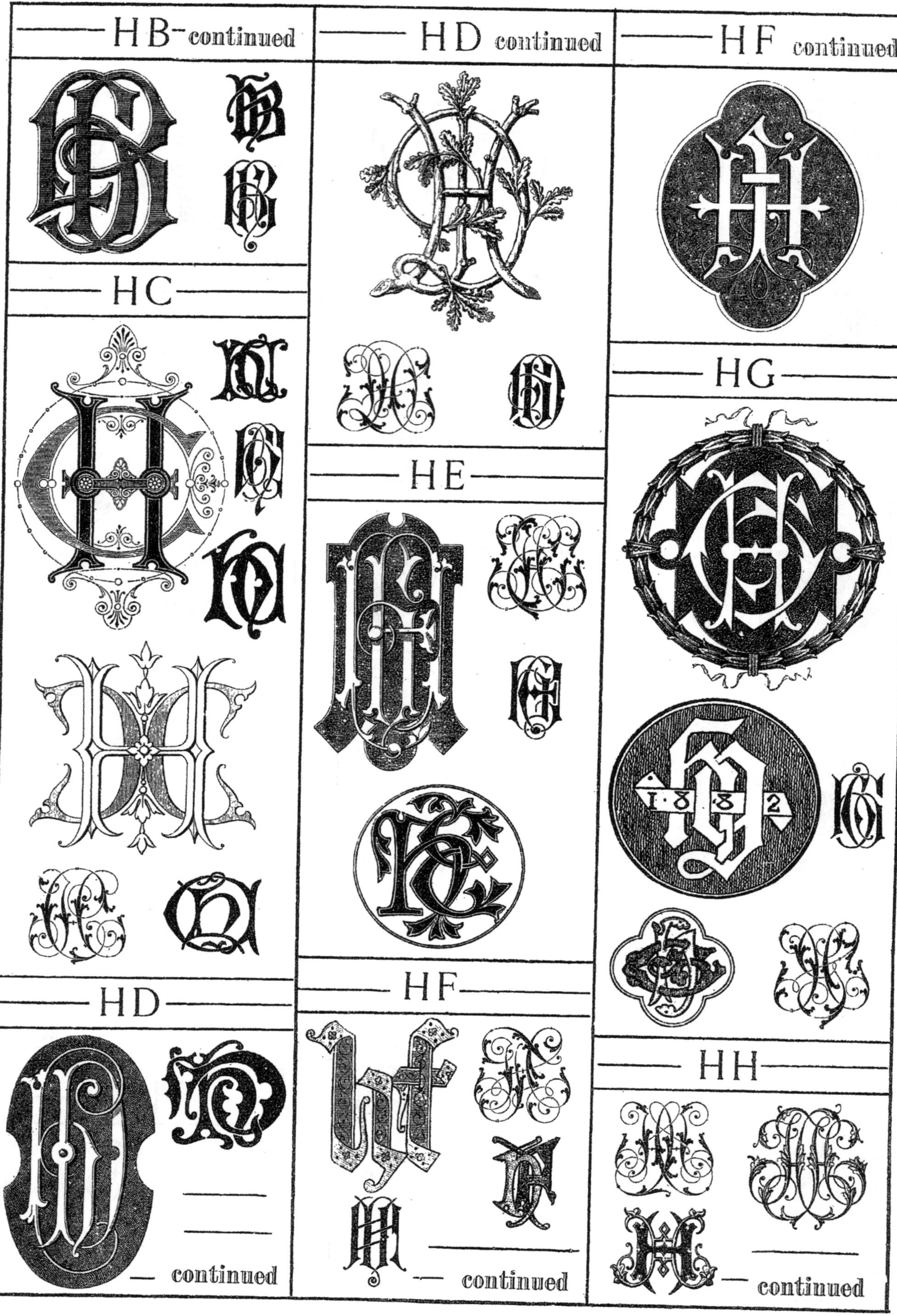

HB–continued
HC
HD
continued
HD continued
HE
HF
continued
HF continued
HG
1882
HH
continued

PLATE 42

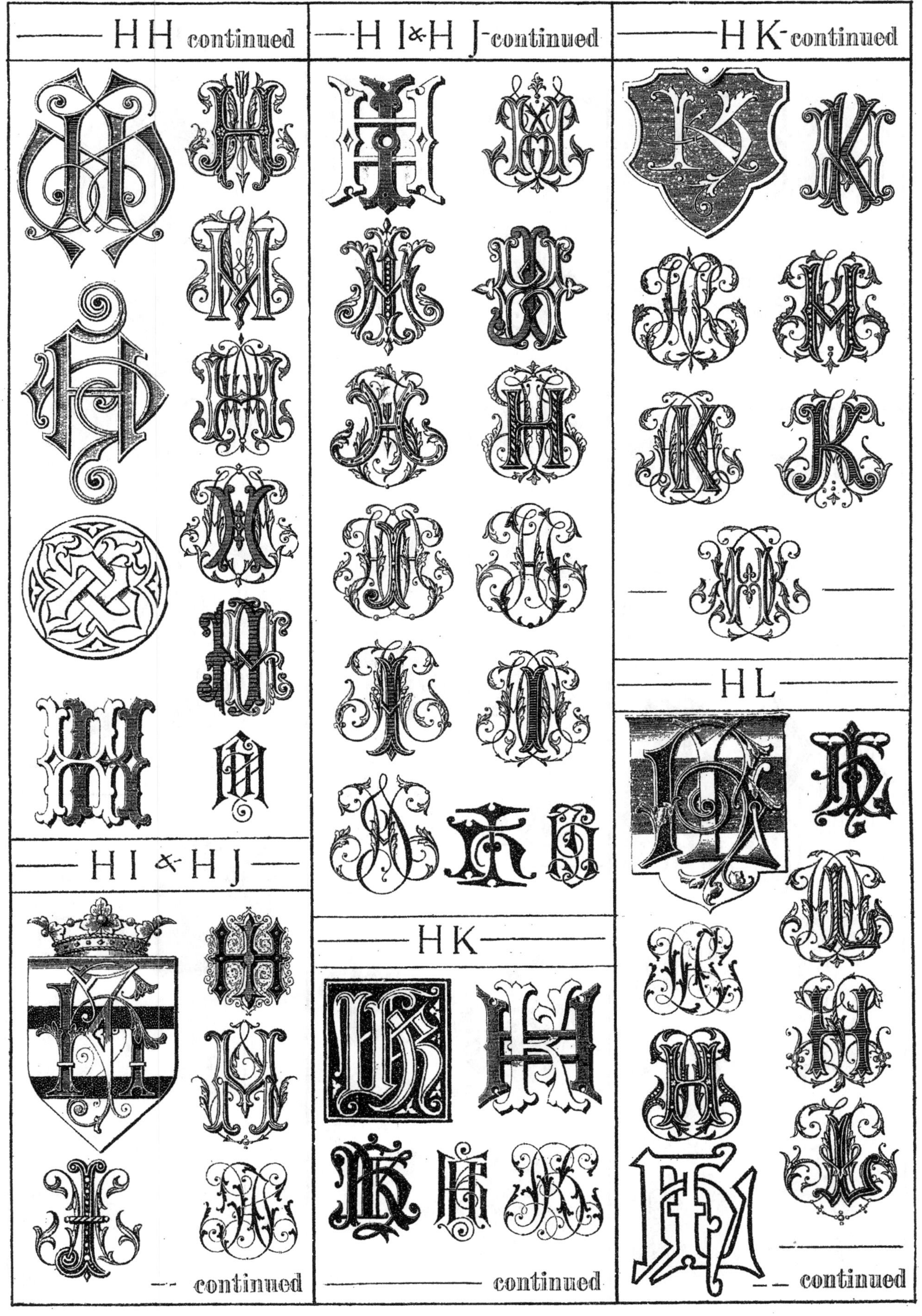
H H continued
H I & H J continued
H K continued
H I & H J
continued
H K
continued
H L
continued

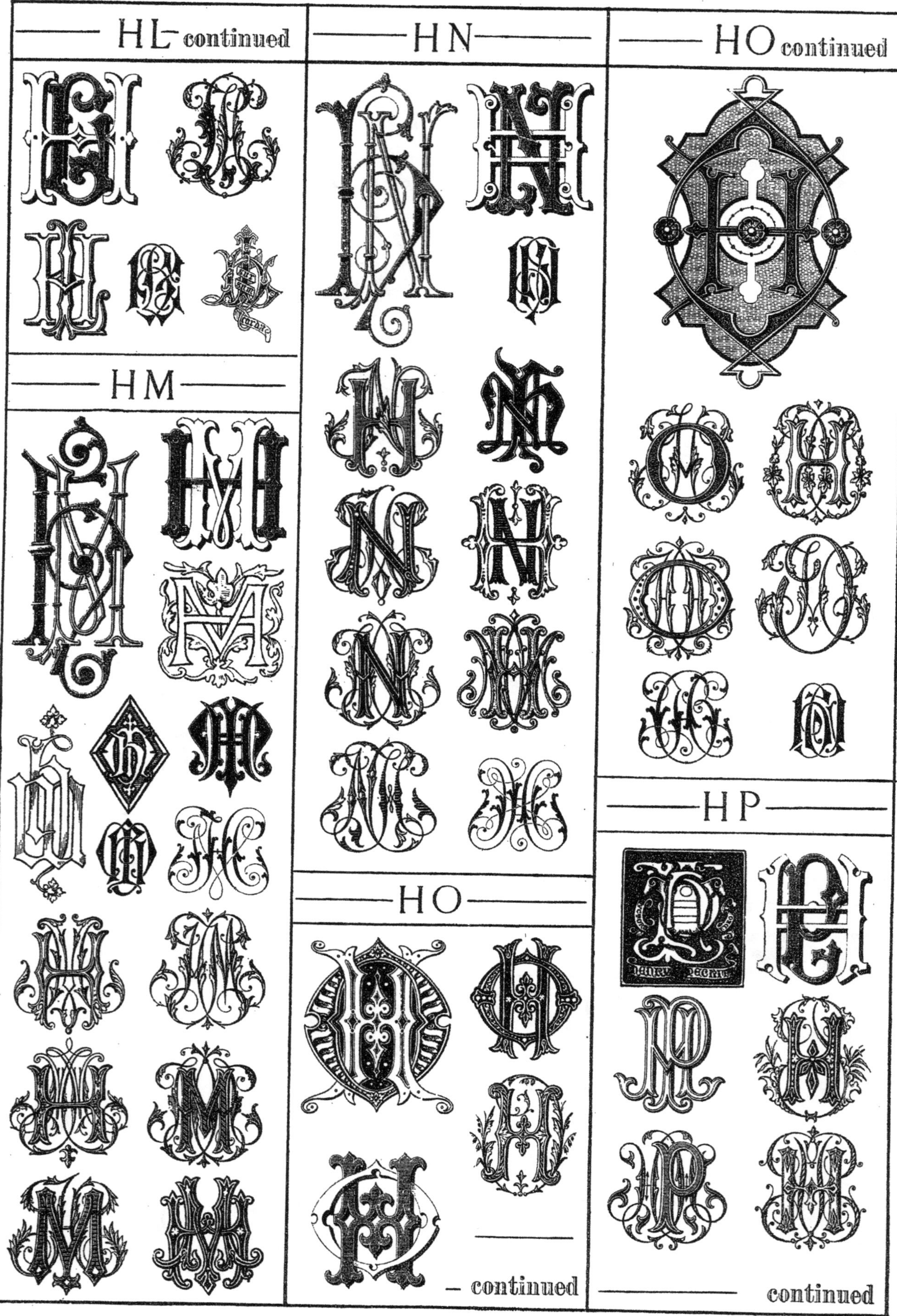

Plate 44

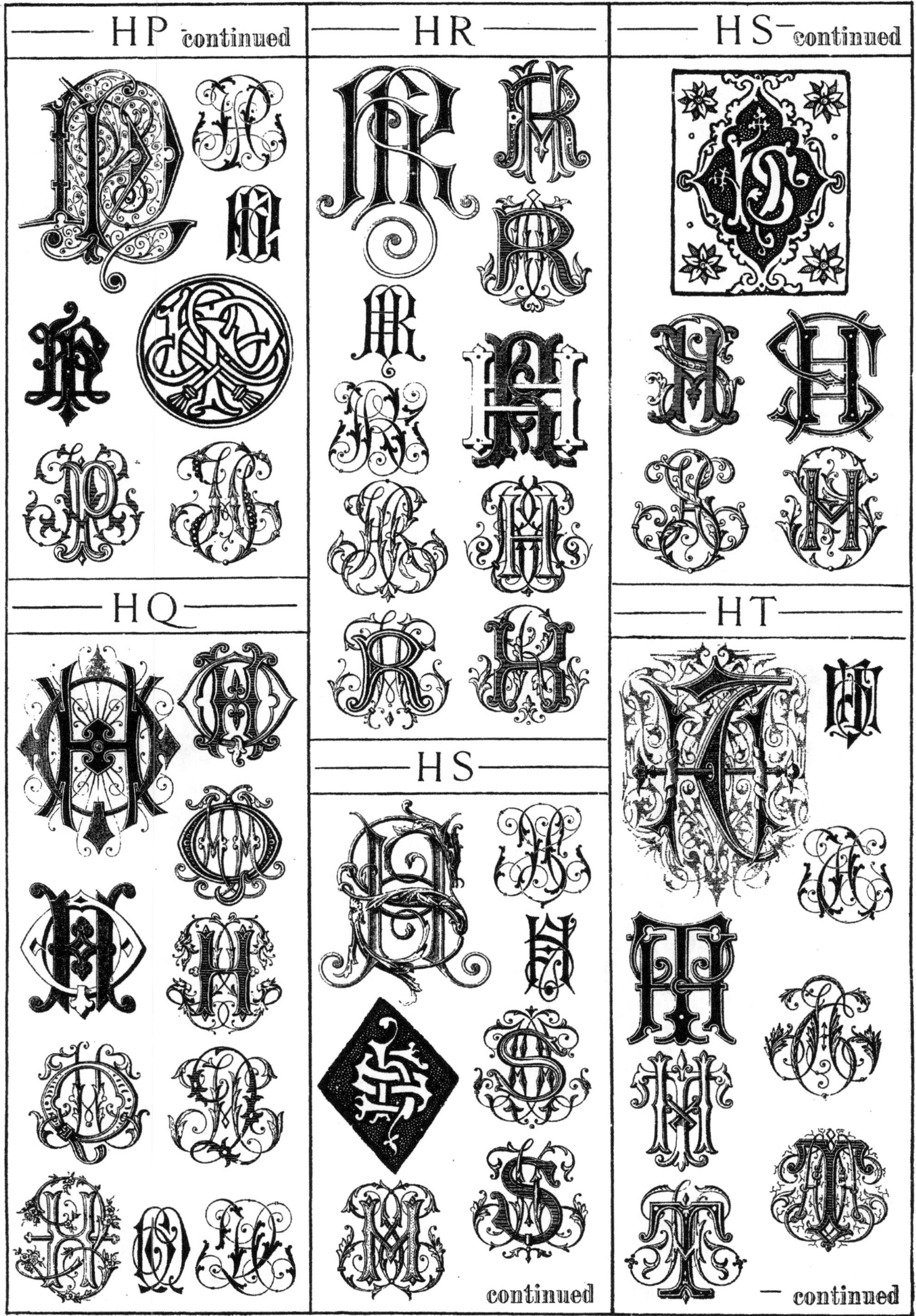
HP continued
HR
HS–continued
HQ
HS
HT
continued
– continued

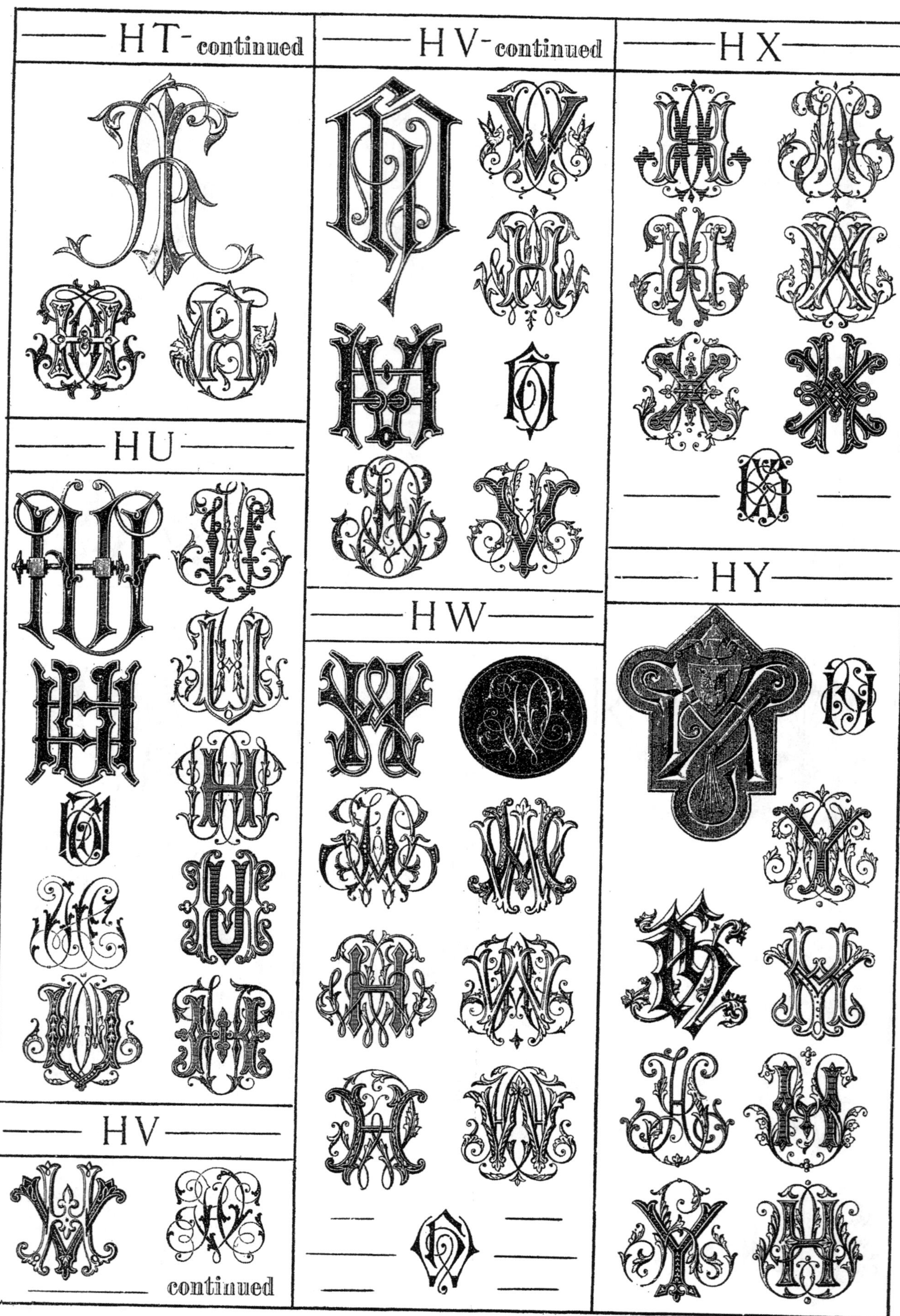
HT-continued
HV-continued
HX
HU
HW
HY
HV
continued

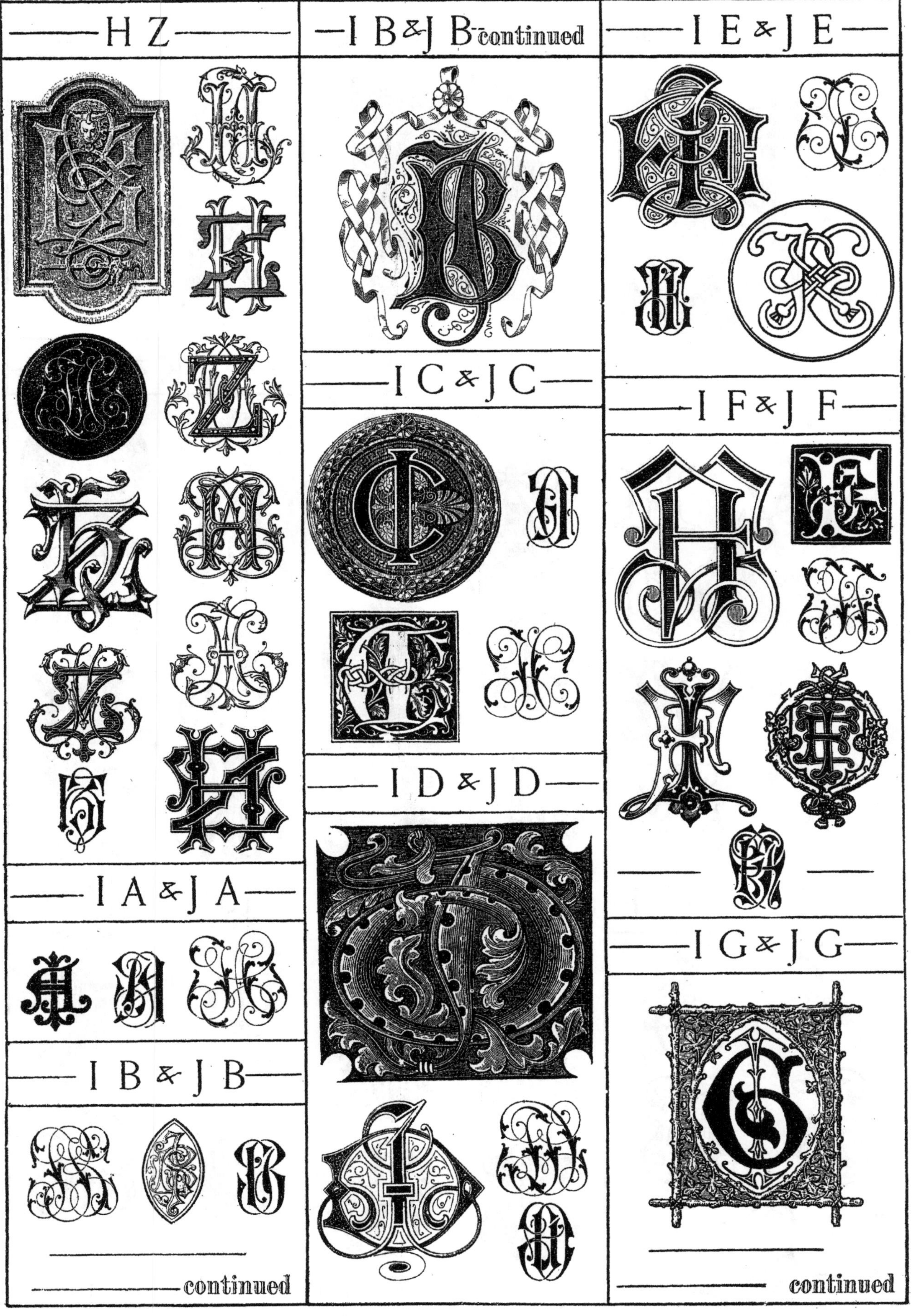
H Z
I B & J B continued
I E & J E
I C & J C
I F & J F
I D & J D
I A & J A
I G & J G
I B & J B
continued
continued

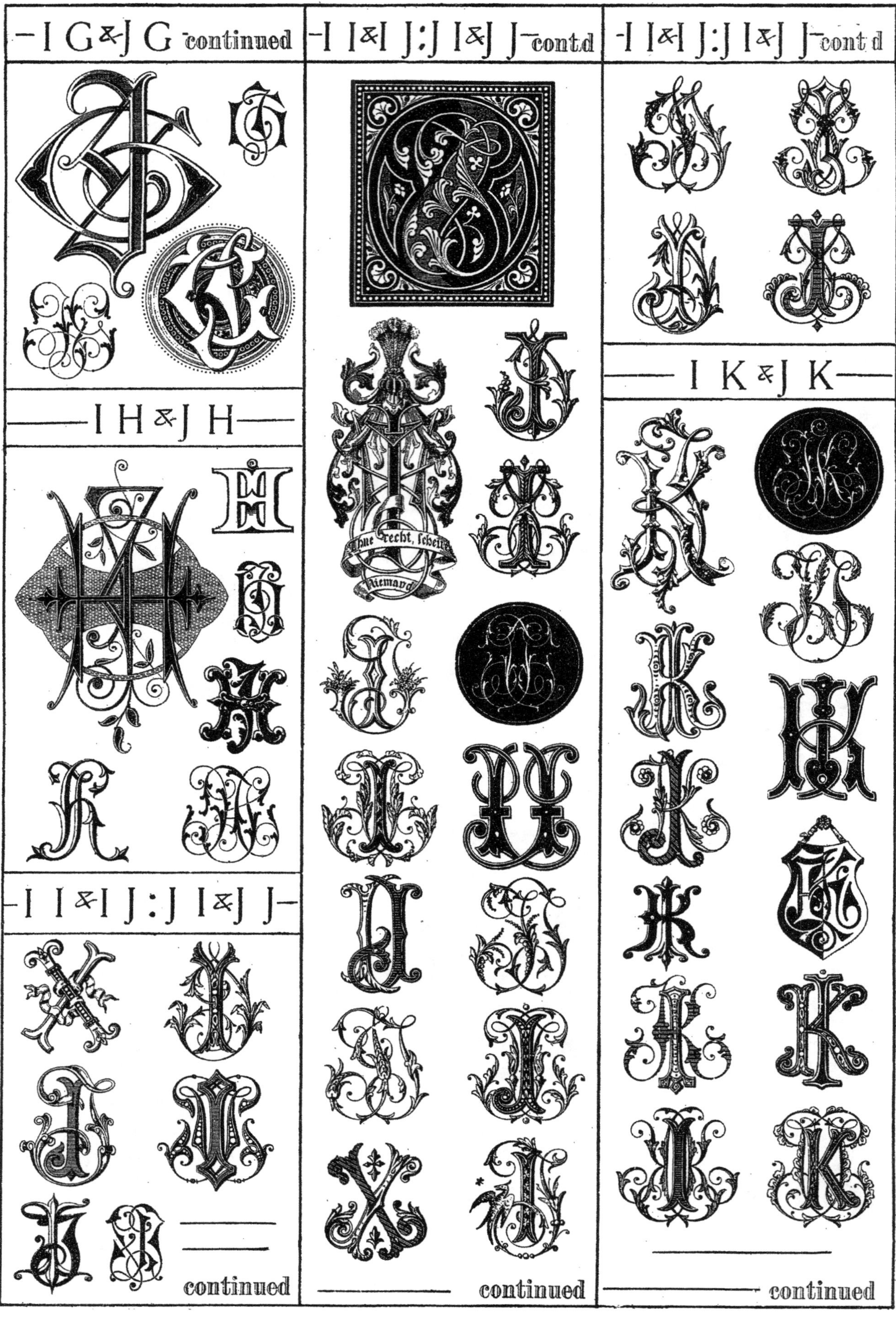
–I G & J G continued
–I H & J H–
–I I & I J : J I & J J–
continued
–I I & I J : J I & J J–cont.d
Ohne recht, scheinen
Niemand
continued
–I I & I J : J I & J J–cont.d
–I K & J K–
continued

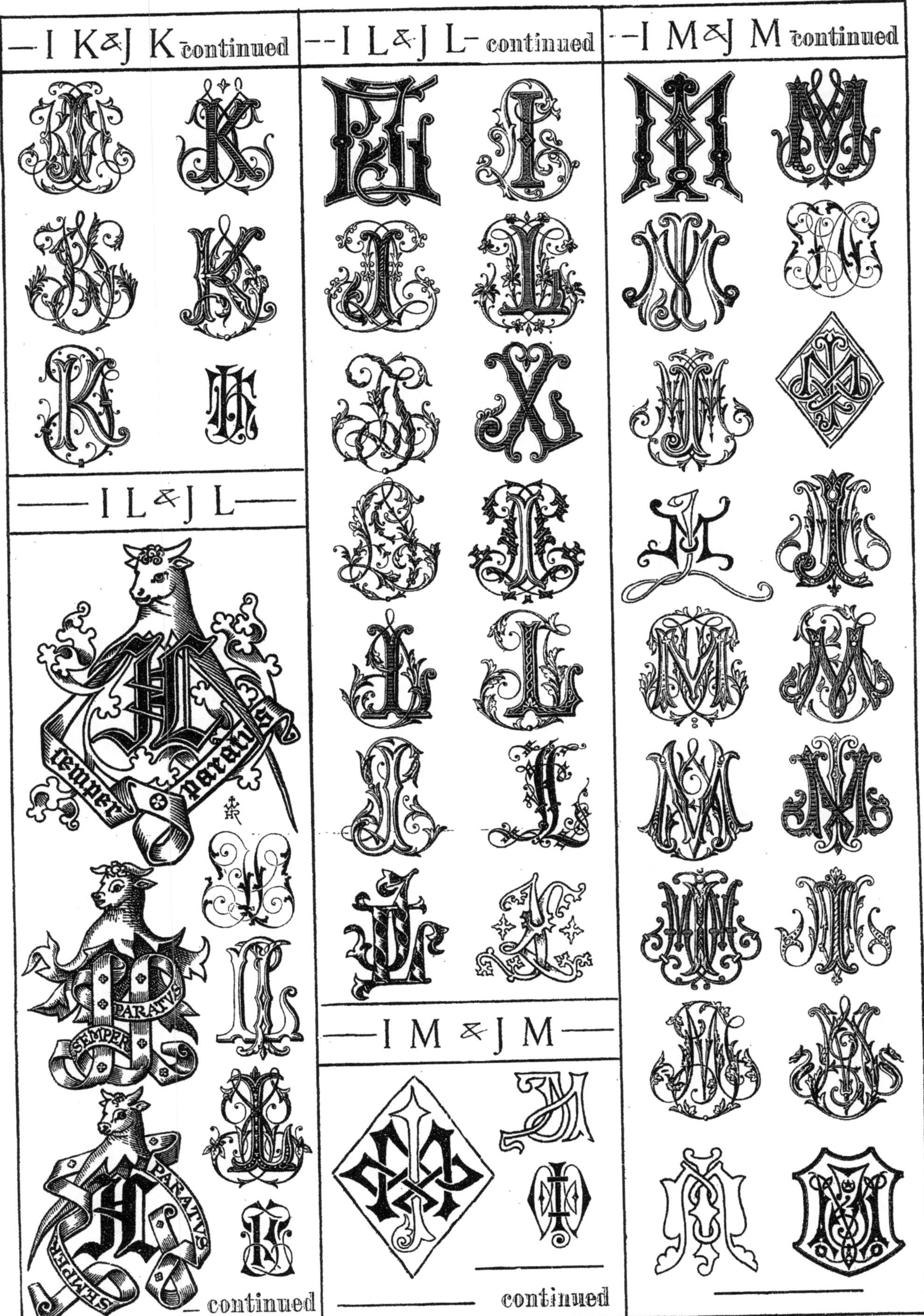
I K & J K continued
I L & J L continued
I M & J M continued
I L & J L
semper paratus
SEMPER PARATVS
SEMPER PARATVS
continued
I M & J M
continued

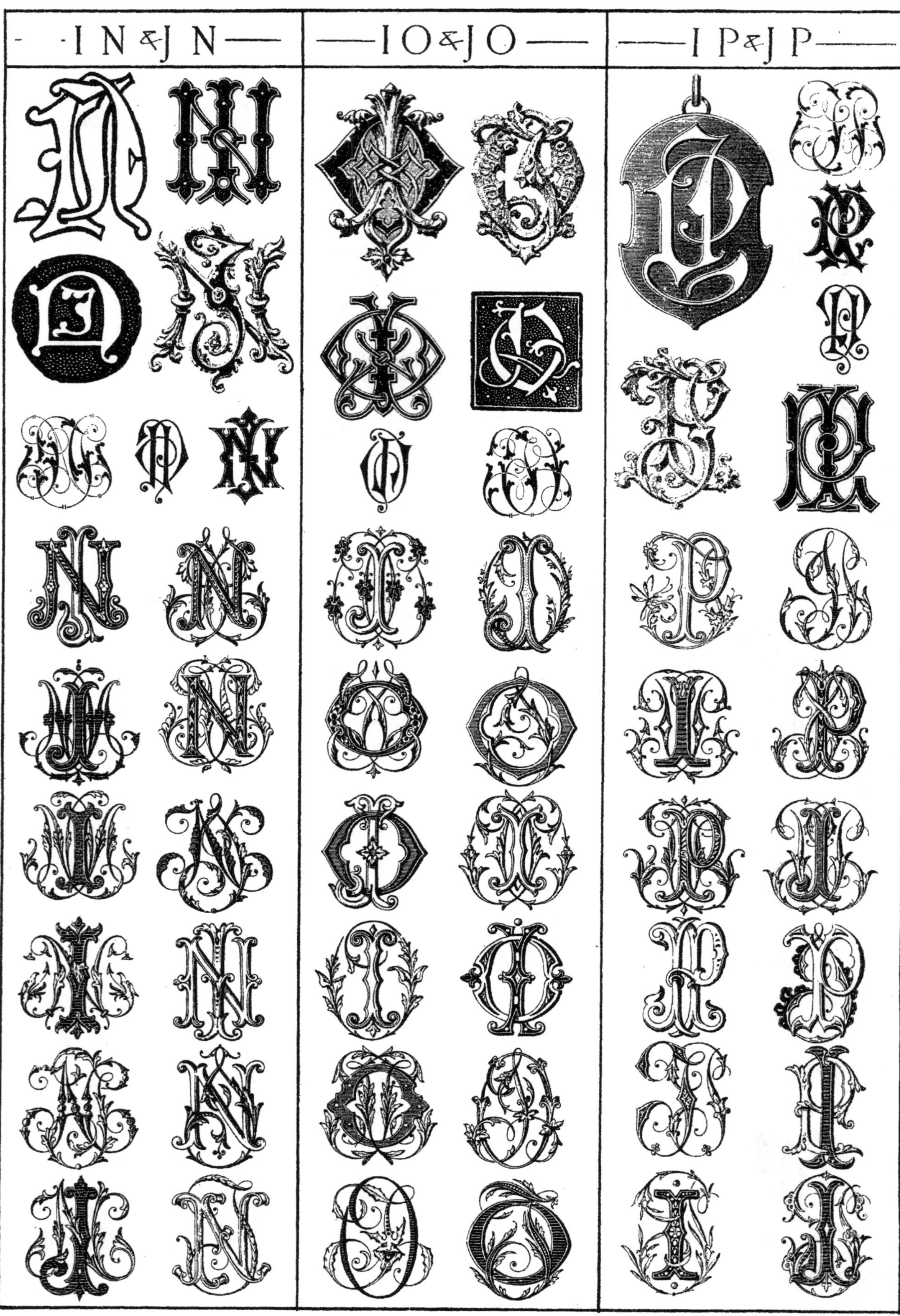
I N & J N
I O & J O
I P & J P

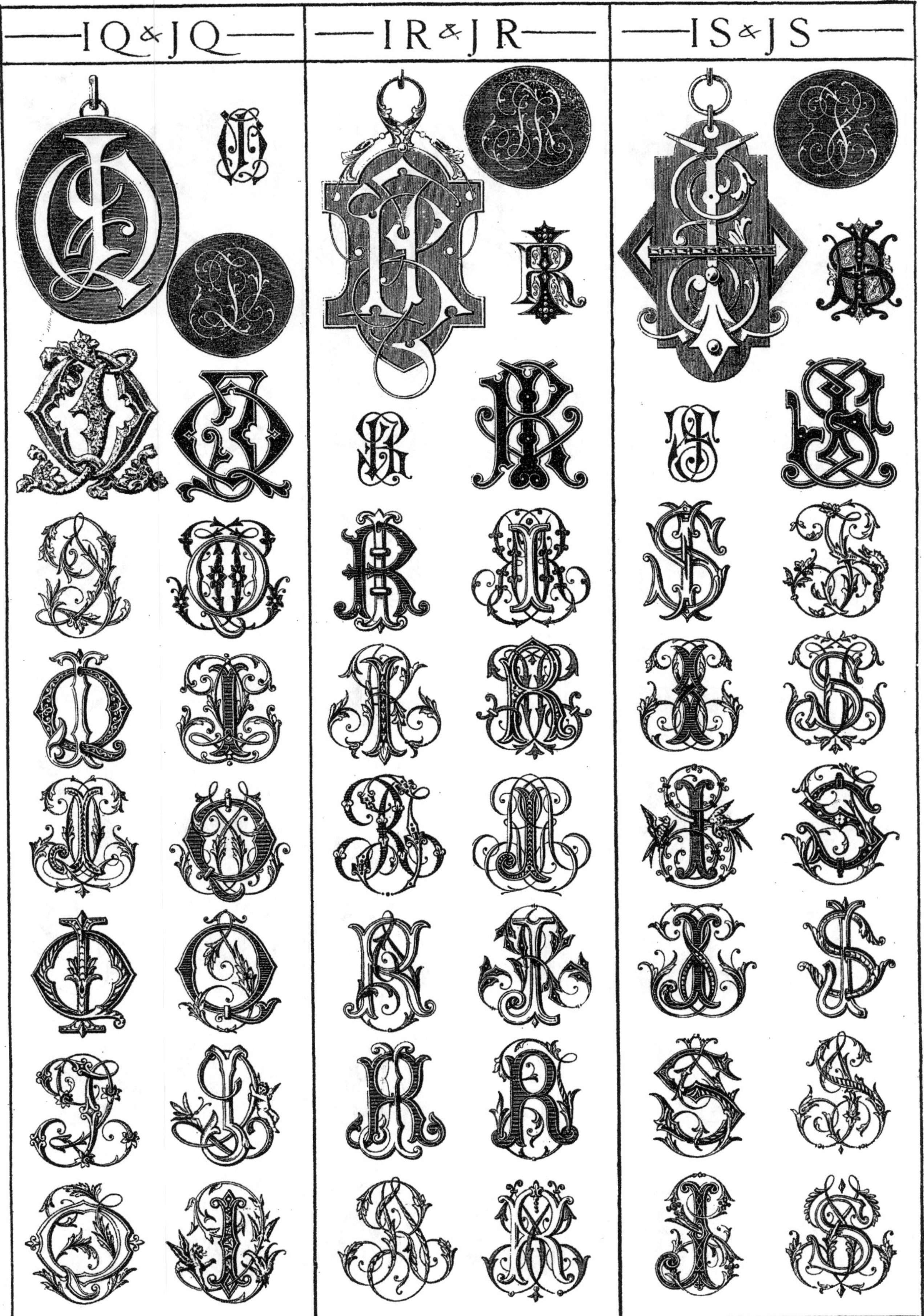
IQ & JQ
IR & JR
IS & JS

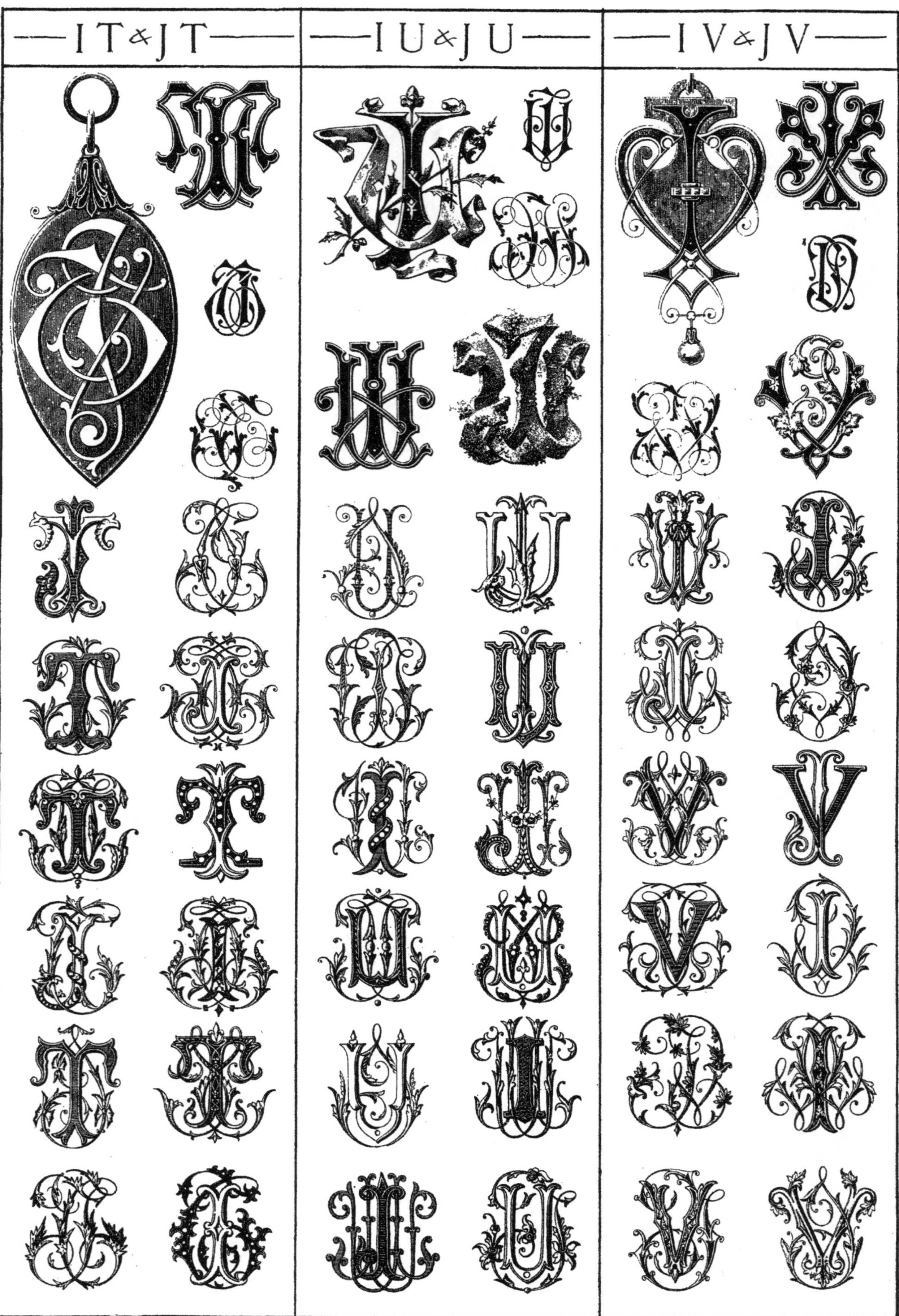
IT & JT
IU & JU
IV & JV

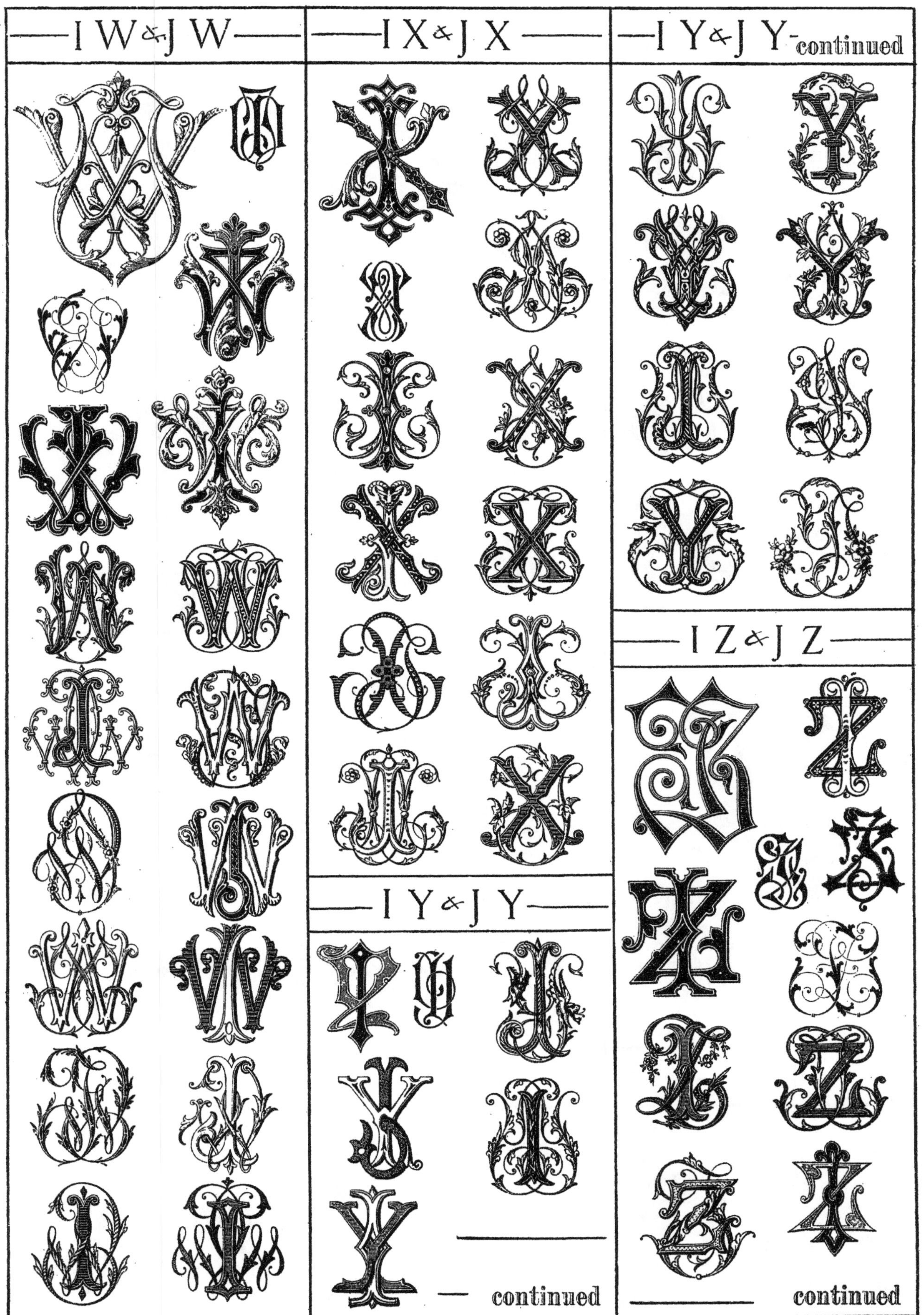

I W & J W
I X & J X
I Y & J Y- continued
I Y & J Y
continued
I Z & J Z
continued

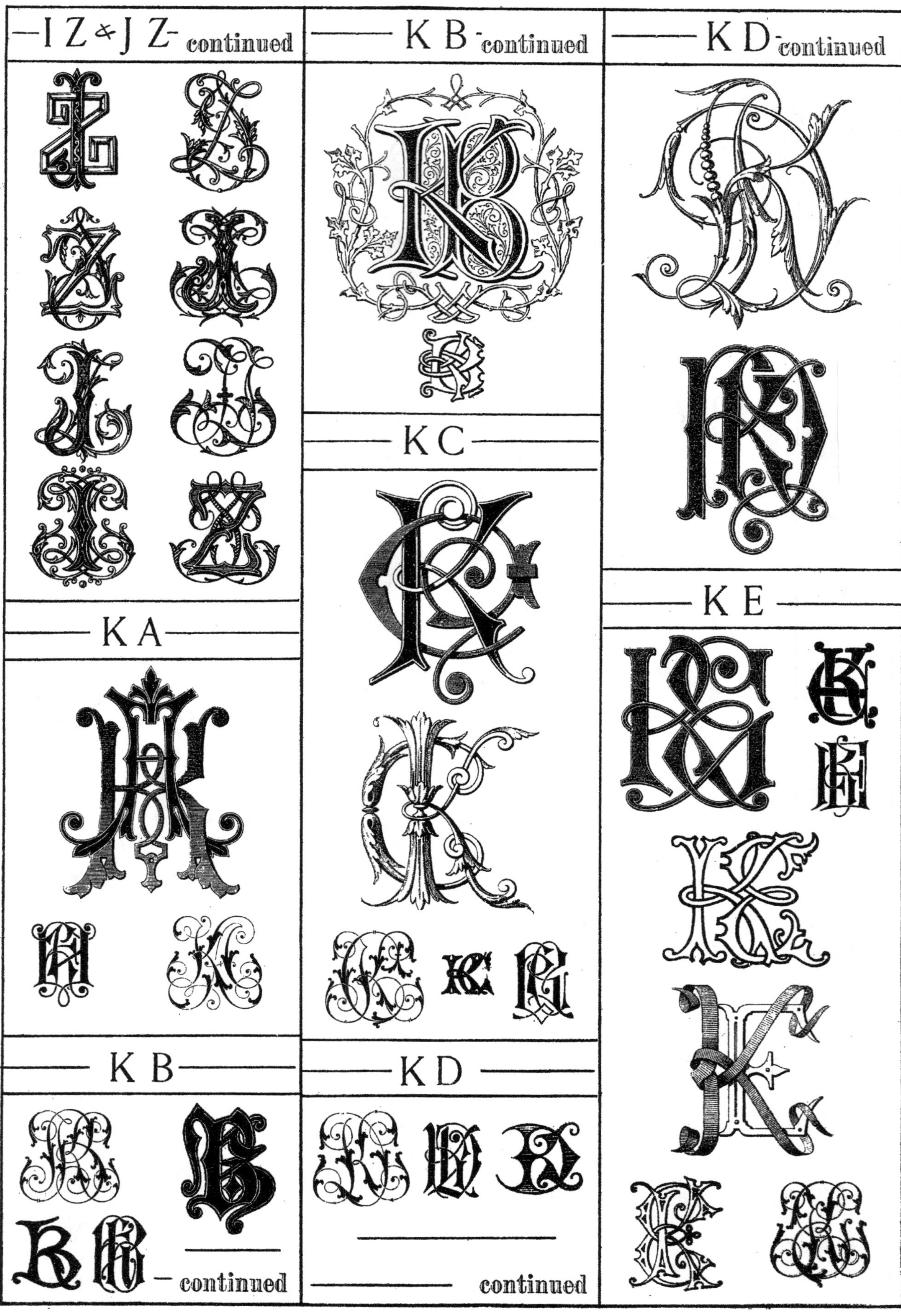

I Z & J Z continued
K B continued
K D continued
K A
K C
K E
K B
K D
continued
continued

KF
KH
KK continued
KG
KI & KJ
KL
KK
continued
continued

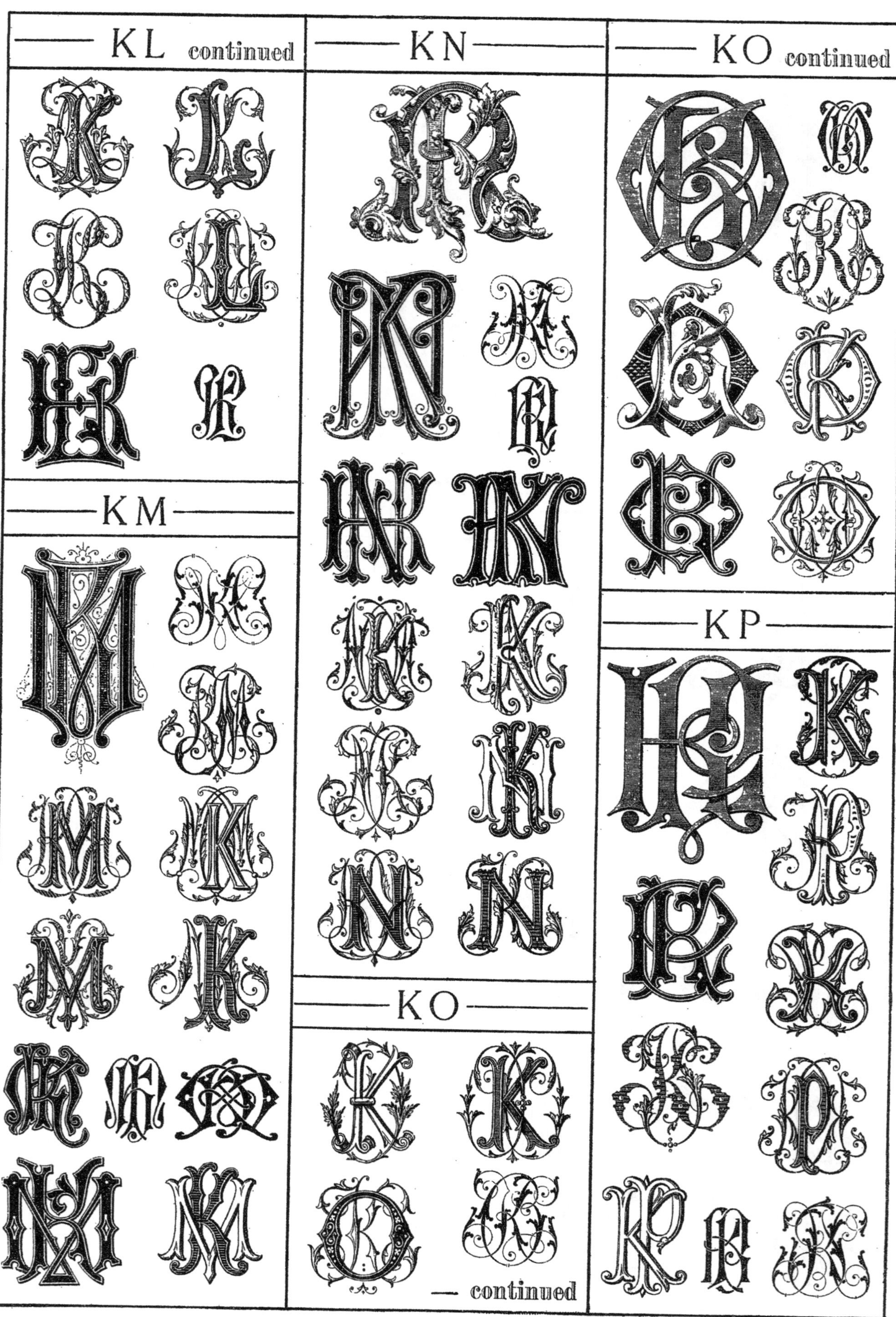
KL continued
KN
KO continued
KM
KO
— continued
KP

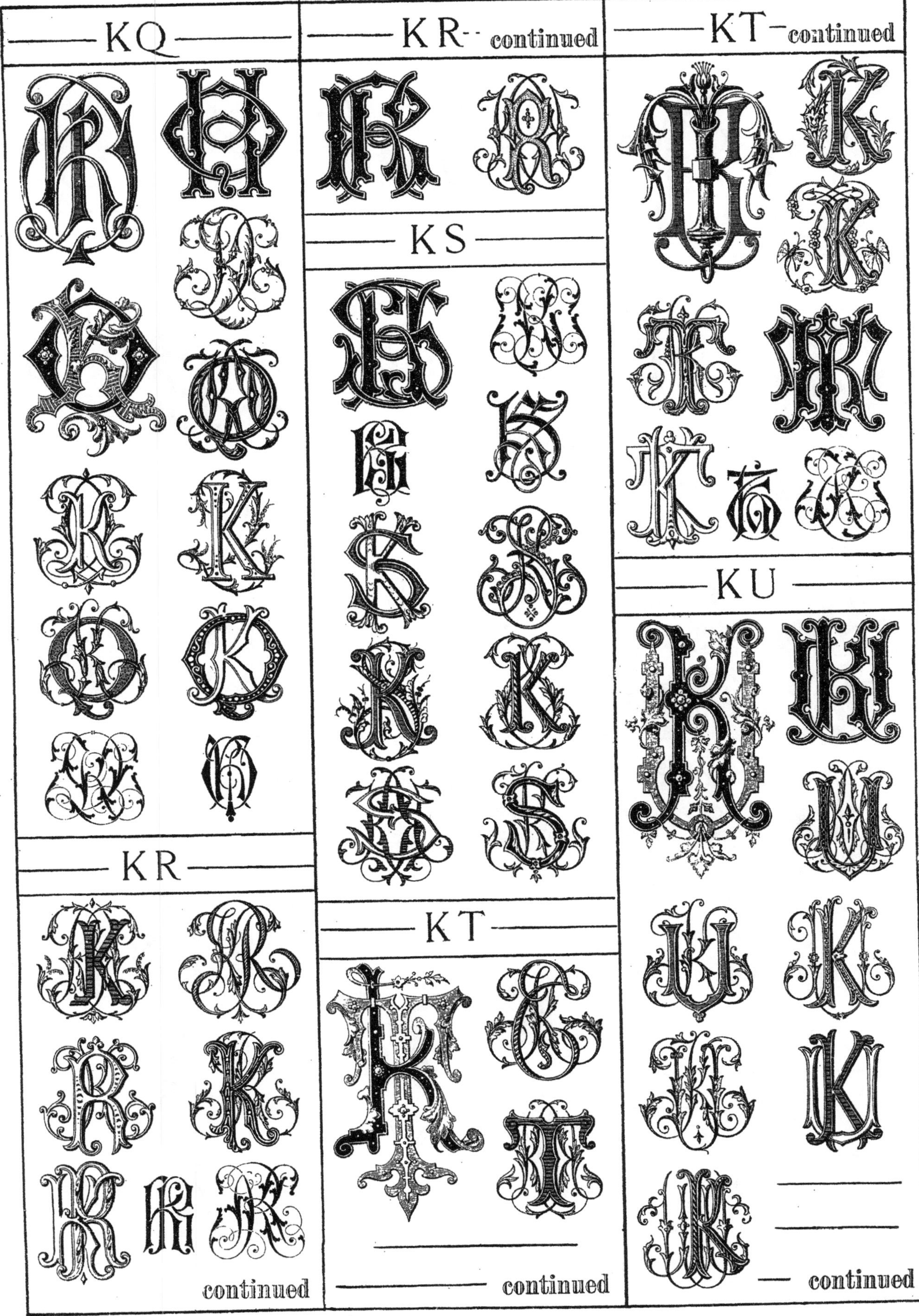
KQ
KR-- continued
KS
KT–continued
KU
KR
KT
continued
continued
continued

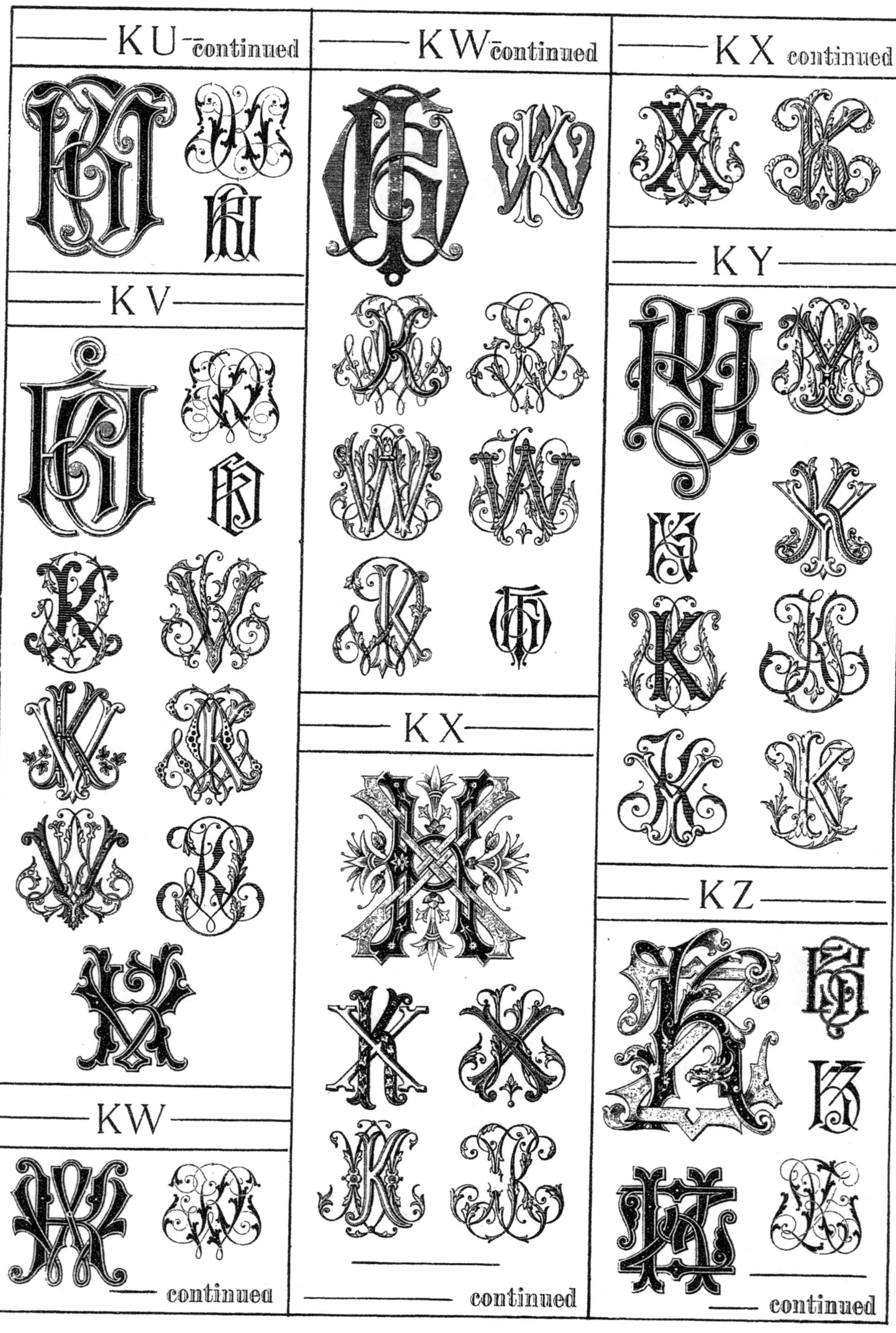
KU—continued
KV
KW
continued
KW—continued
KX
continued
KX continued
KY
KZ
continued

Plate 58

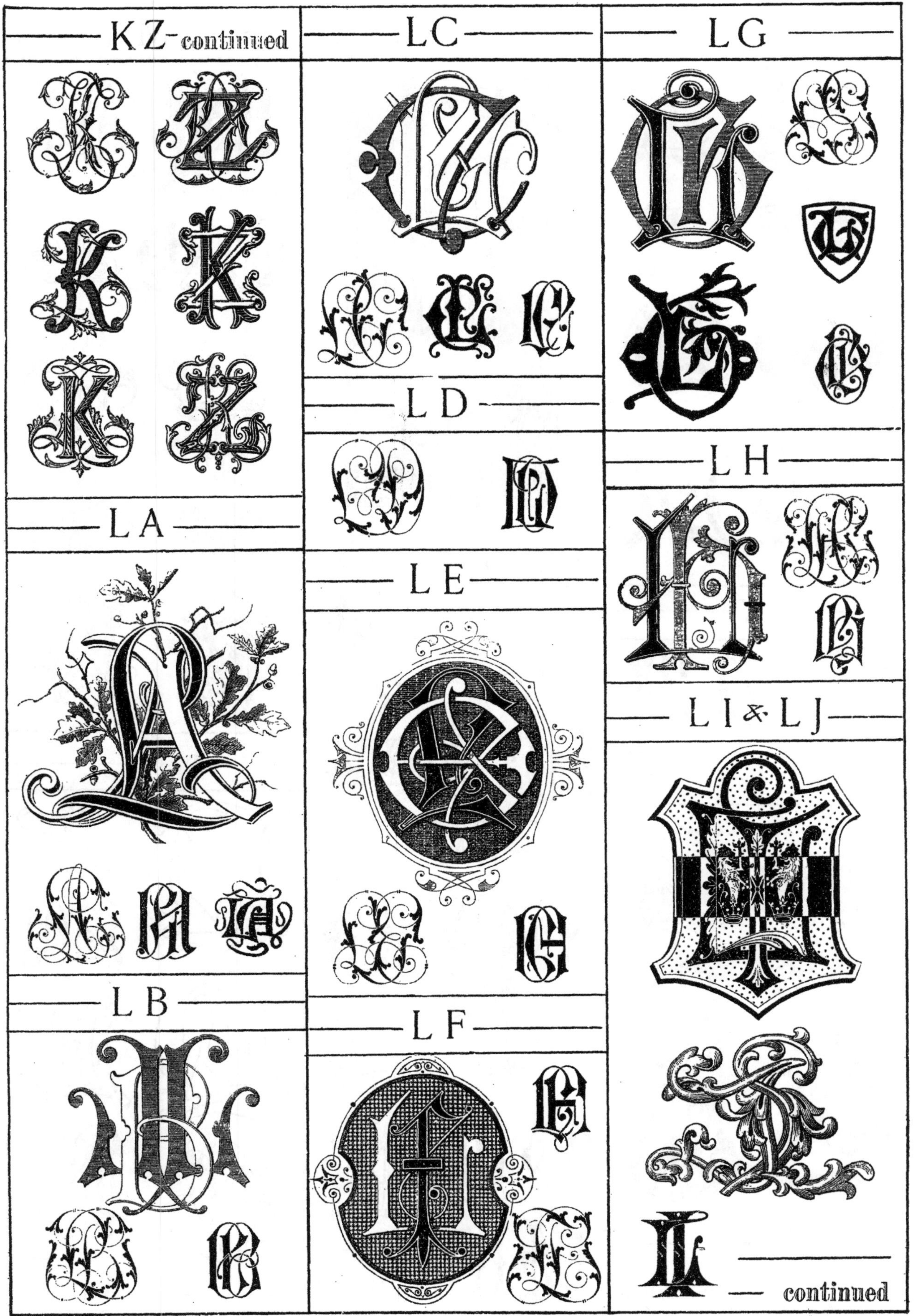
KZ-continued
LC
LG
LD
LH
LA
LE
LI & LJ
LB
LF
continued

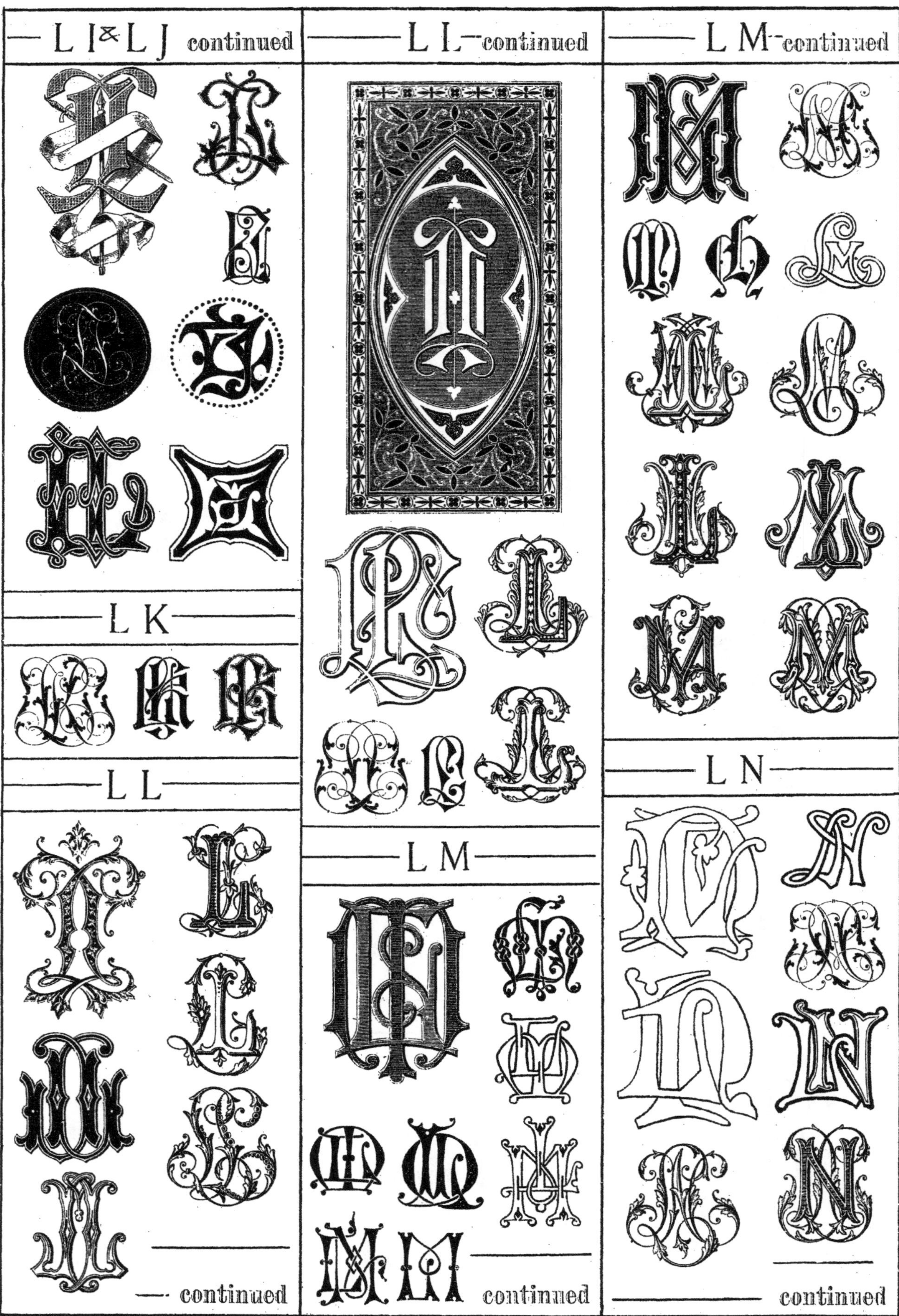
L I & L J continued
L L continued
L M continued
L K
L L
L M
L N
continued
continued
continued

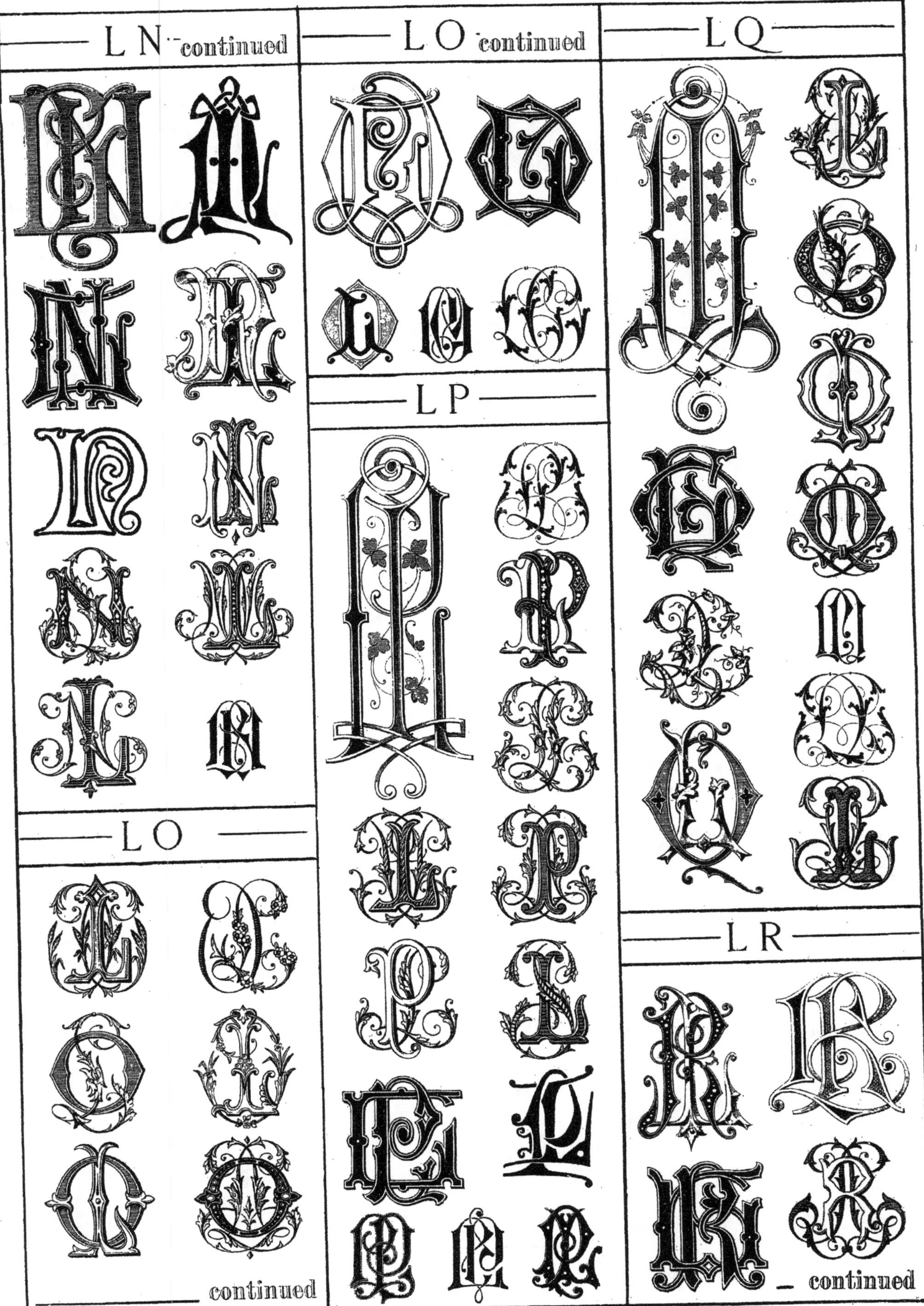
LN continued
LO continued
LQ
LP
LO
LR
continued
continued

LR—continued
LS—continued
LU—continued
LT
LS
LU
LV
— continued
continued
— continued
continued

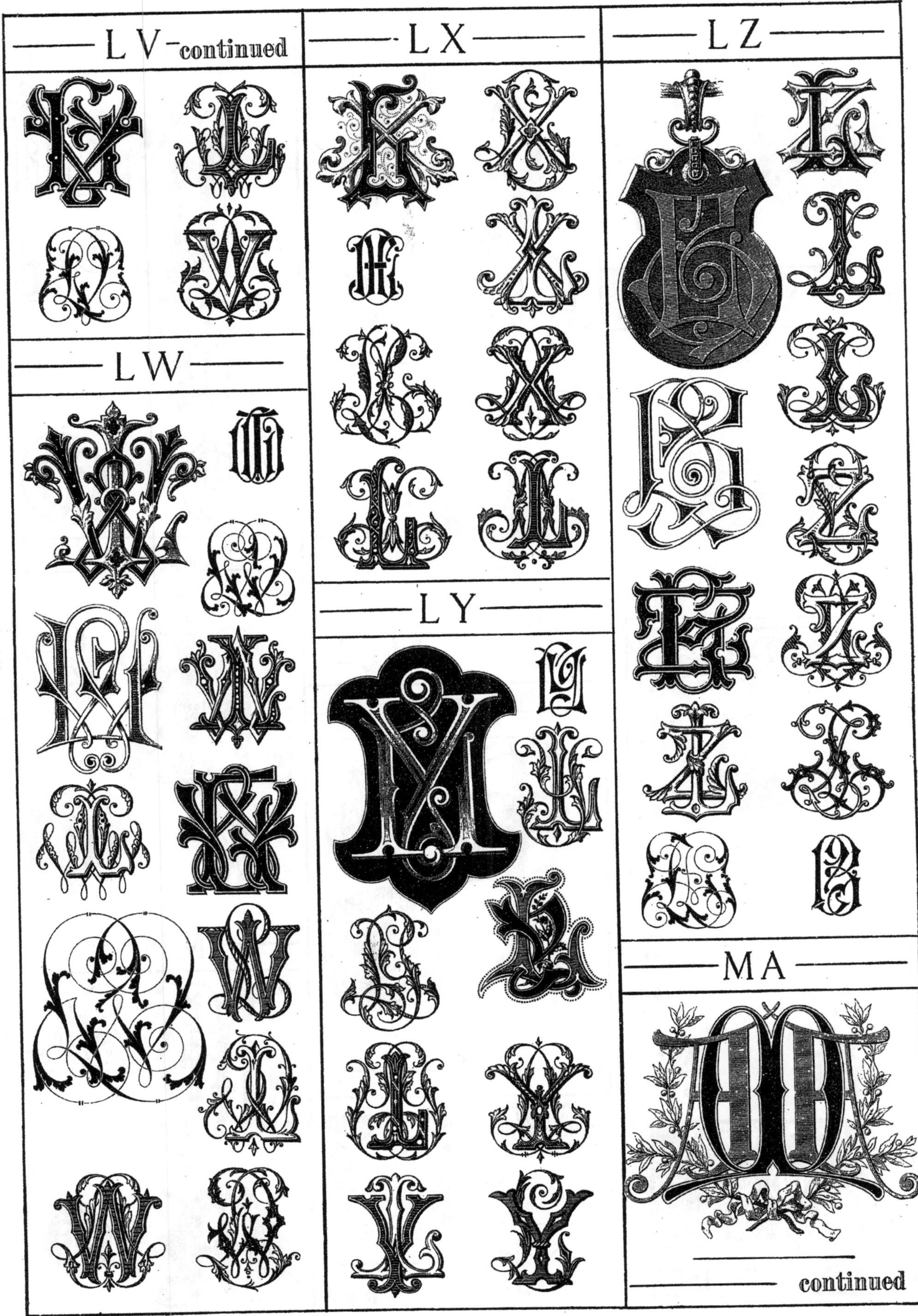

LV continued
LX
LZ
LW
LY
MA
continued

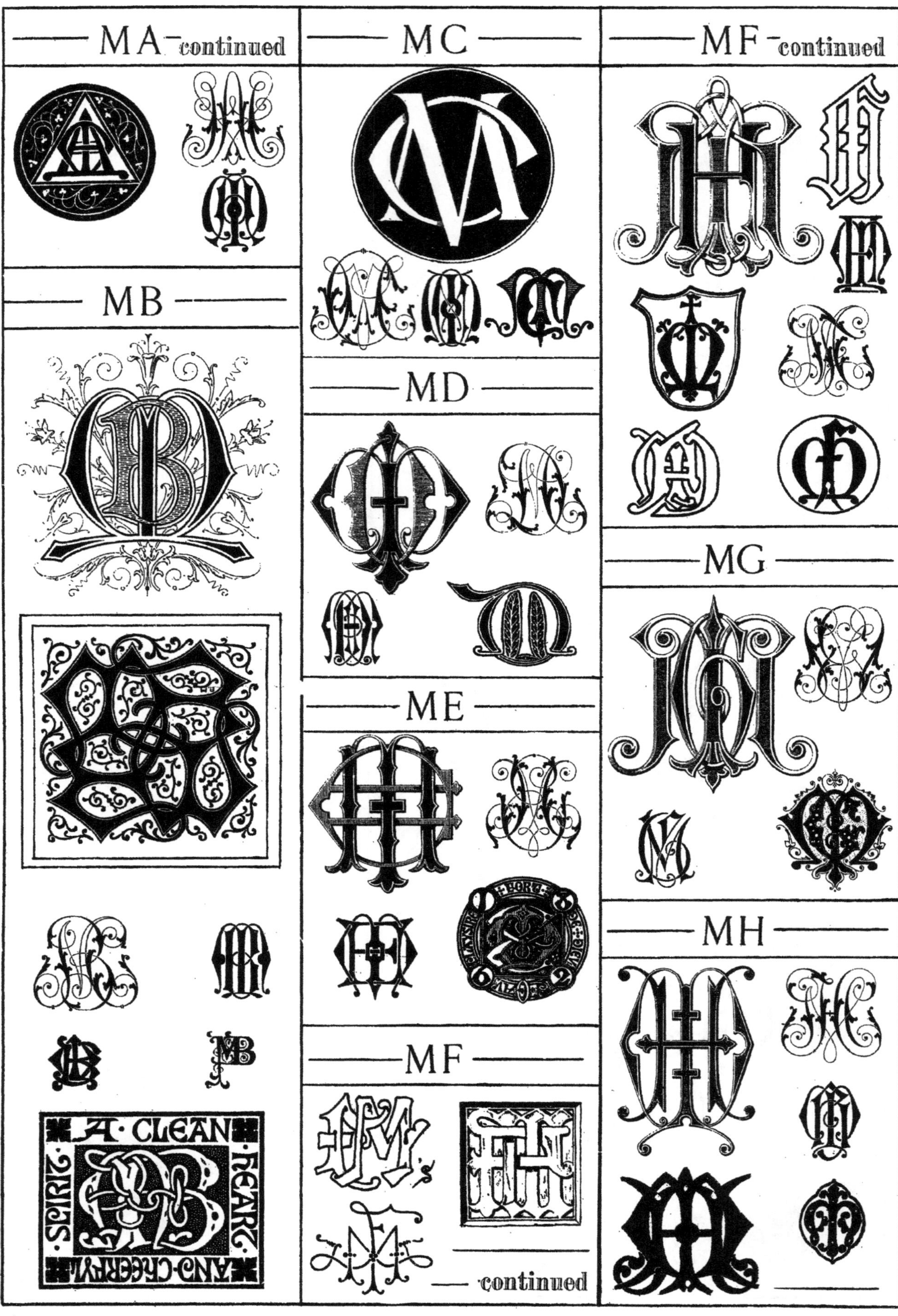
MA continued
MB
MC
MD
ME
MF
continued
MF continued
MG
MH
A CLEAN HEART AND CHEERFUL SPIRIT

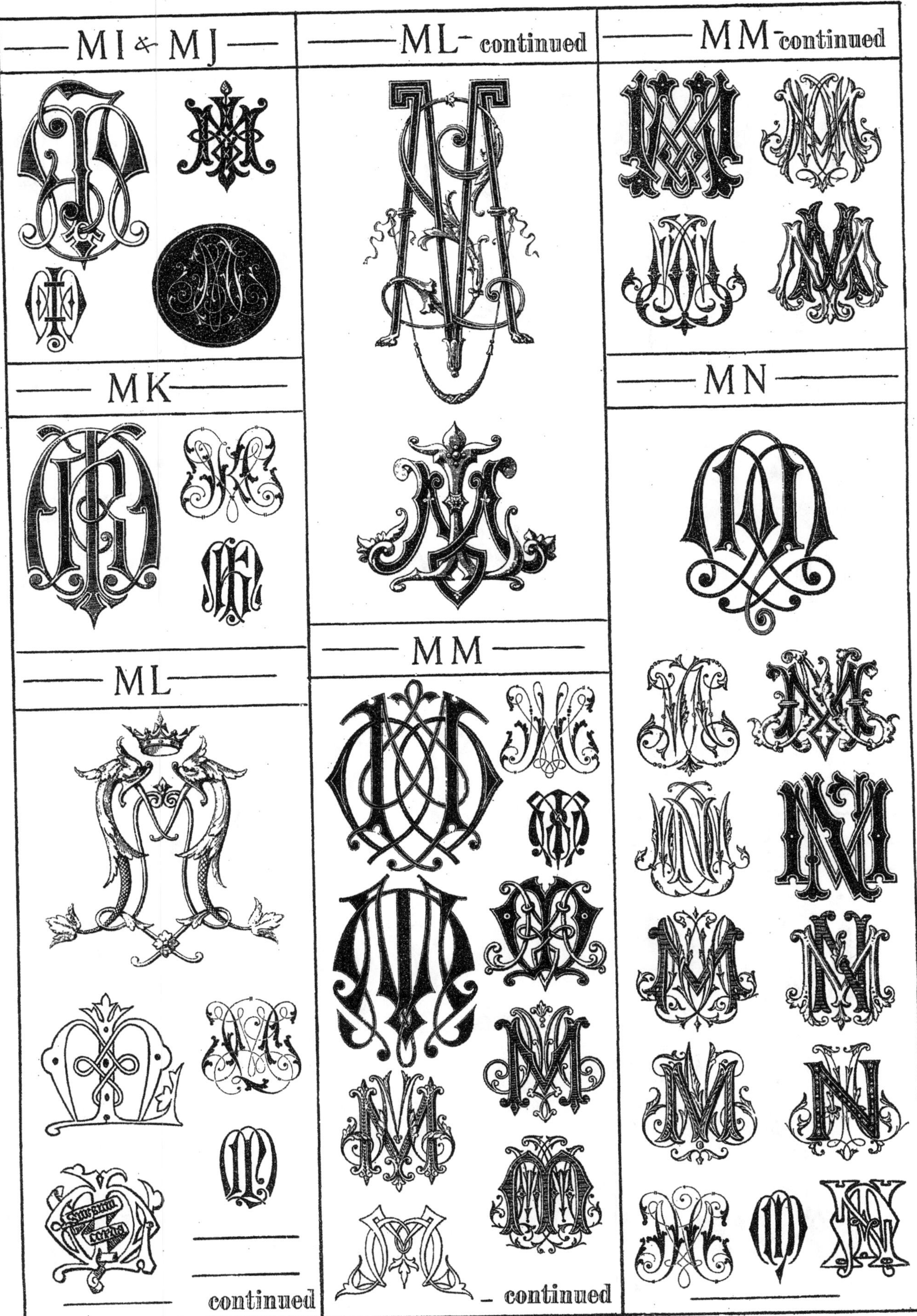
MI & MJ
ML- continued
MM- continued
MK
MN
ML
MM
continued
- continued

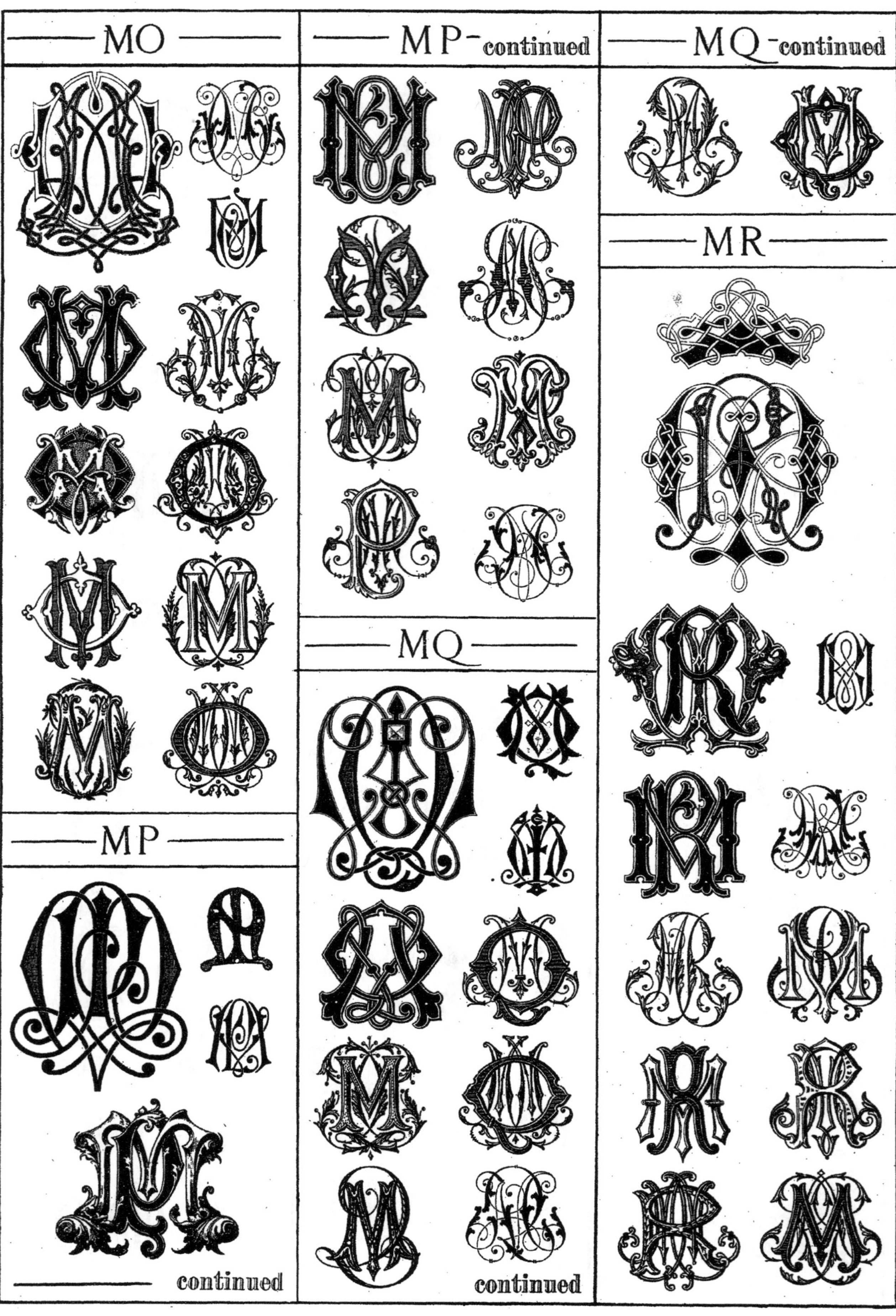
MO
MP–continued
MQ–continued
MR
MQ
MP
continued
continued

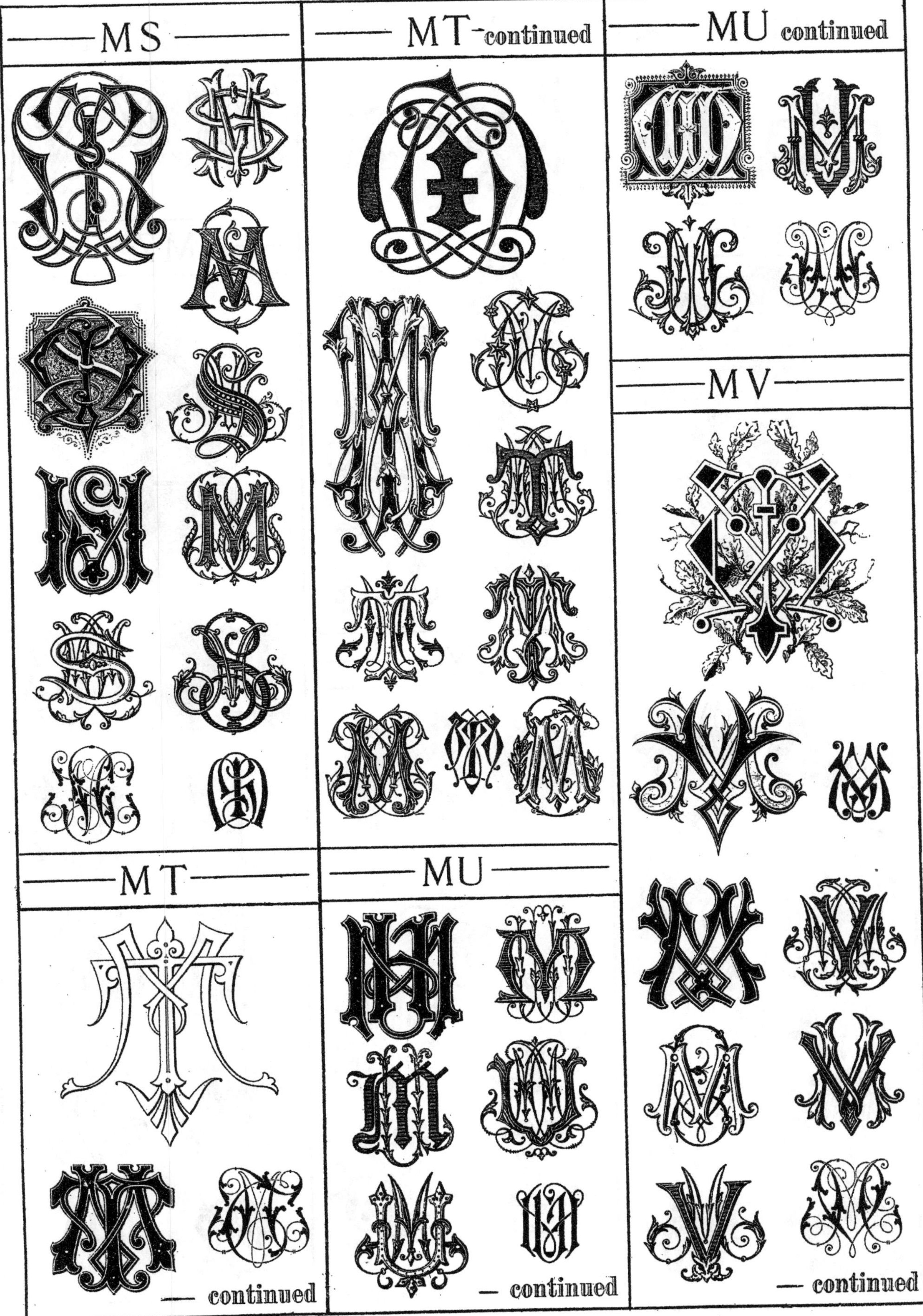
MS
MT continued
MU continued
MV
MT
MU
continued
continued
continued

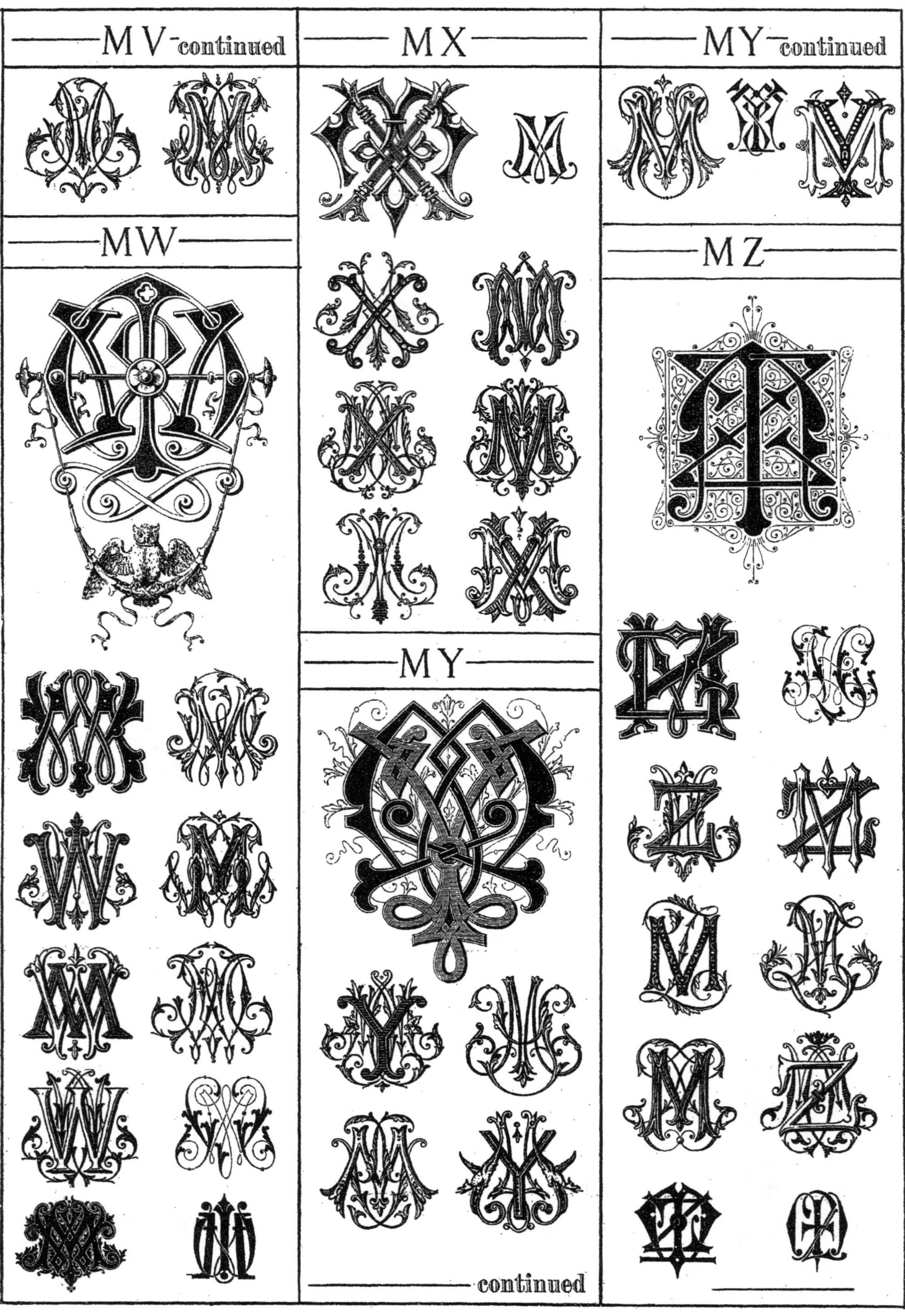
MV continued
MX
MY continued
MW
MZ
MY
continued

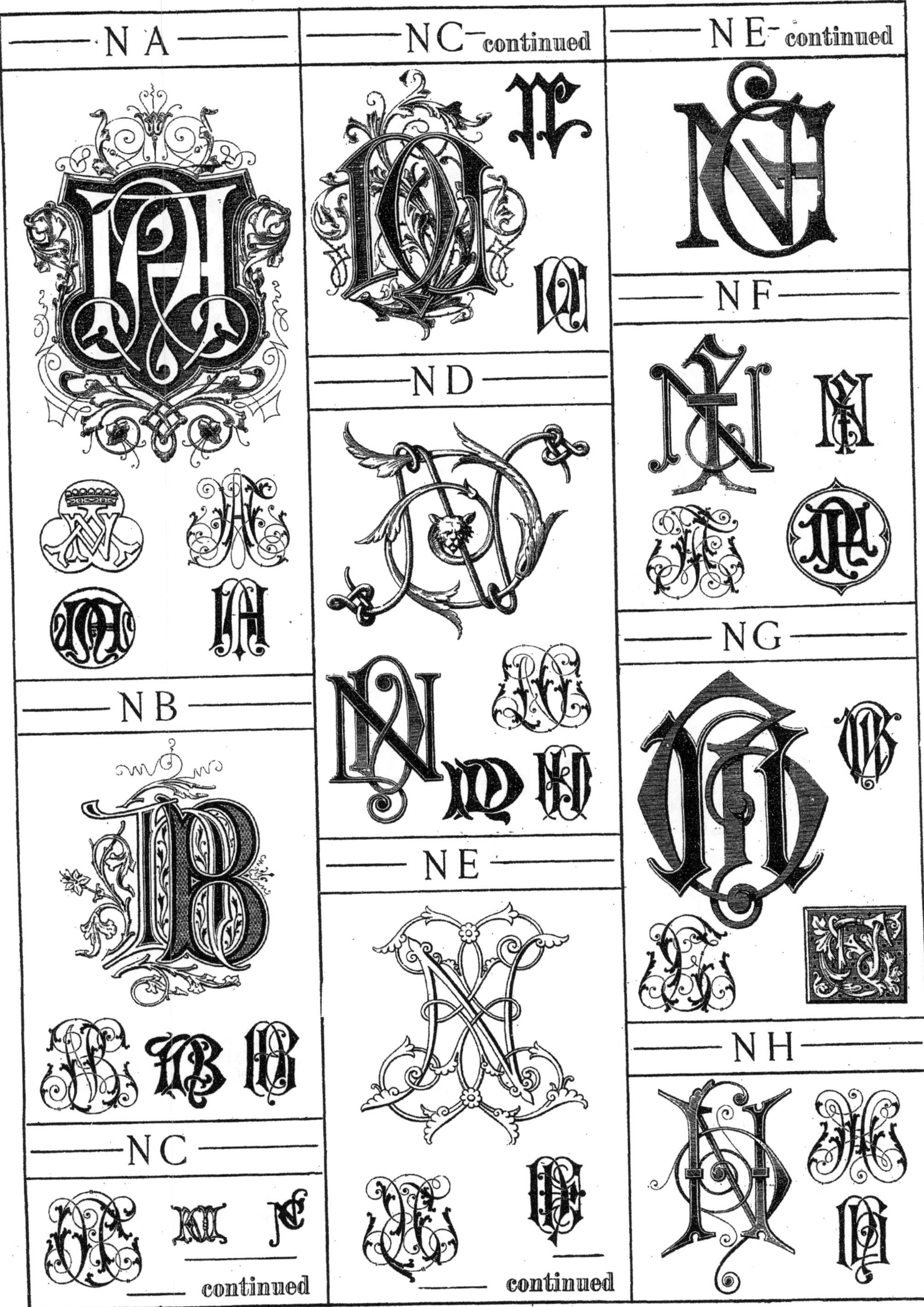
N A
N C continued
N E continued
N F
N D
N G
N B
N E
N H
N C
continued
continued

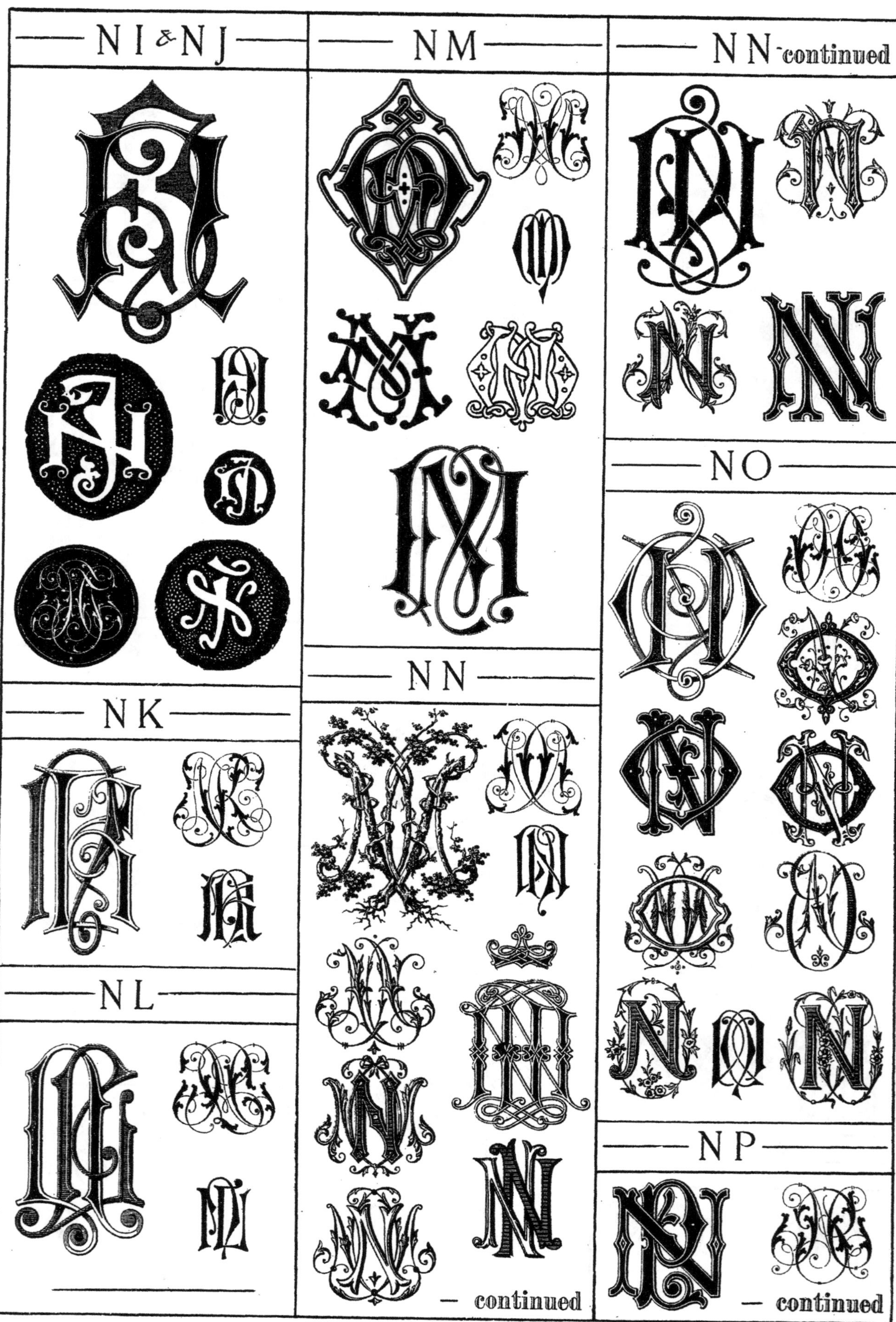

PLATE 70

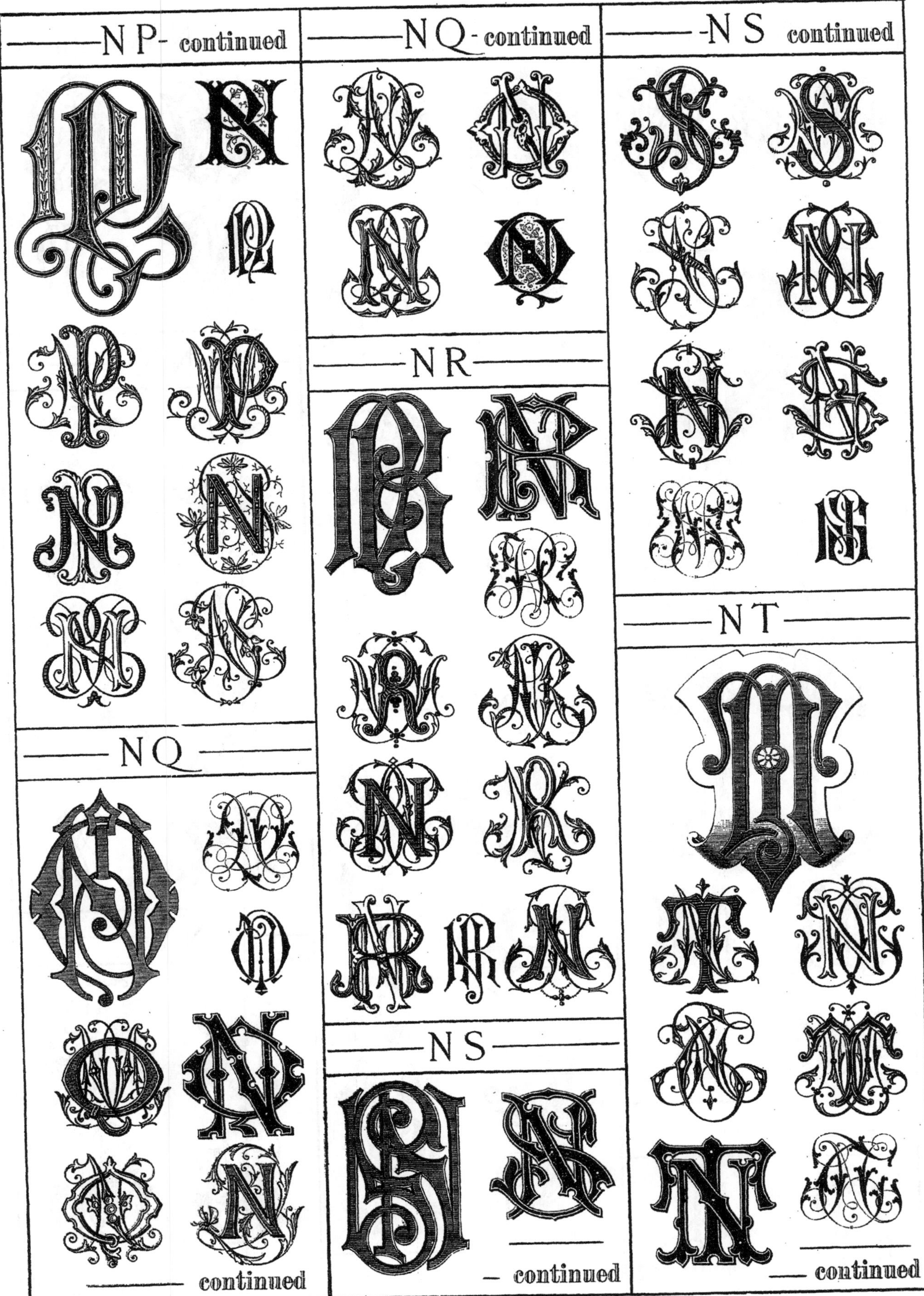
NP- continued
NQ- continued
-NS continued
NQ
NR
NT
NS
continued
- continued
continued

NT- continued
NV- continued
NW continued
NU
NX
NW
NY
NV
continued
continued
continued

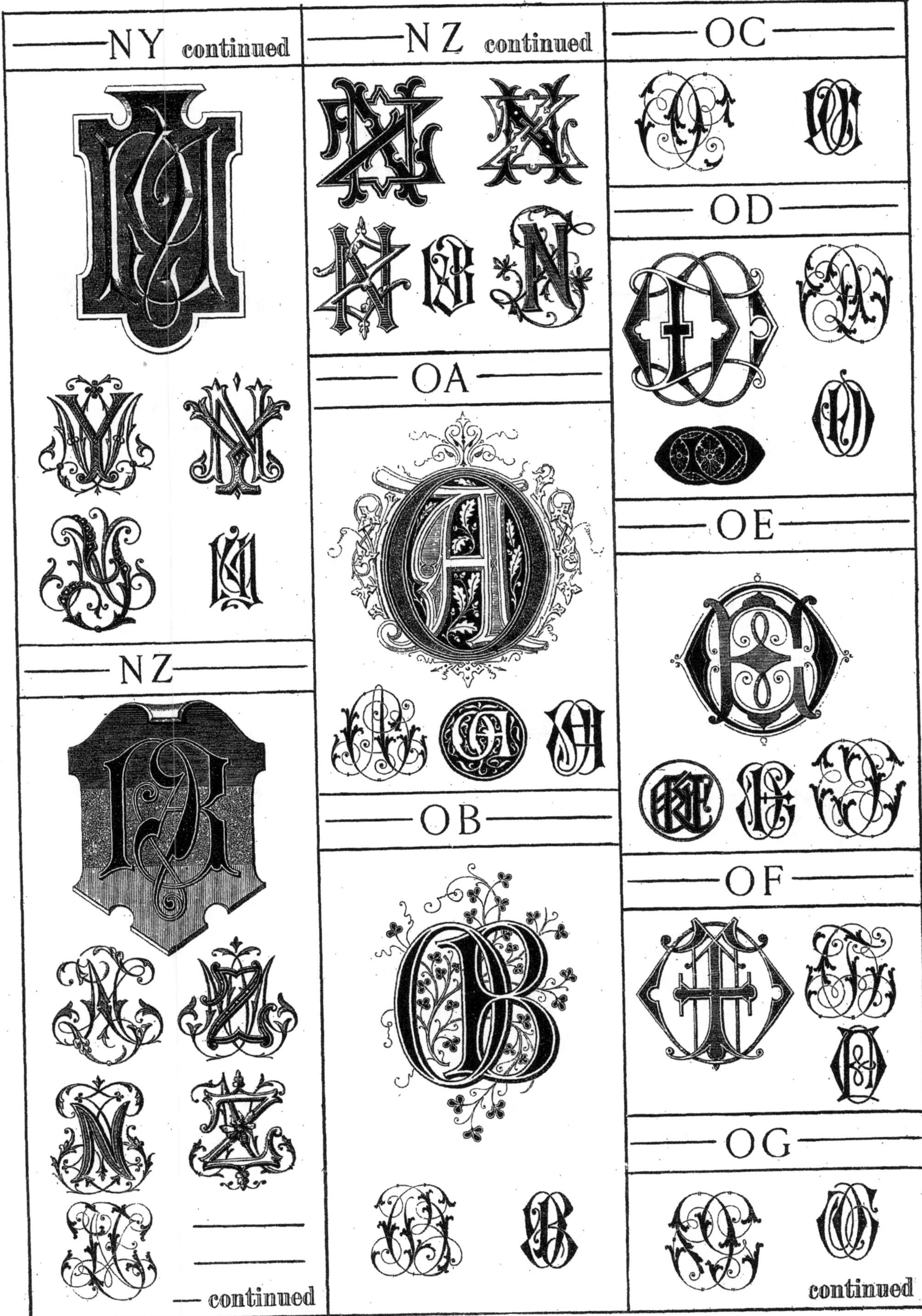

NY continued
NZ continued
OC
OD
OA
OE
NZ
OB
OF
OG
continued
continued

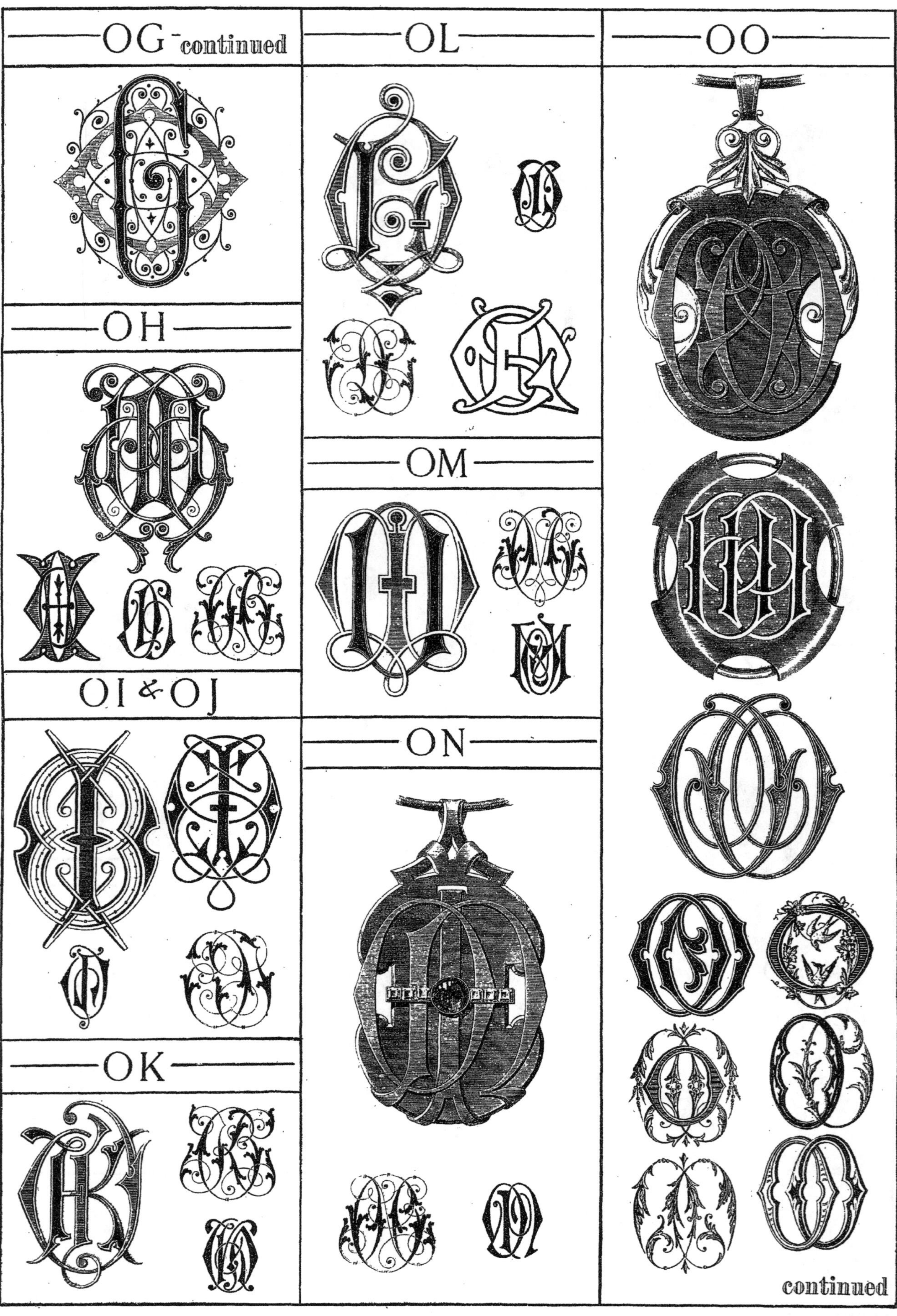
OG continued
OL
OO
OH
OM
OI & OJ
ON
OK
continued

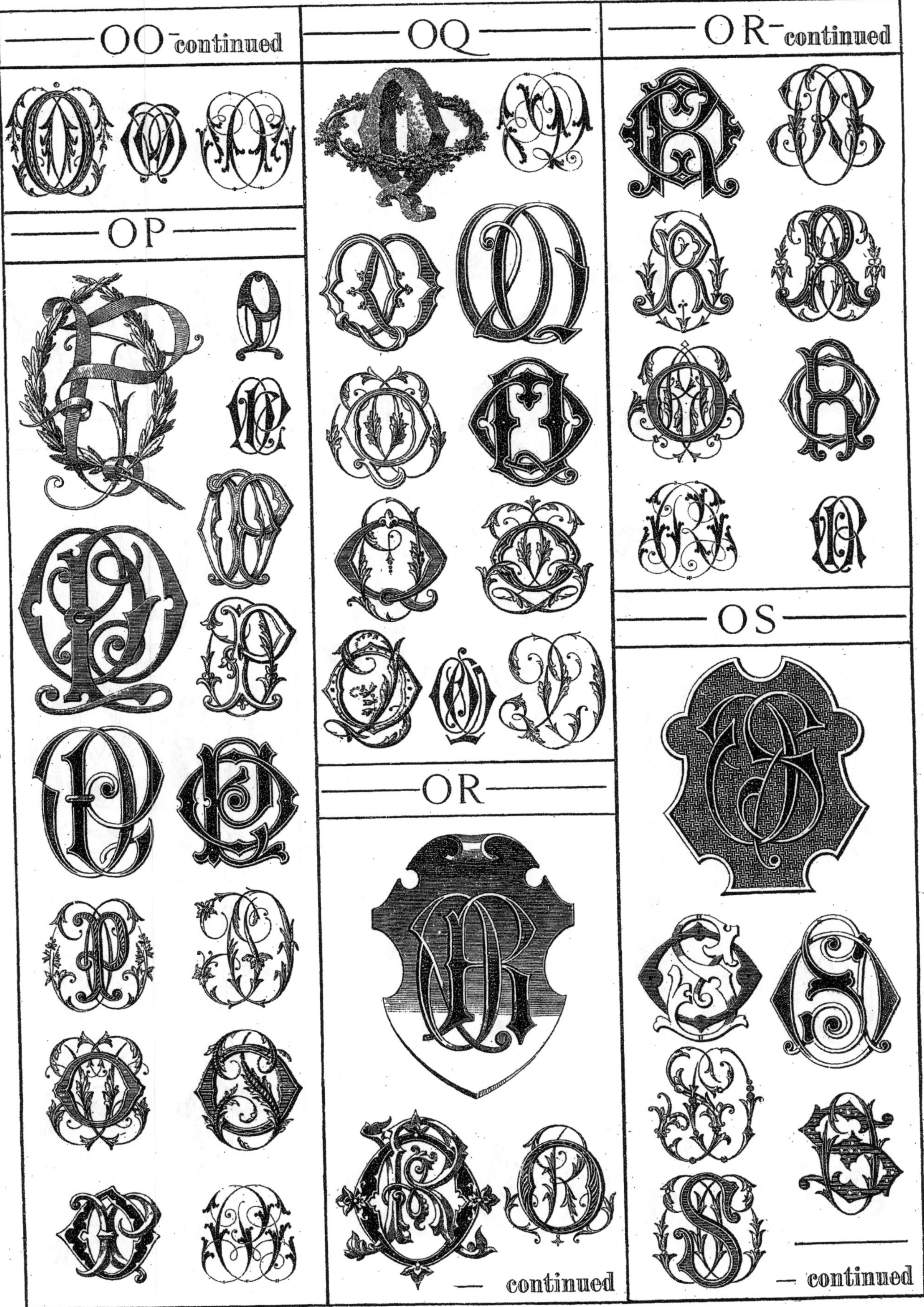

OO–continued
OP
OQ
OR
– continued
OR–continued
OS
– continued

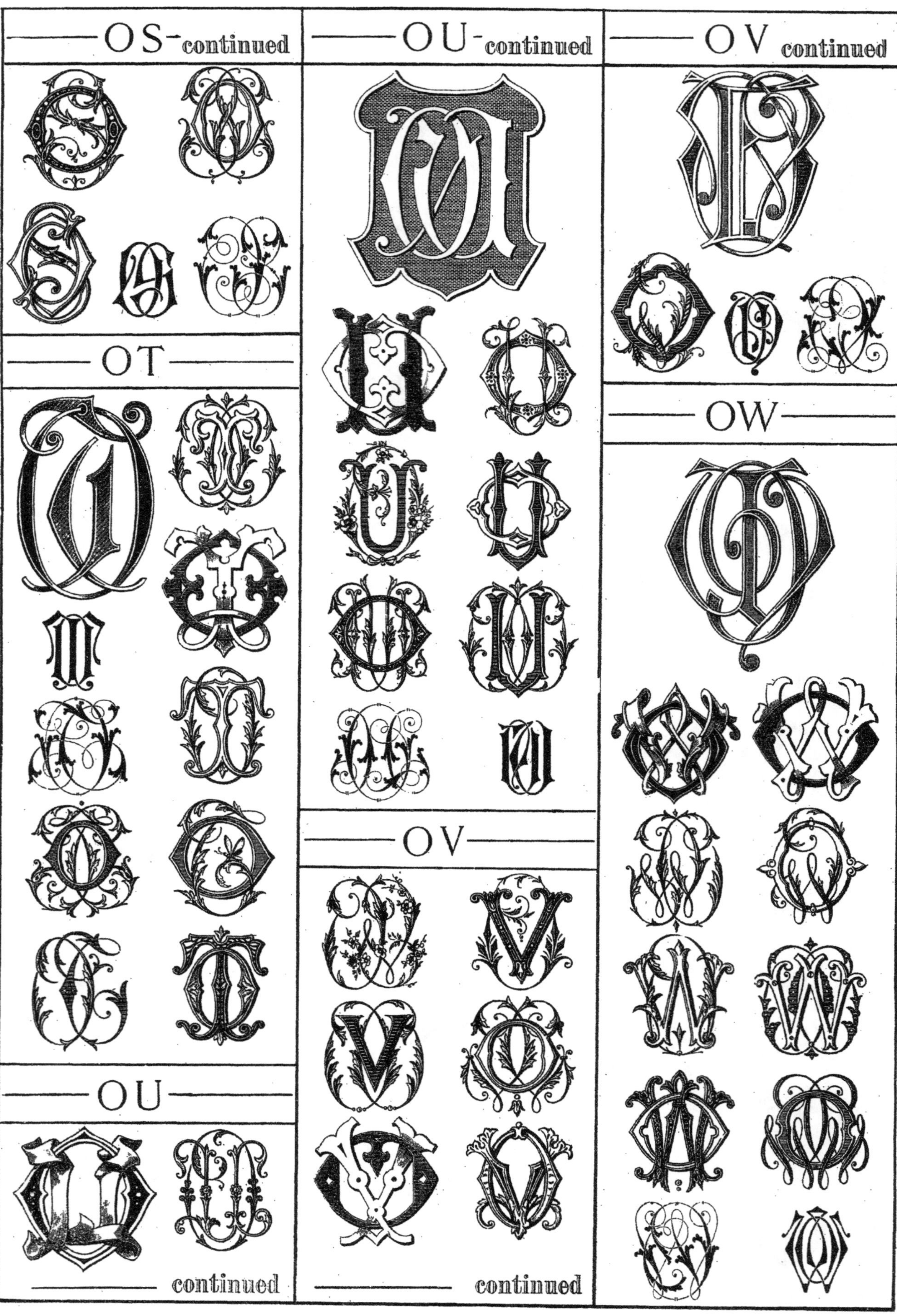

OS-continued
OU-continued
OV continued
OT
OW
OV
OU
continued
continued

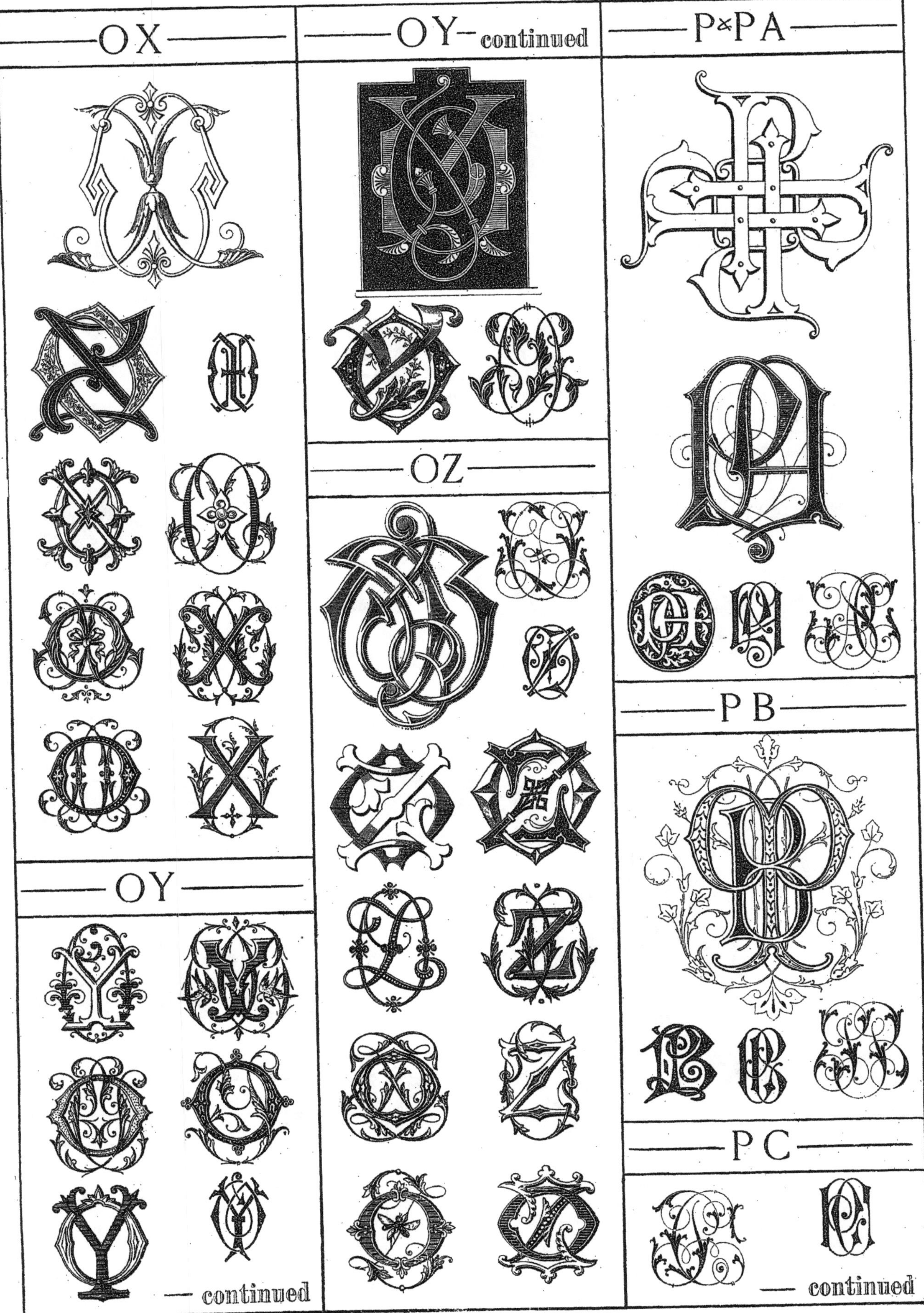
OX
OY — continued
P & PA
OZ
OY
— continued
PB
PC
— continued

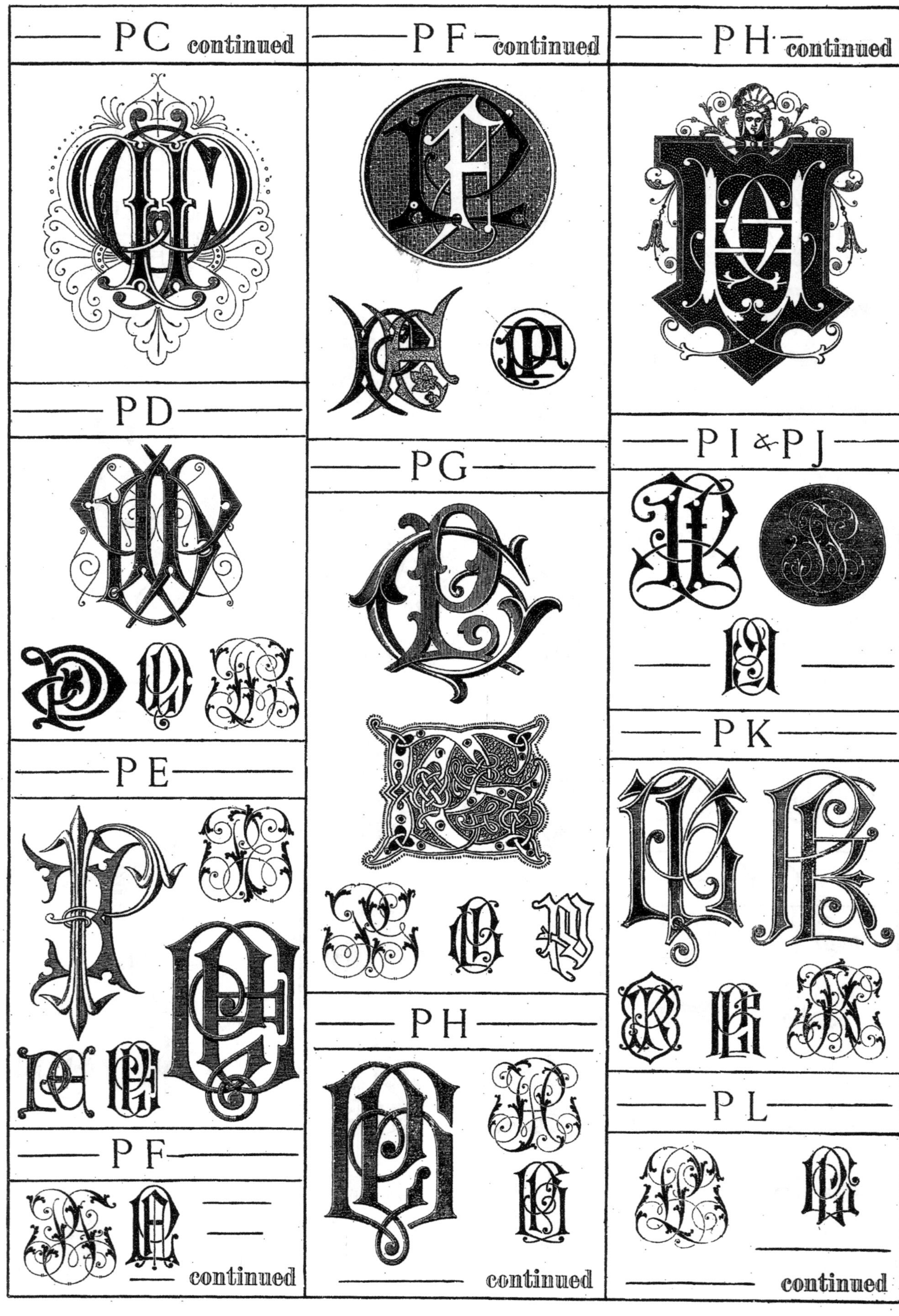
PC continued
PF continued
PH continued
PD
PG
PI & PJ
PE
PK
PH
PL
PF
continued
continued
continued

P L- continued
P O continued
P P-- continued
P M
P P
P N
P Q
P O
continued
- continued

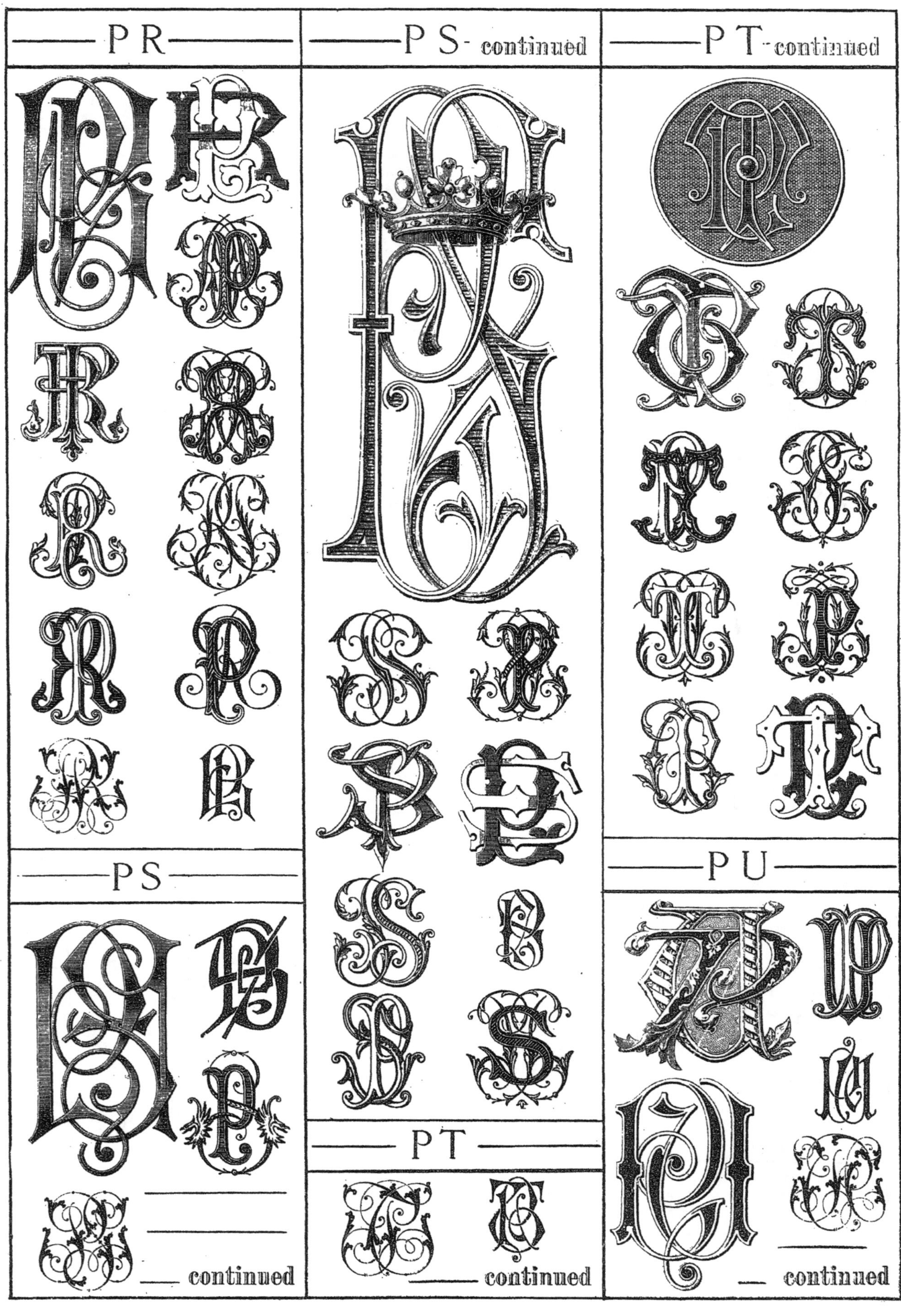
PR
PS- continued
PT- continued
PS
continued
PT
continued
PU
continued

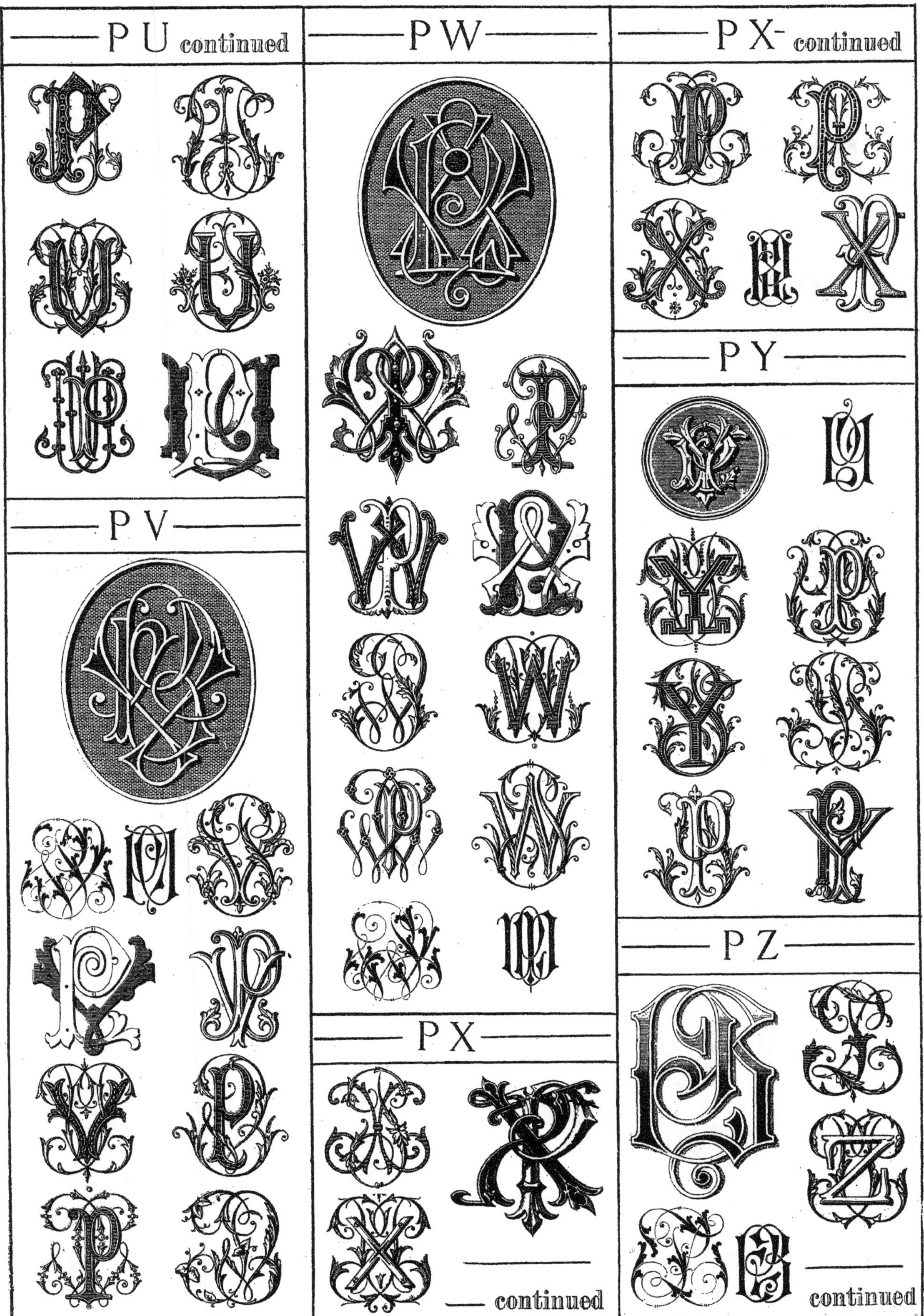
P U continued
P W
P X- continued
P V
P Y
P X
P Z
continued
continued

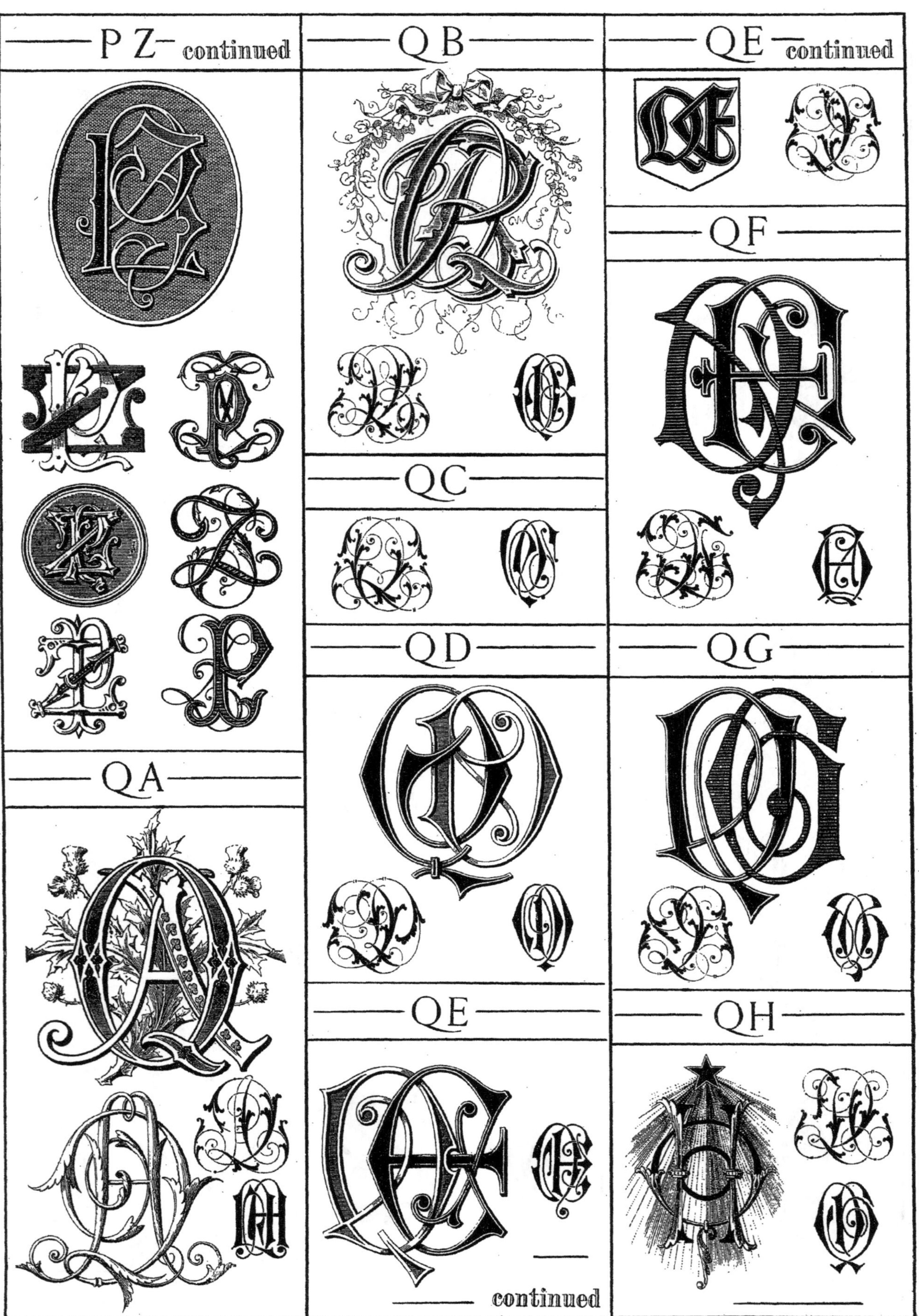
P Z continued
Q B
Q E continued
Q F
Q C
Q D
Q G
Q A
Q E
Q H
continued

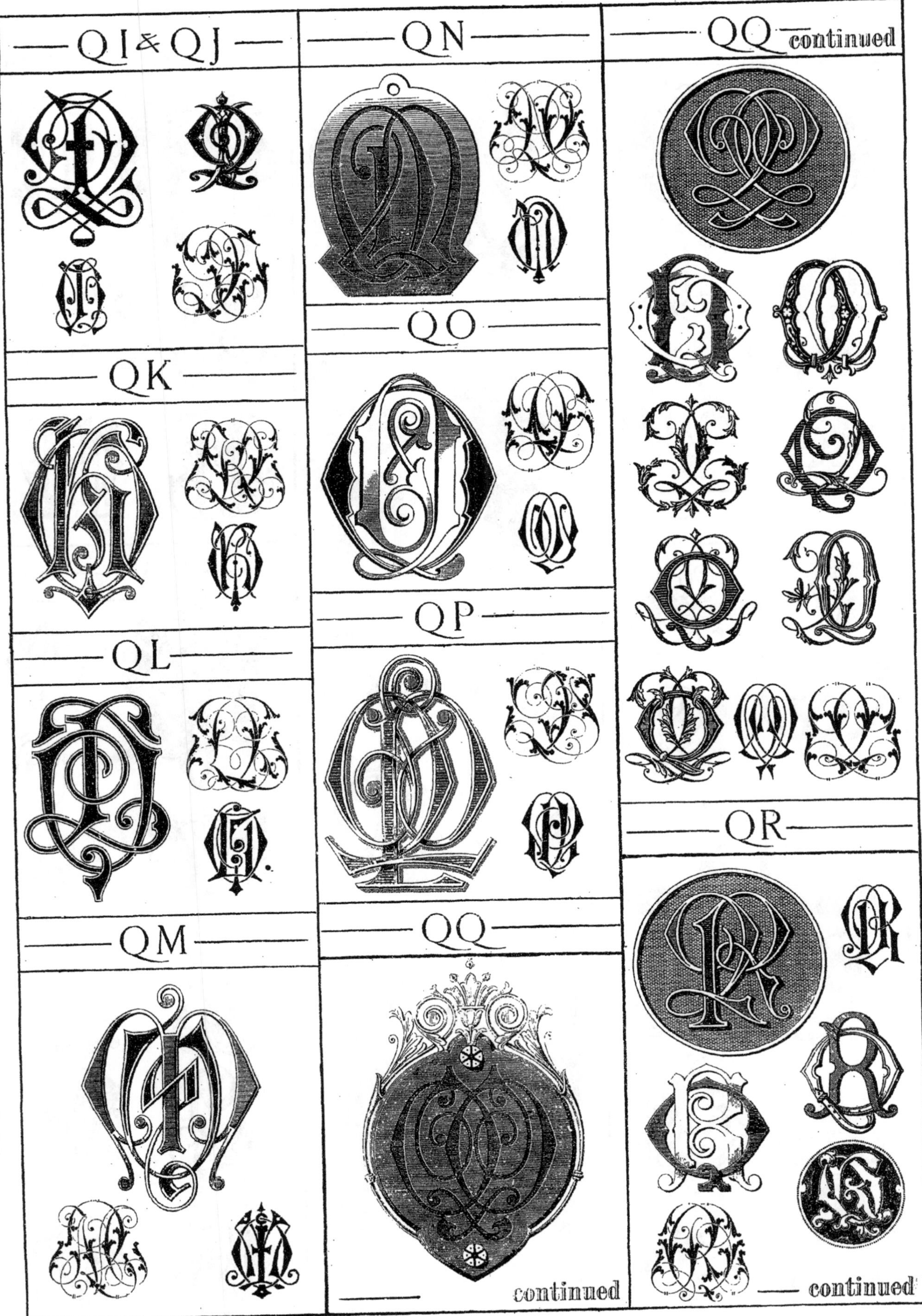
QI & QJ
QK
QL
QM
QN
QO
QP
QQ
continued
QQ continued
QR
continued

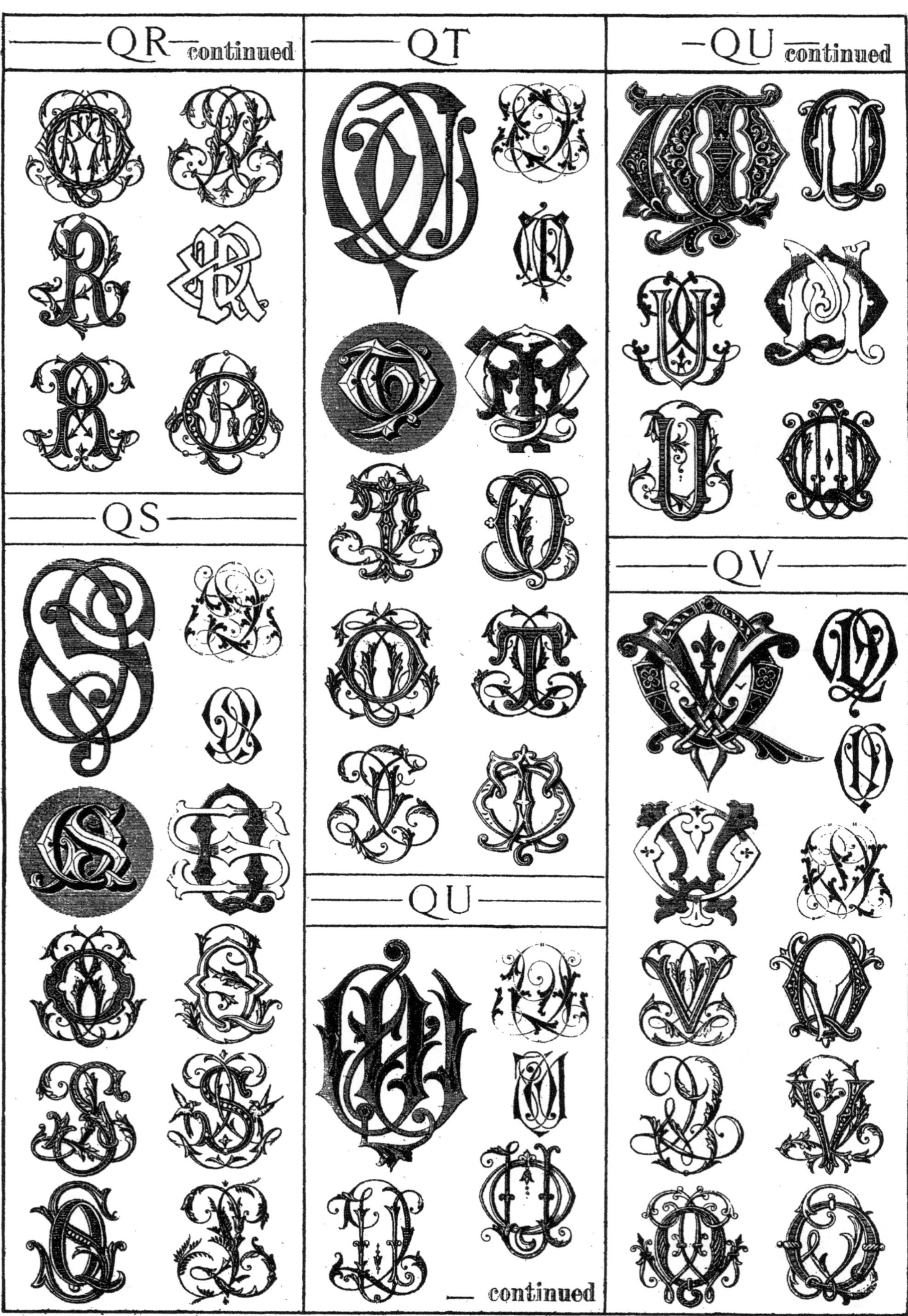
QR continued
QT
QU continued
QS
QU
continued
QV

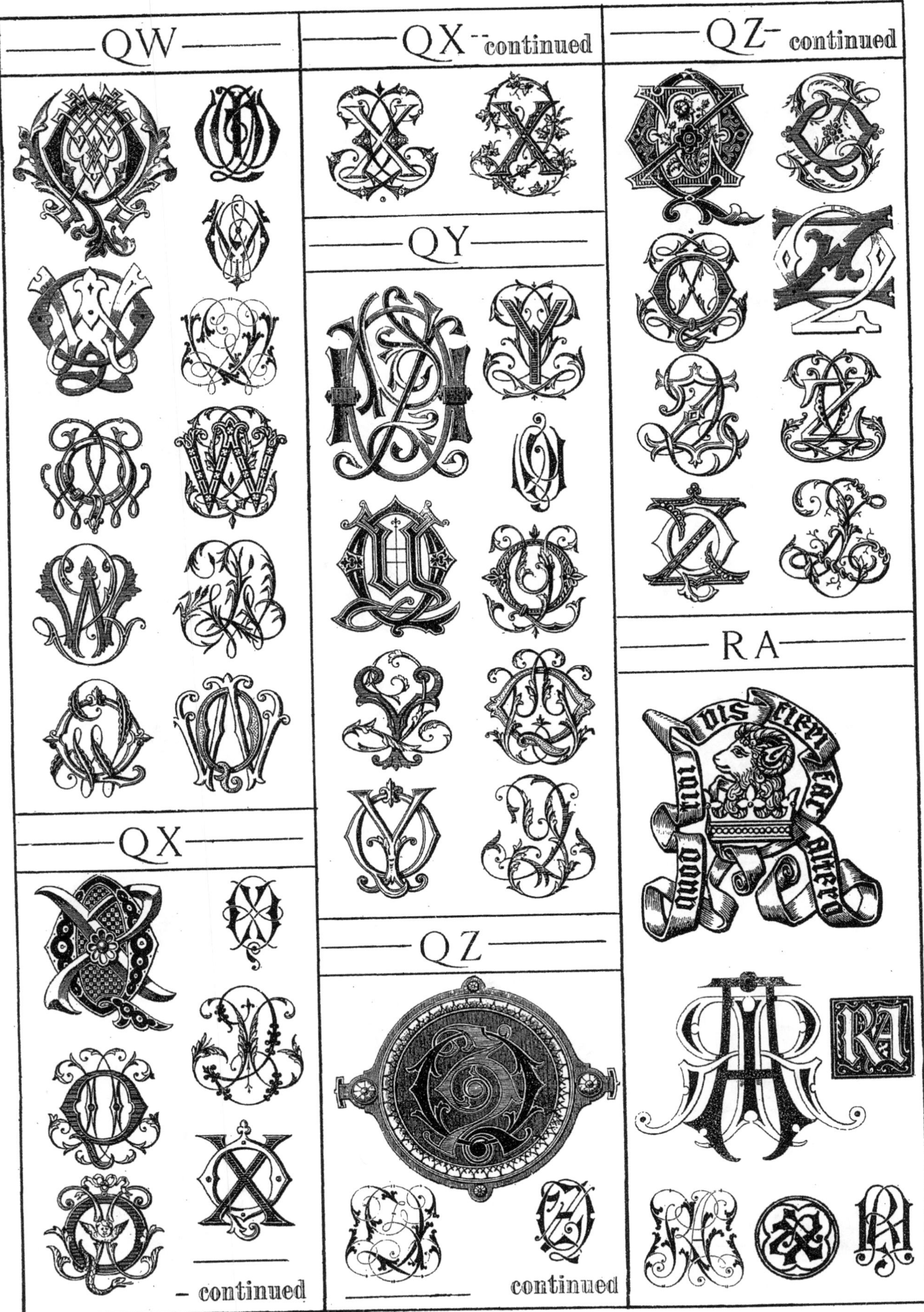

QW
QX-- continued
QZ- continued
QY
QX
- continued
QZ
continued
RA
vis fieri
tibi
fac
quod
altero

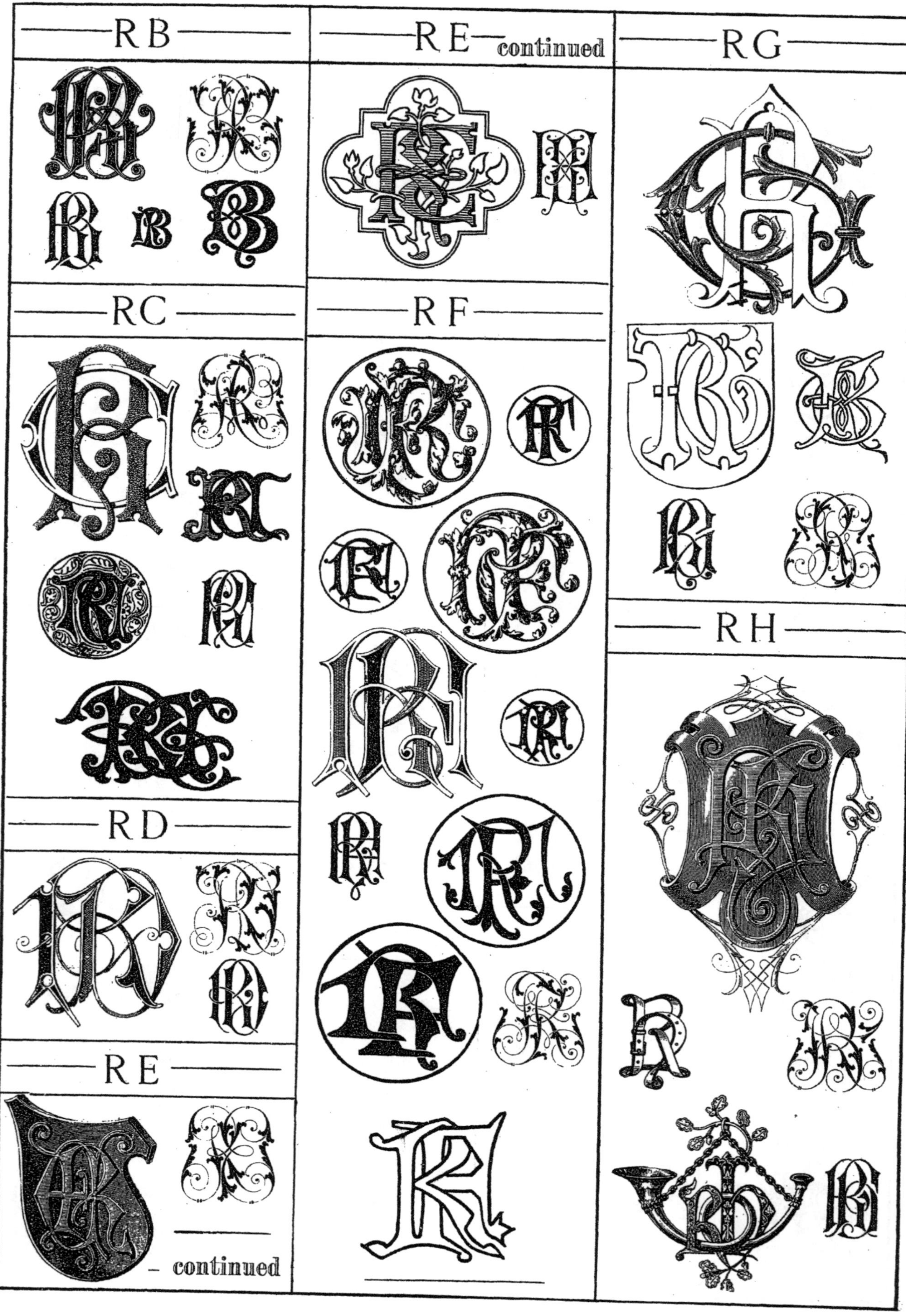
RB
RE continued
RG
RC
RF
RD
RH
RE
continued

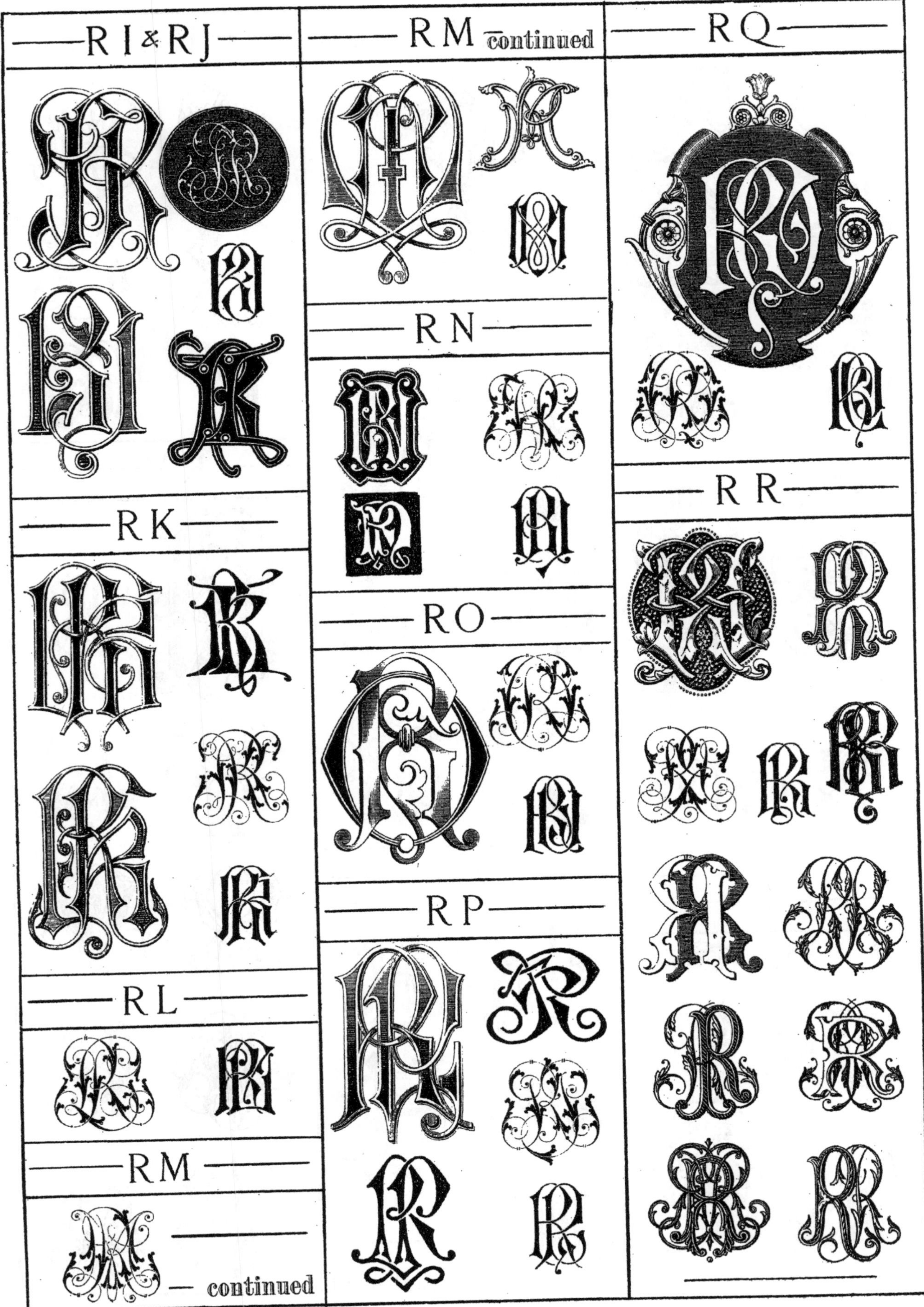
RI & RJ
RM continued
RQ
RN
RK
RO
RR
RP
RL
RM
continued

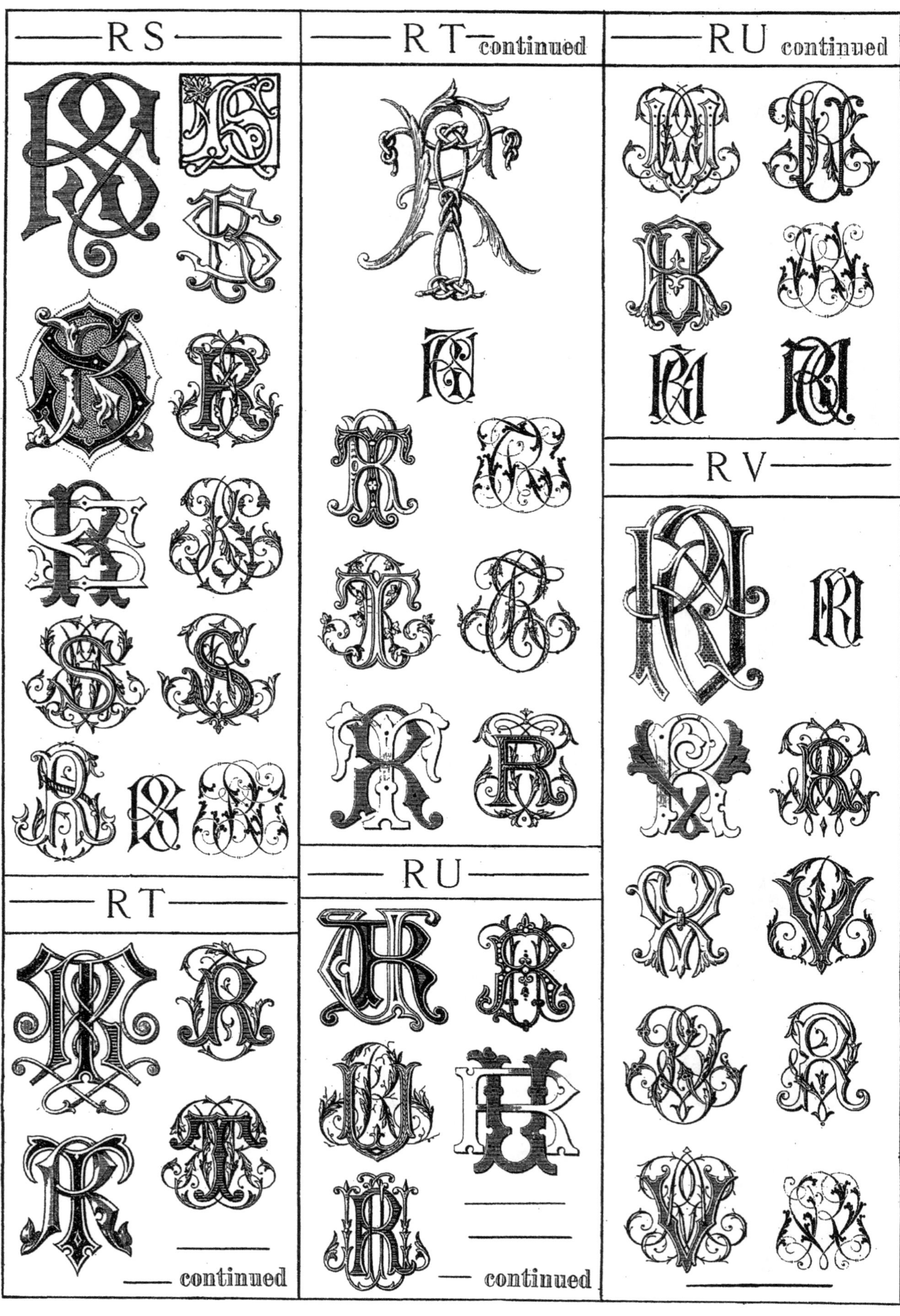
RS
RT—continued
RU continued
RV
RT
RU
continued
continued

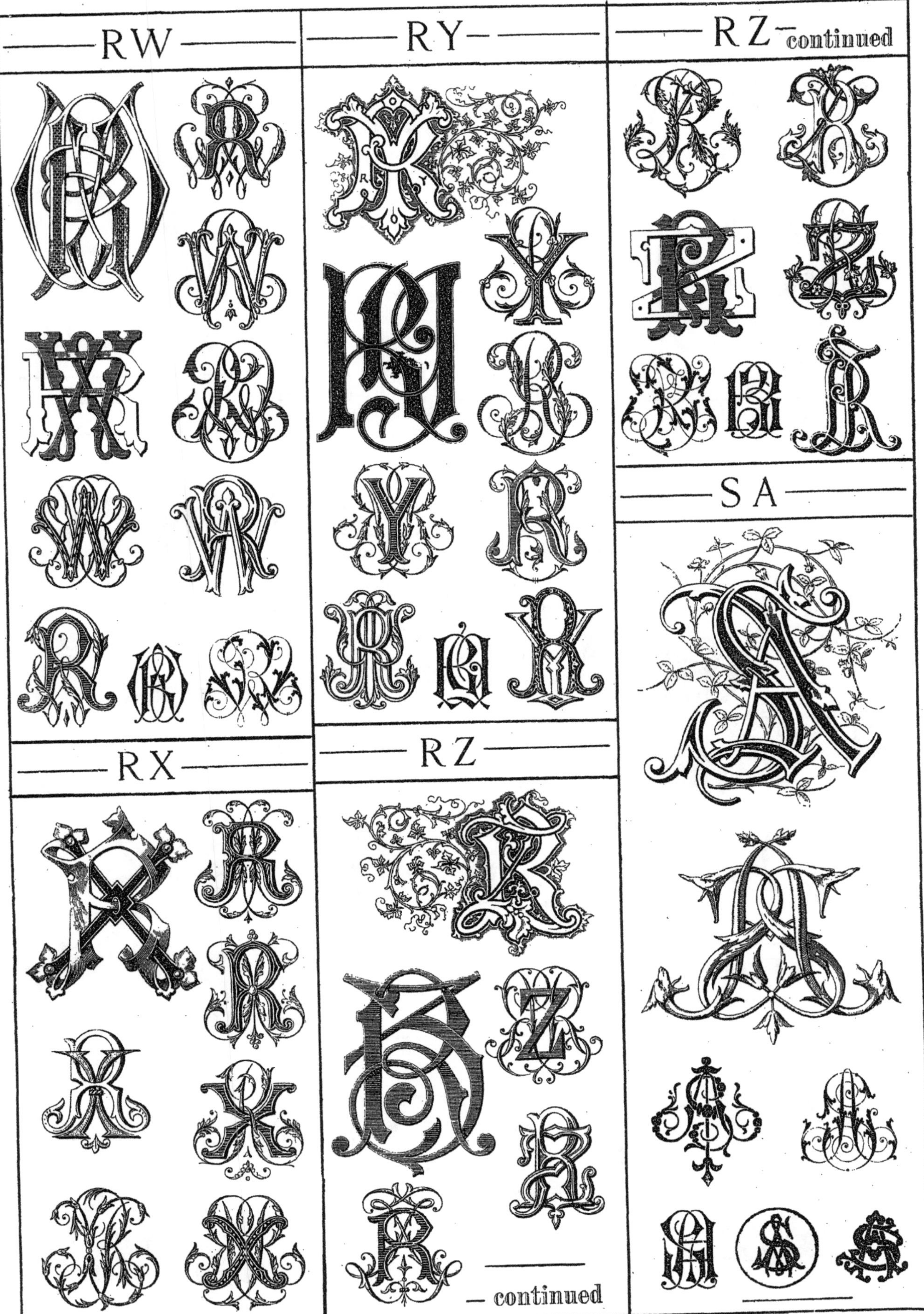
RW
RY
RZ—continued
SA
RX
RZ
— continued

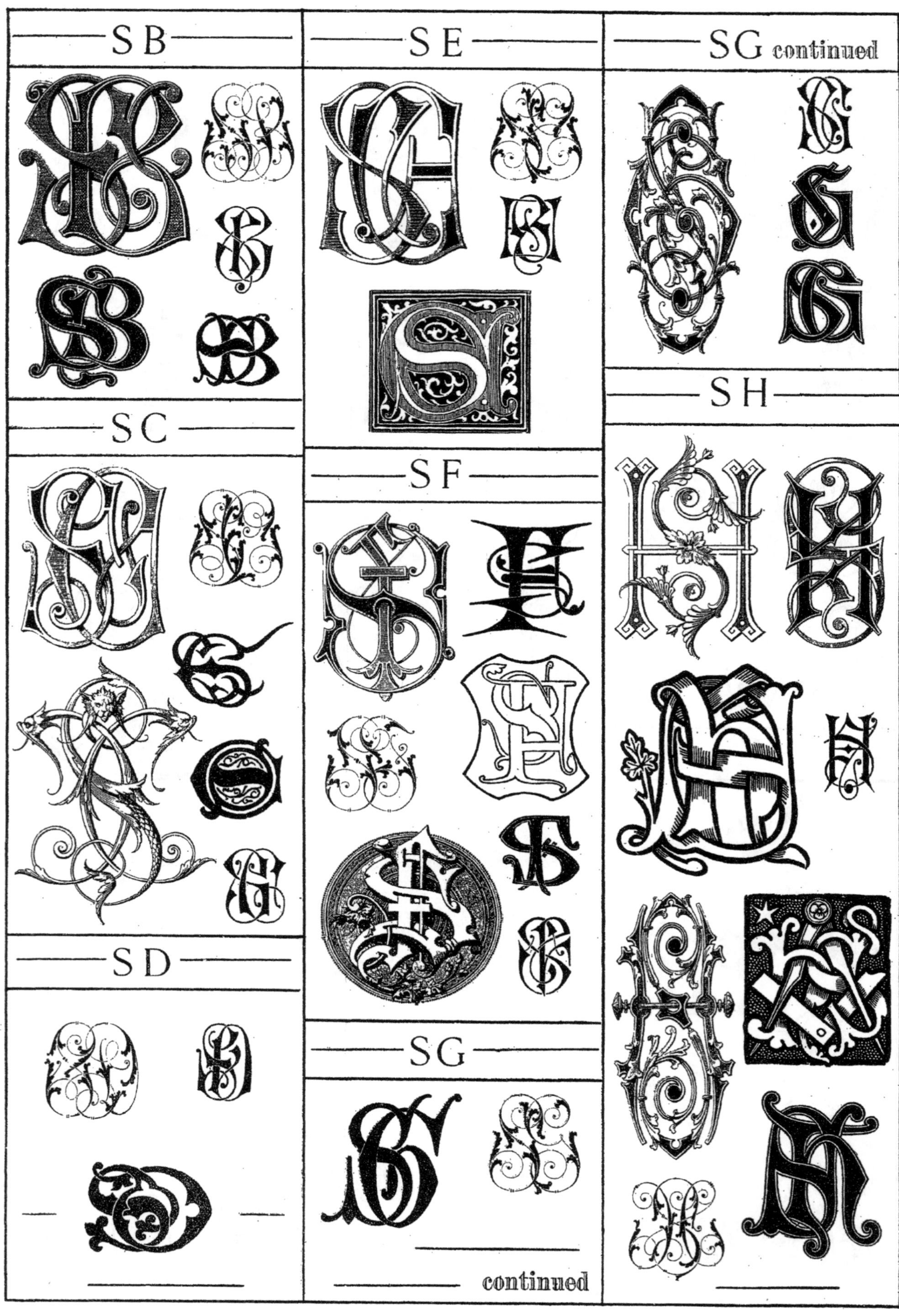
SB
SE
SG continued
SC
SF
SH
SD
SG
continued

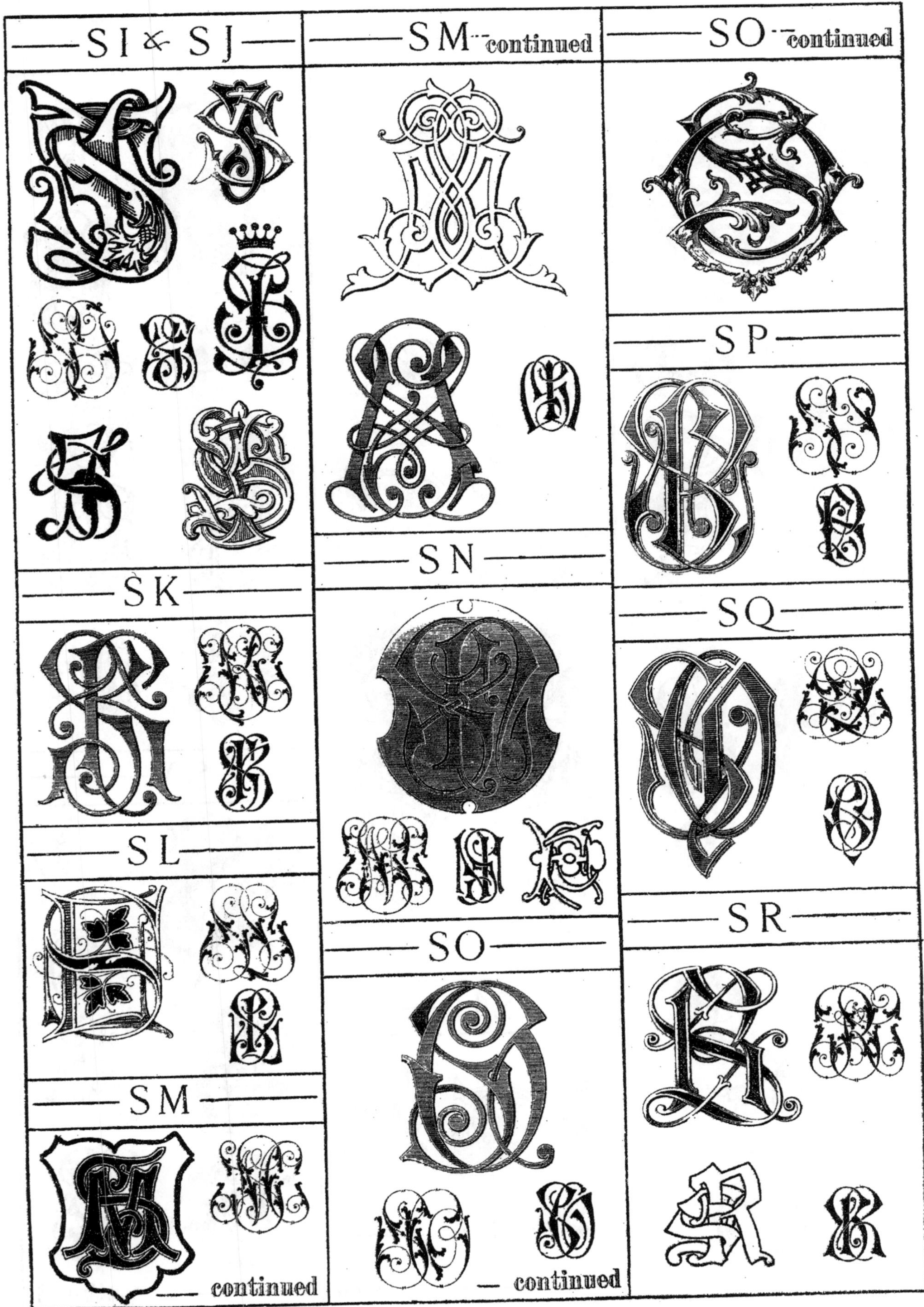
SI & SJ
SM continued
SO continued
SK
SL
SM
continued
SN
SO
continued
SP
SQ
SR

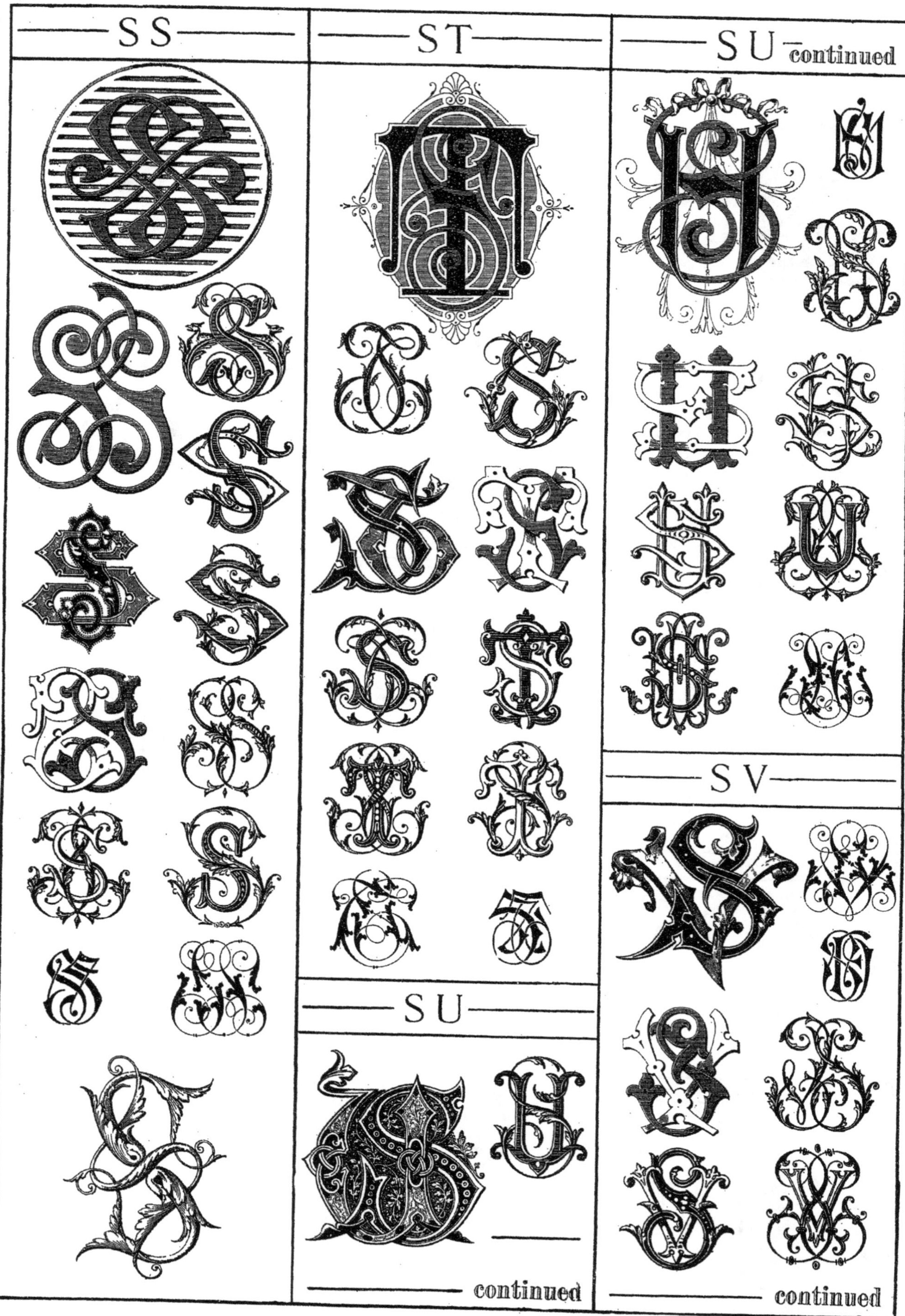

Plate 92

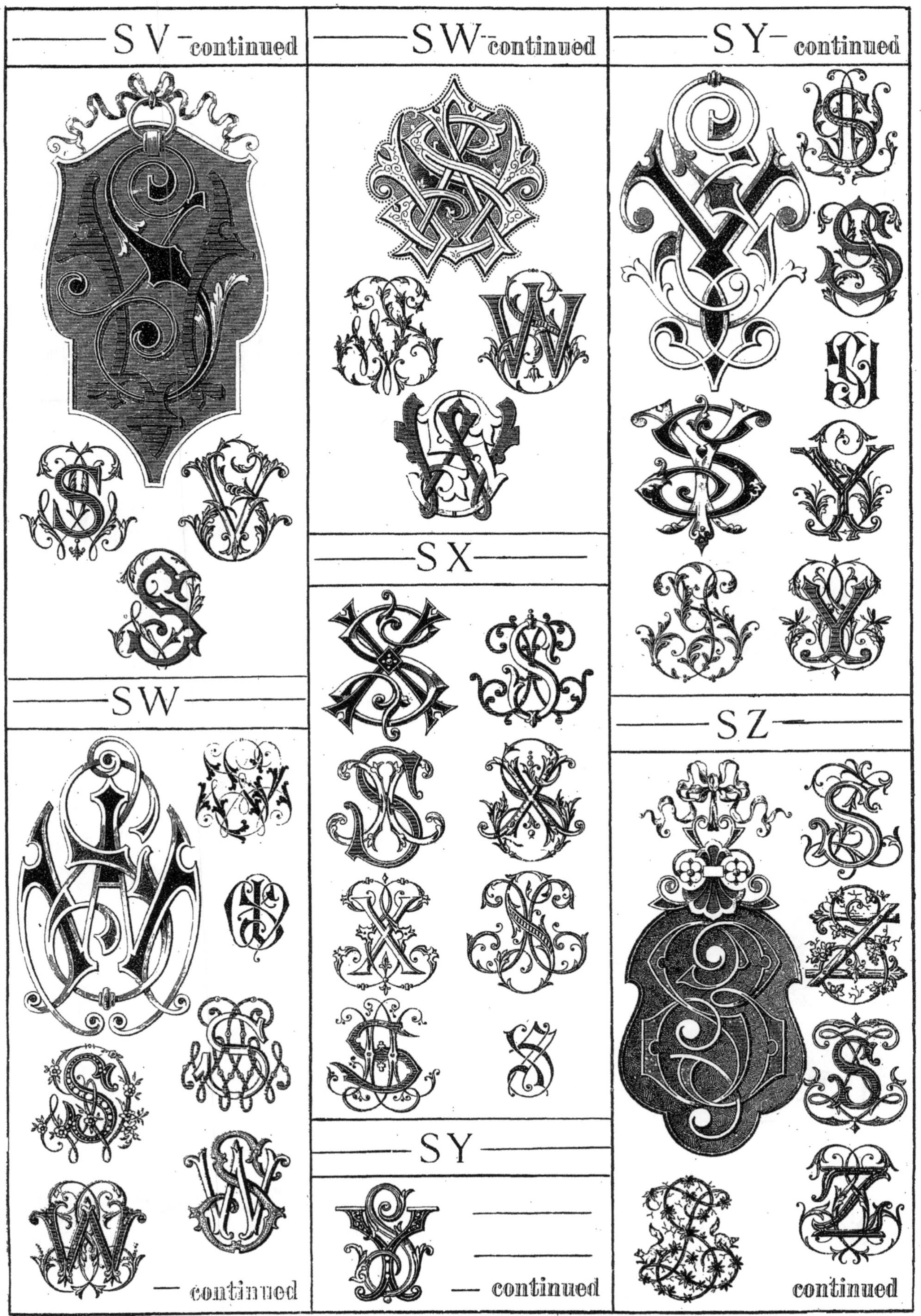
SV continued
SW continued
SY continued
SX
SW
SZ
SY
continued
continued
continued

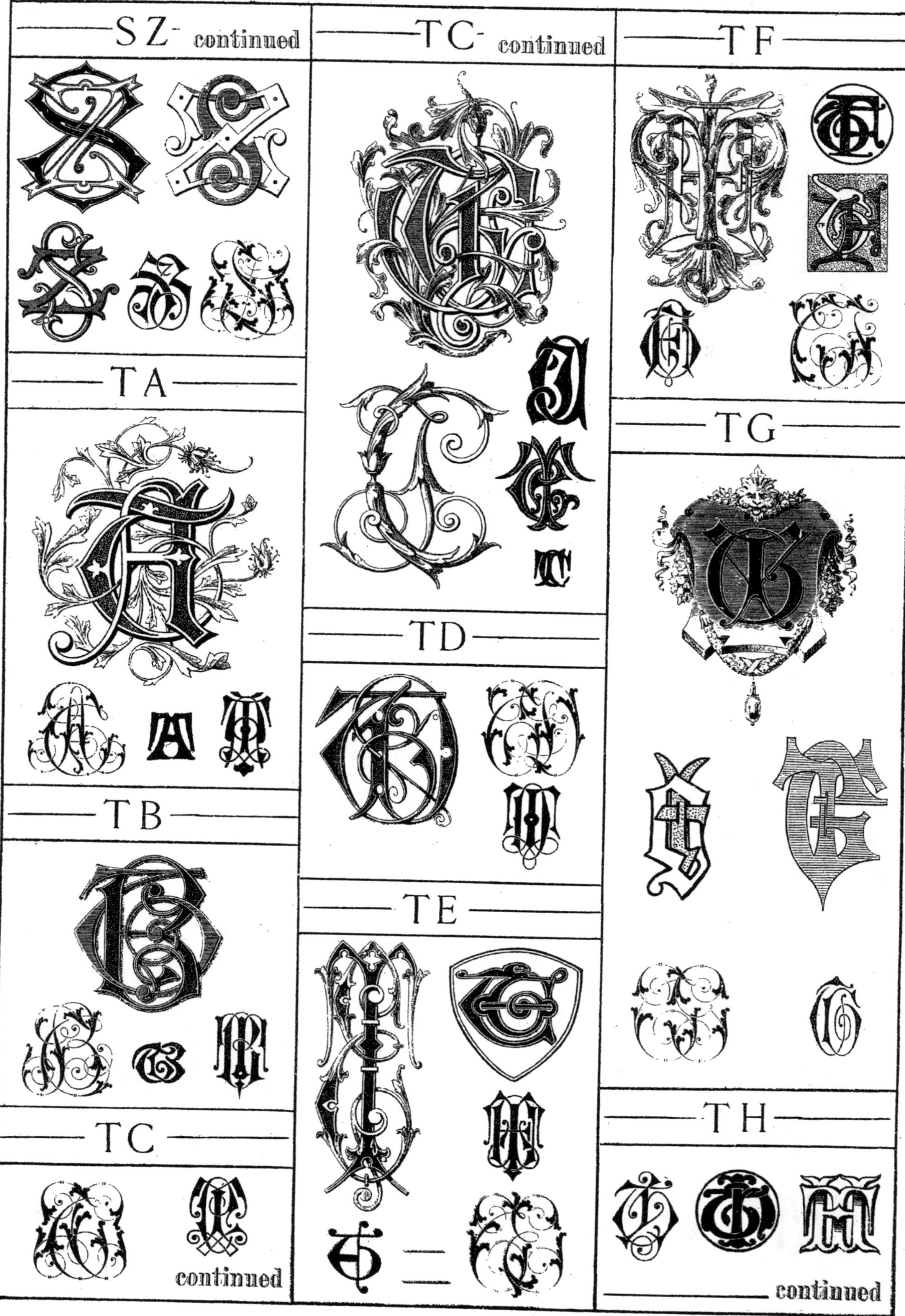
SZ- continued
TC- continued
TF
TA
TG
TD
TB
TE
TC
continued
TH
continued

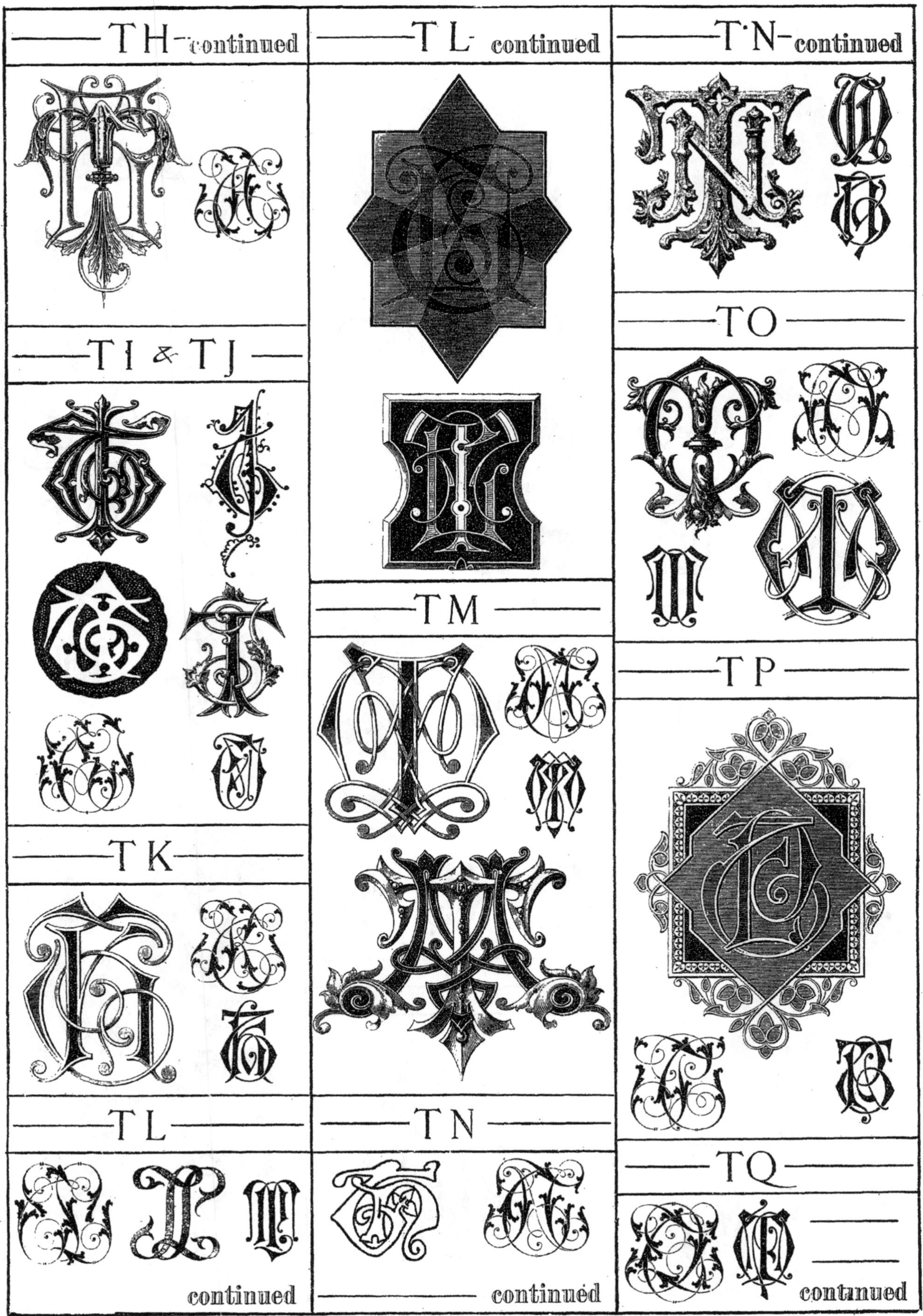
TH—continued
TL—continued
TN—continued
TI & TJ
TO
TM
TP
TK
TL
TN
TQ
continued
continued
continued

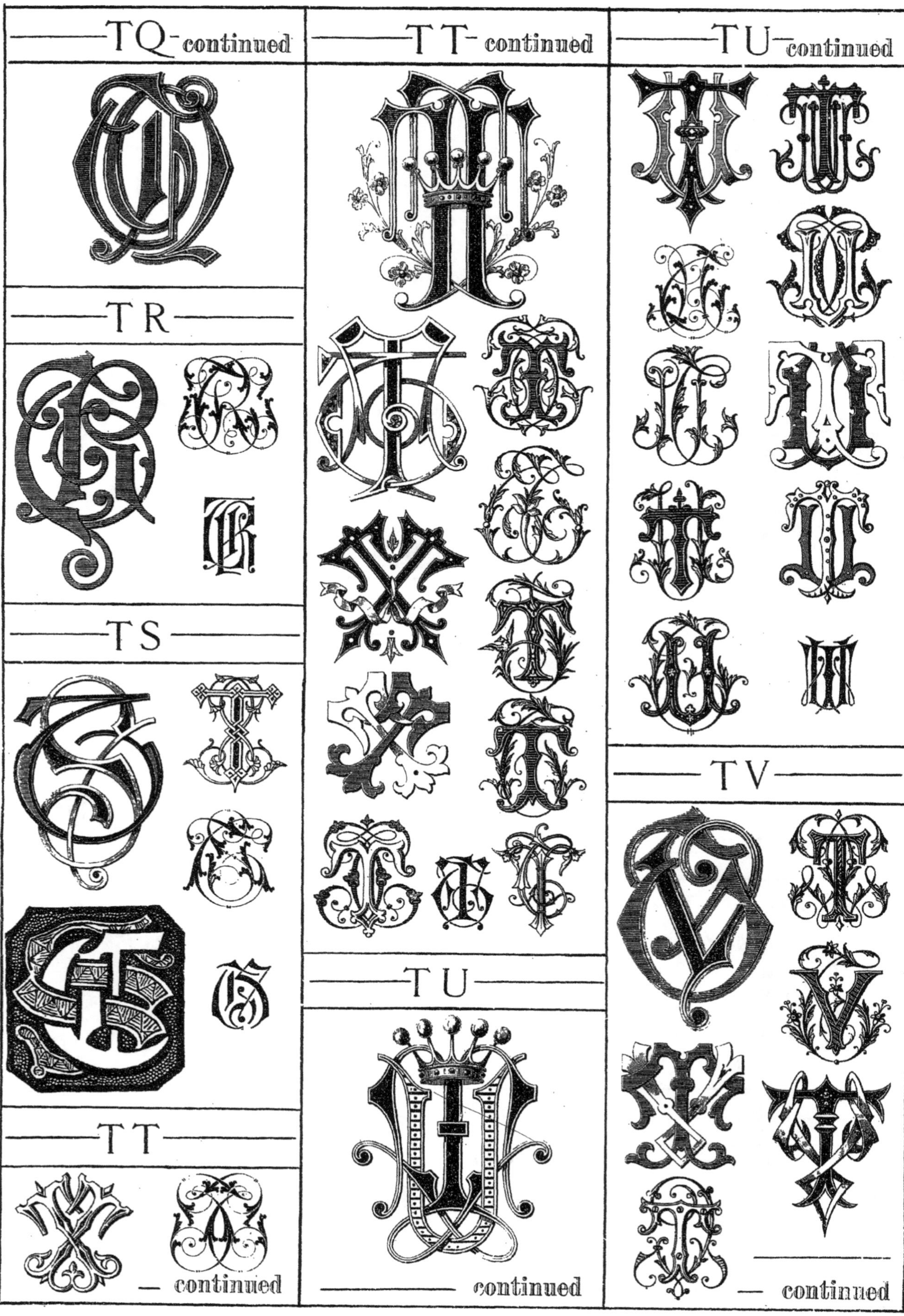

TQ- continued
TR
TS
TT
— continued
TT- continued
TU
continued
TU- continued
TV
— continued

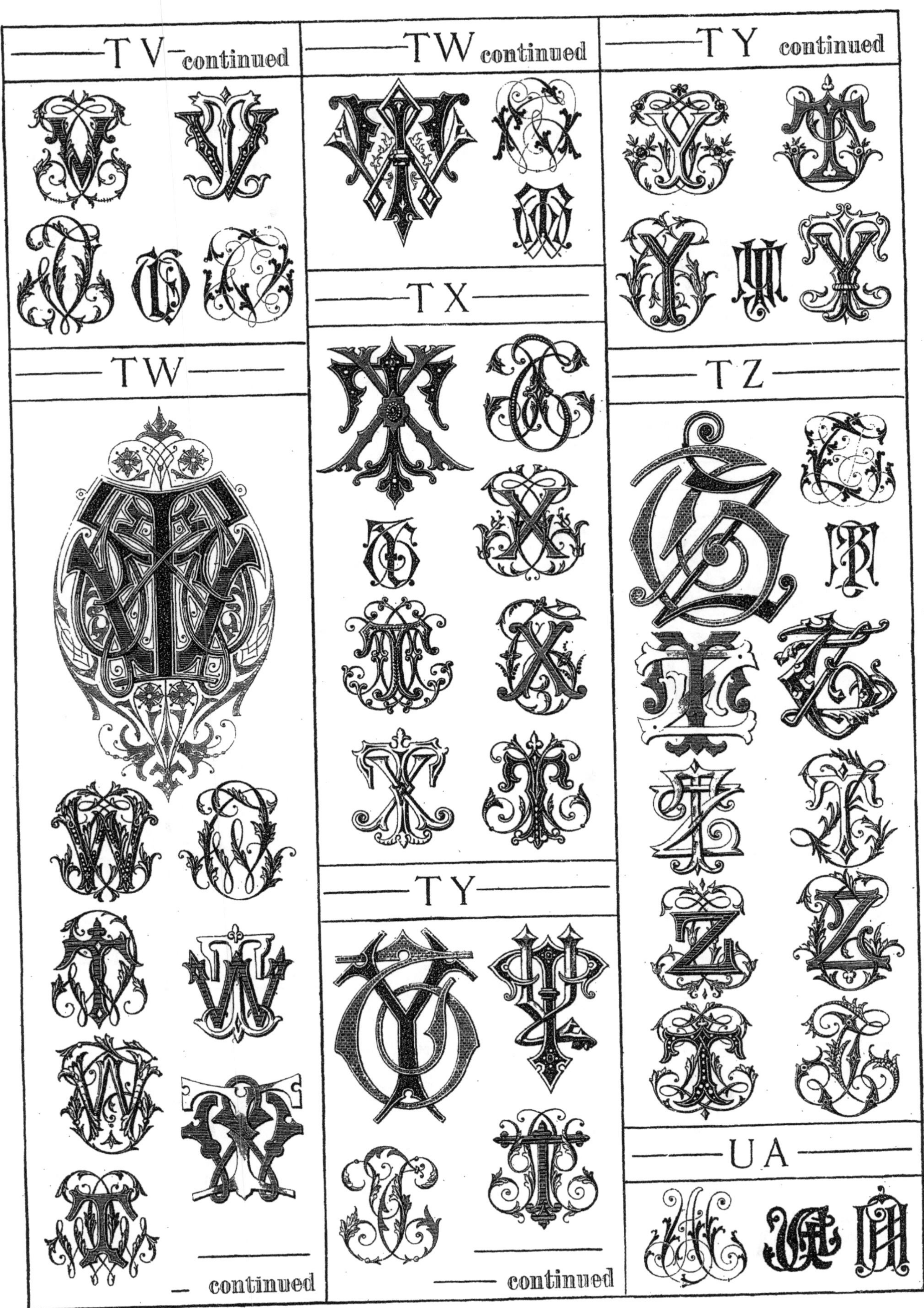
TV continued
TW continued
TY continued
TW
TX
TZ
TY
UA
continued
continued

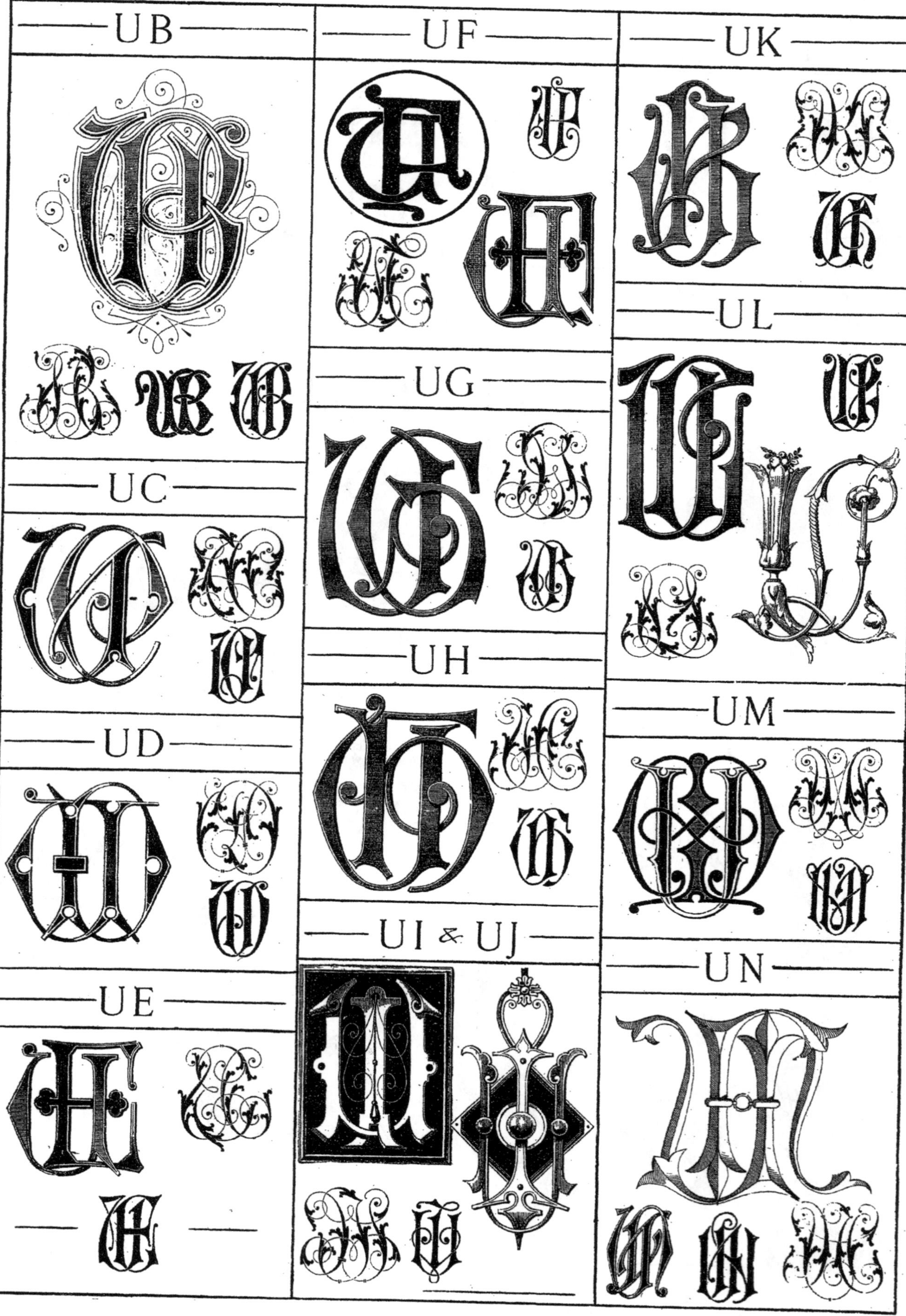

UB
UF
UK
UL
UG
UC
UH
UM
UD
UI & UJ
UN
UE

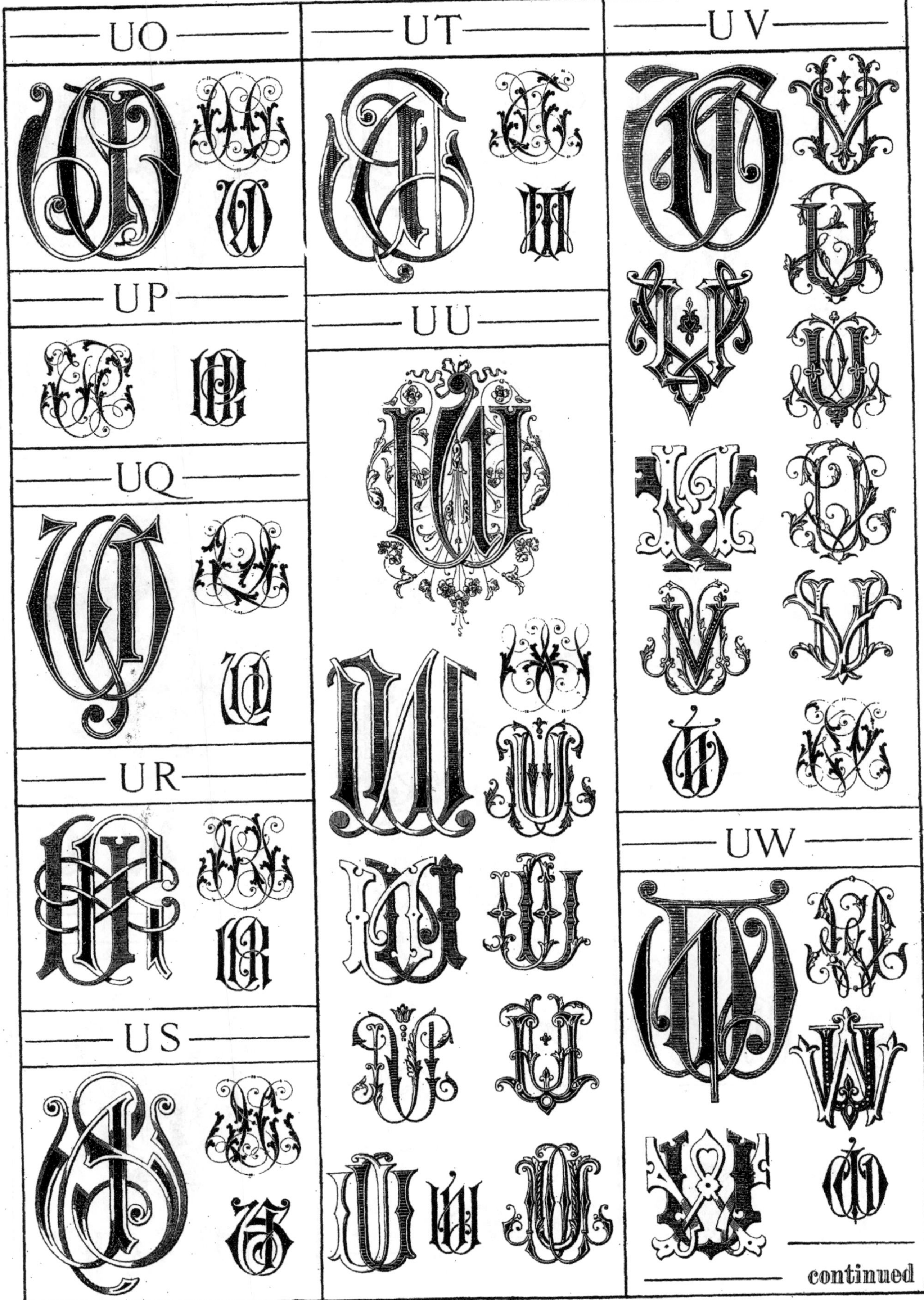
UO
UT
UV
UP
UU
UQ
UR
US
UW
continued

UW continued
UY continued
VA
UX
UZ
VB
VC
UY
continued

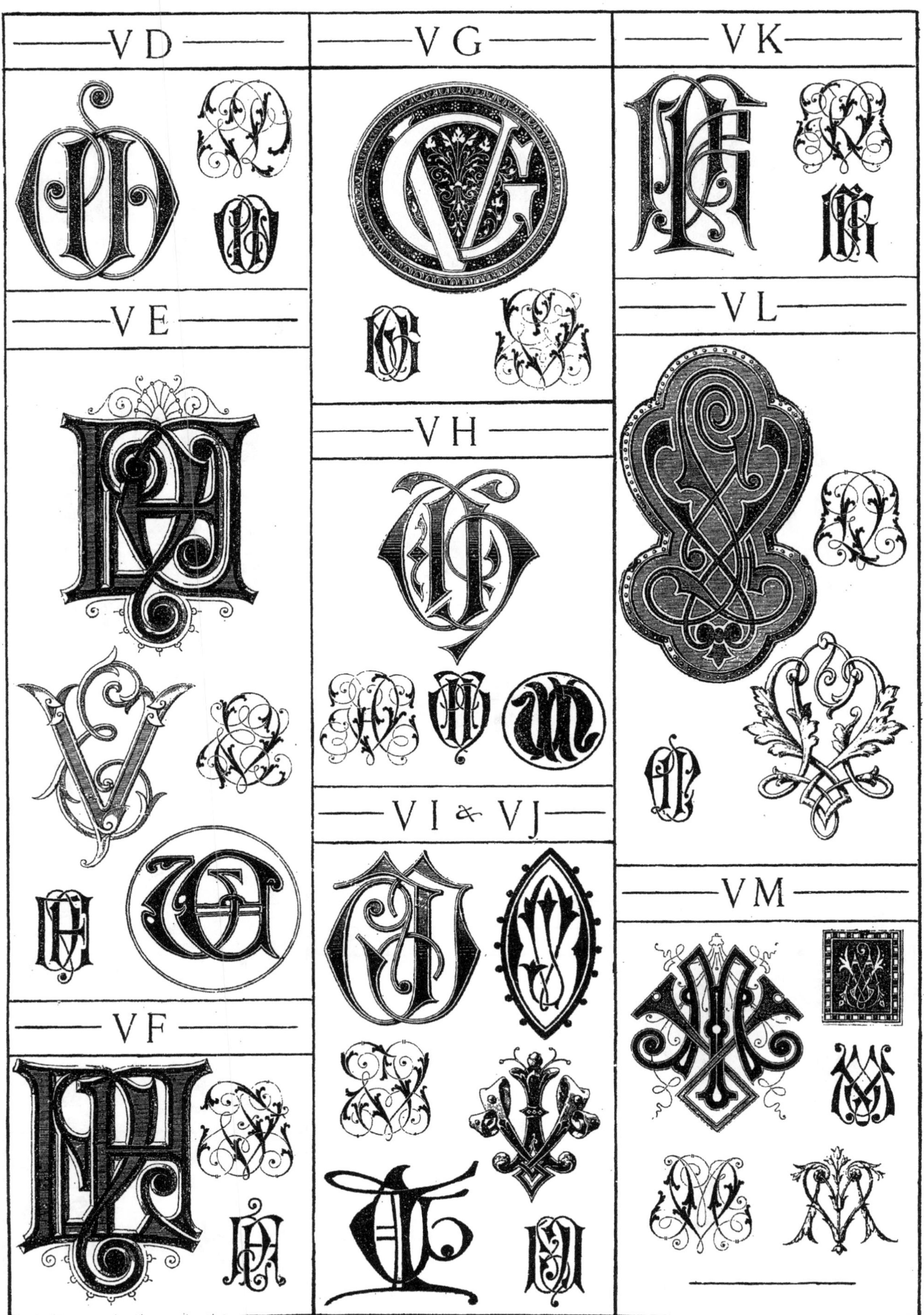
VD
VG
VK
VE
VL
VH
VI & VJ
VM
VF

VN
VP-continued
VR-continued
VO
VQ
VR
VP
VS
VT
continued
continued
continued

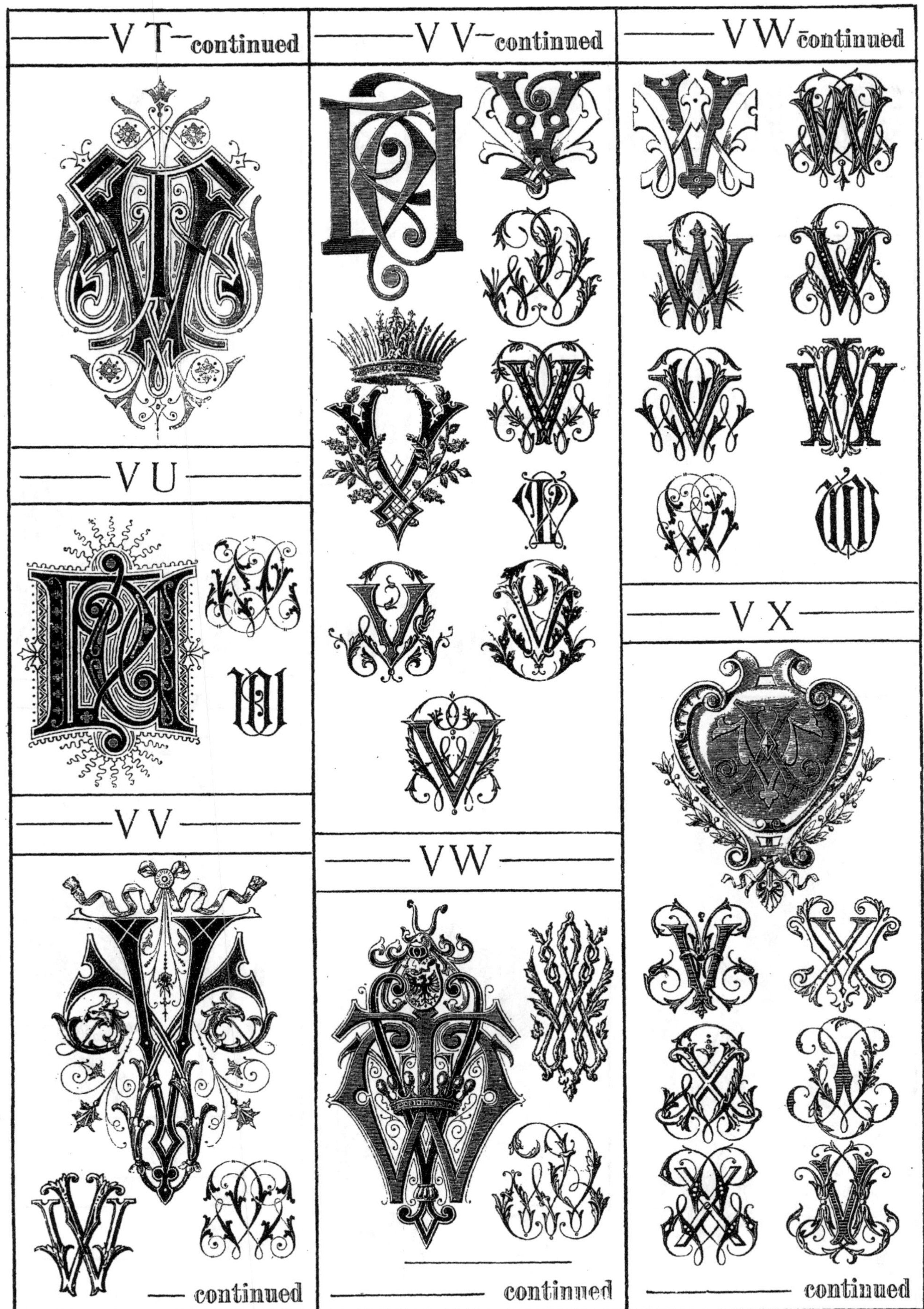
VT—continued
VV—continued
VW—continued
VU
VX
VV
VW
continued
continued
continued

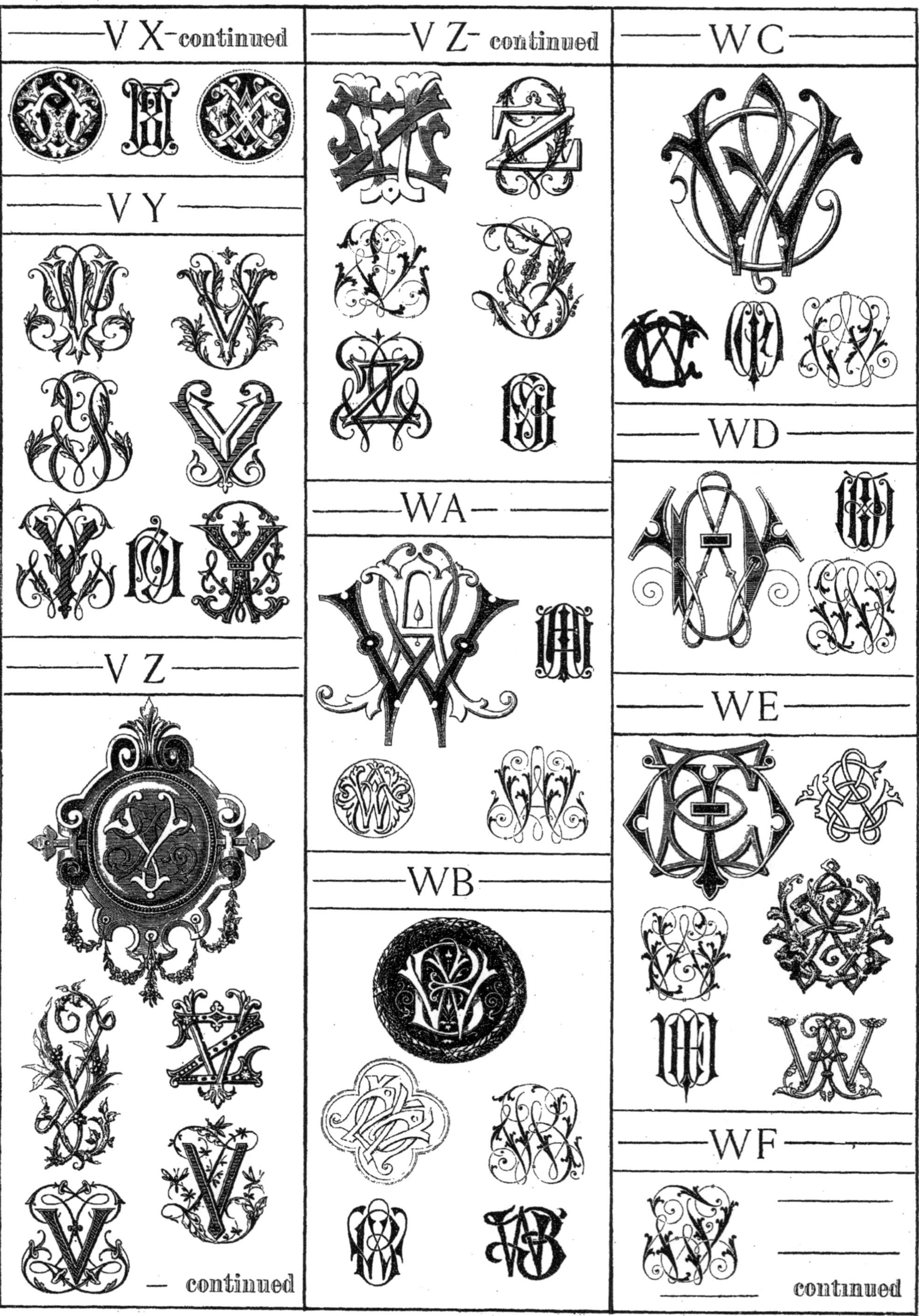
VX-continued
VZ-continued
WC
VY
WD
WA
VZ
WE
WB
WF
continued
continued

PLATE 104

WF continued
WH continued
WK
WG
WI & WJ
WL
WM
WN
WH
continued

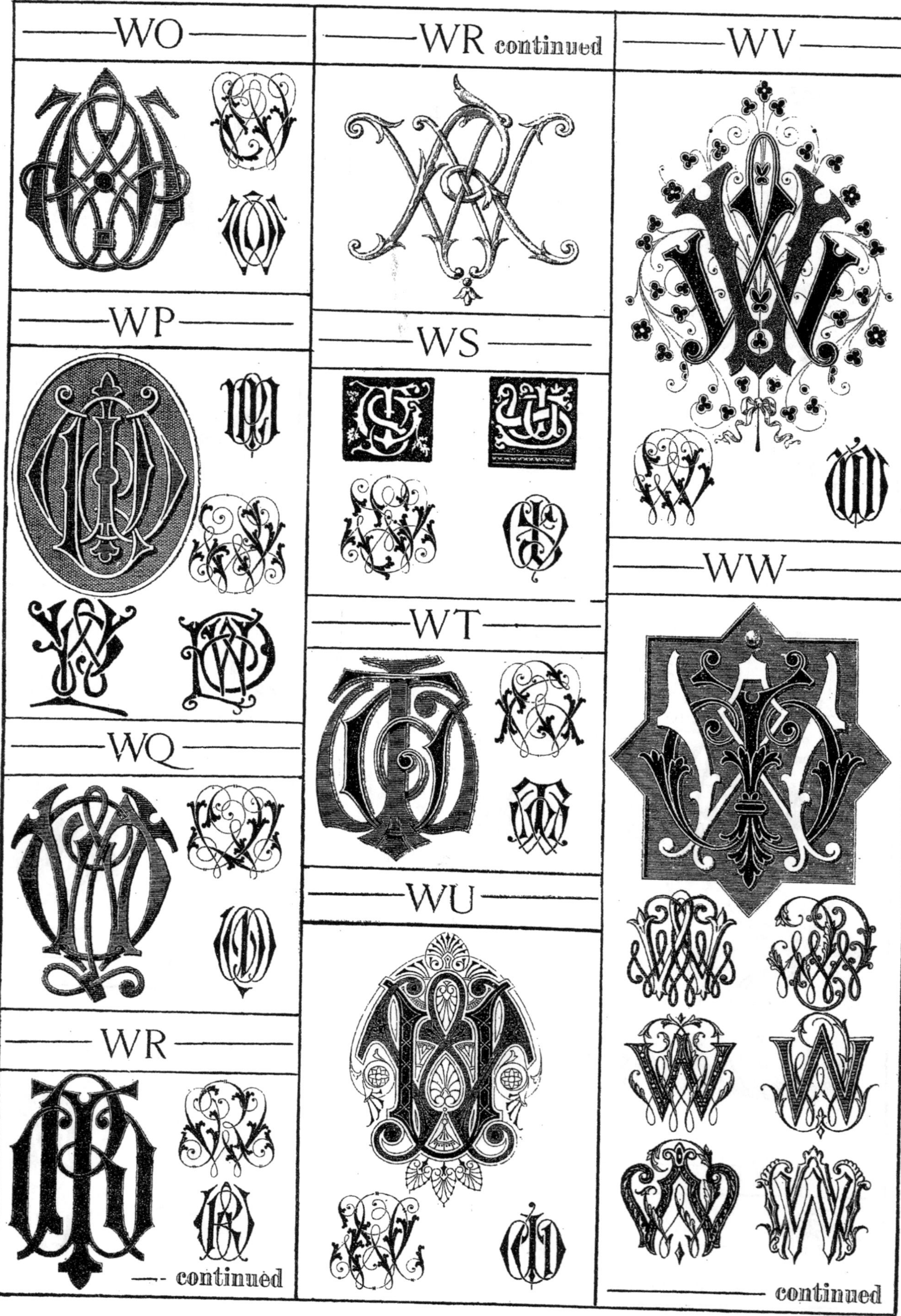
WO
WR continued
WV
WP
WS
WT
WQ
WR
WU
WW
continued
continued

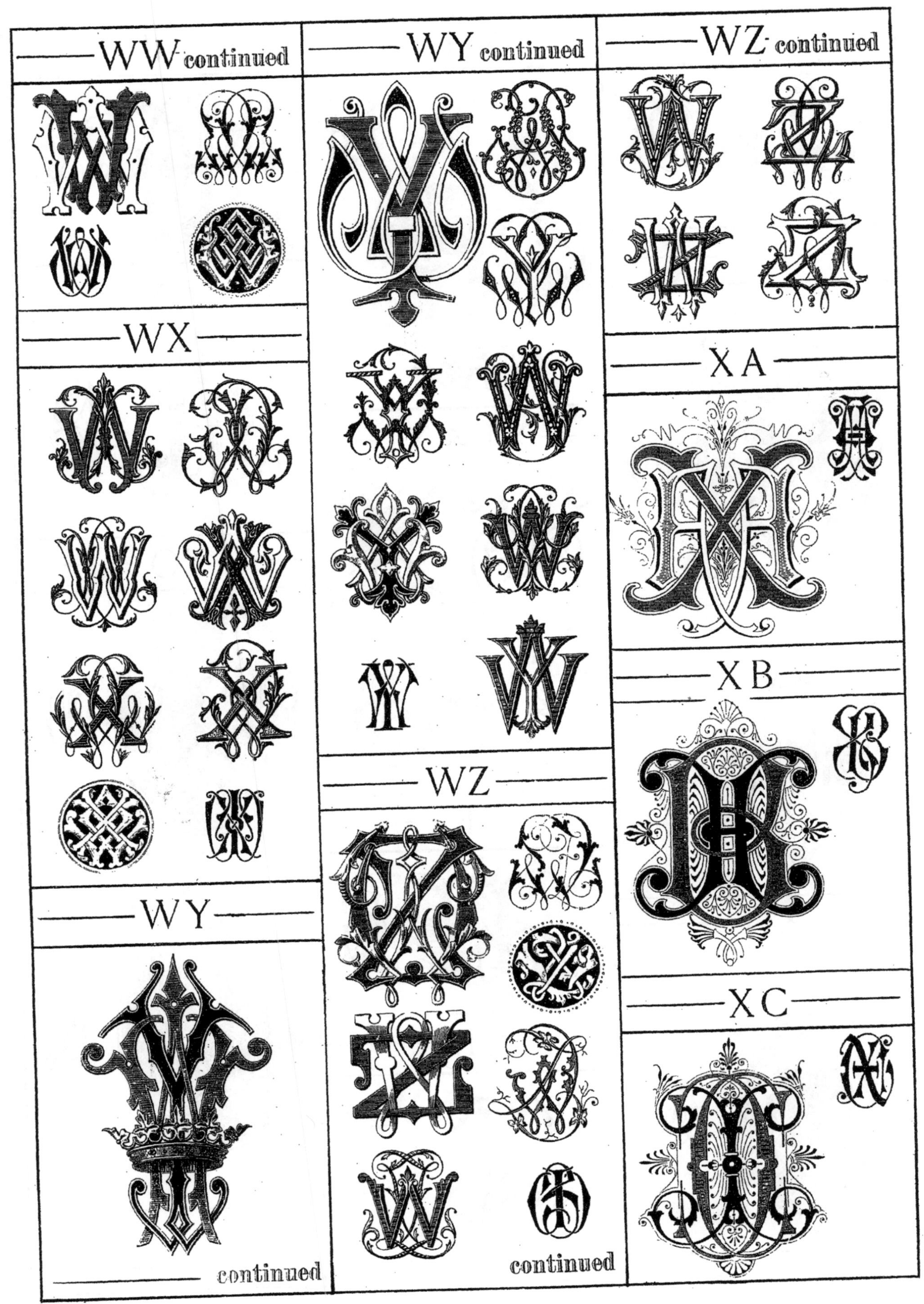
WW continued
WY continued
WZ continued
WX
WY
continued
WZ
continued
XA
XB
XC

XD
XH
XM
XE
XN
XI & XJ
XF
XO
XK
XG
XP
XL

XQ
XR
XS
XT
XU
XV
XW
continued
XW—continued
XX
XY
continued

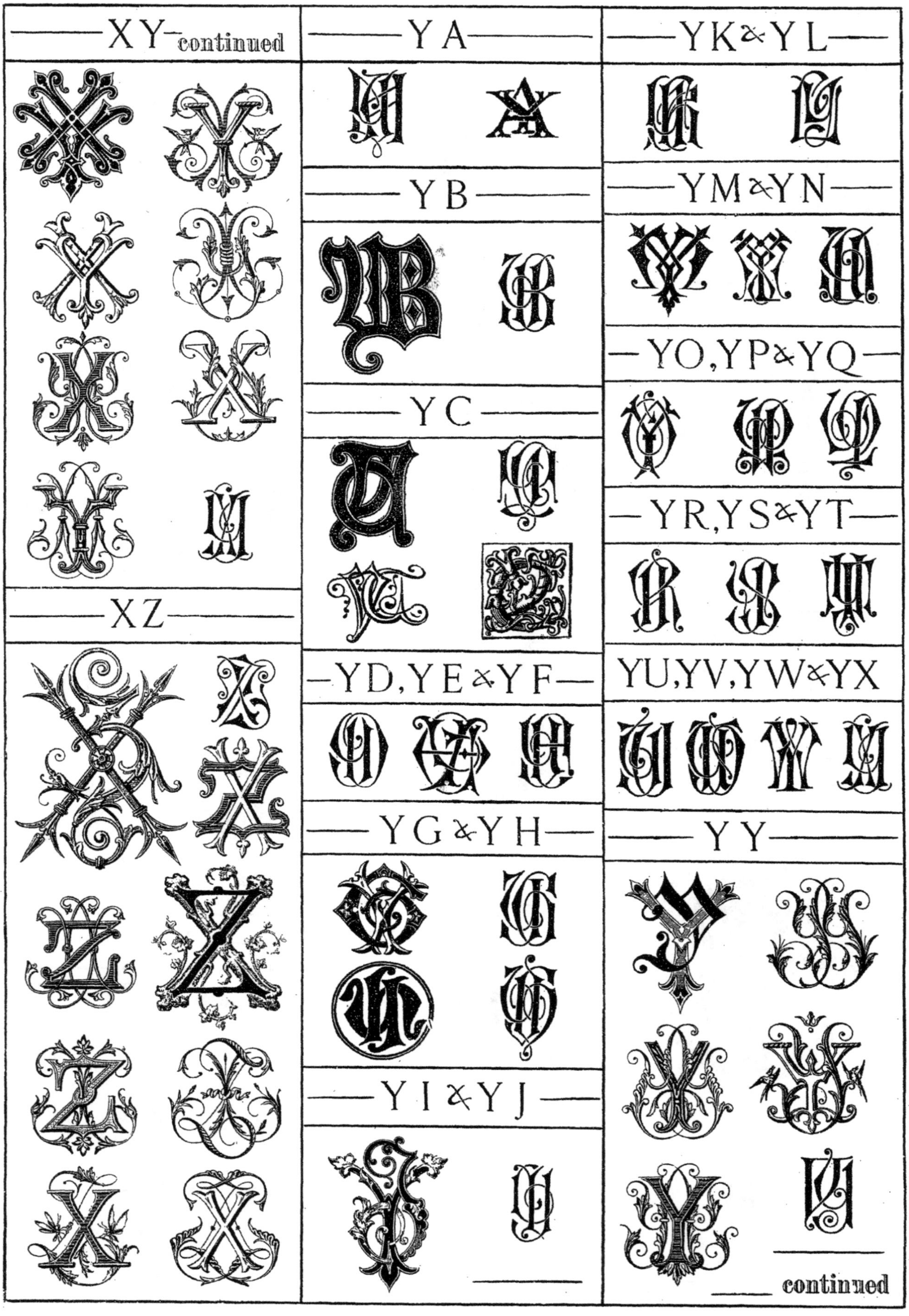

XY—continued

YA

YB

YC

YD, YE & YF

YG & YH

YI & YJ

YK & YL

YM & YN

YO, YP & YQ

YR, YS & YT

YU, YV, YW & YX

YY

continued

XZ

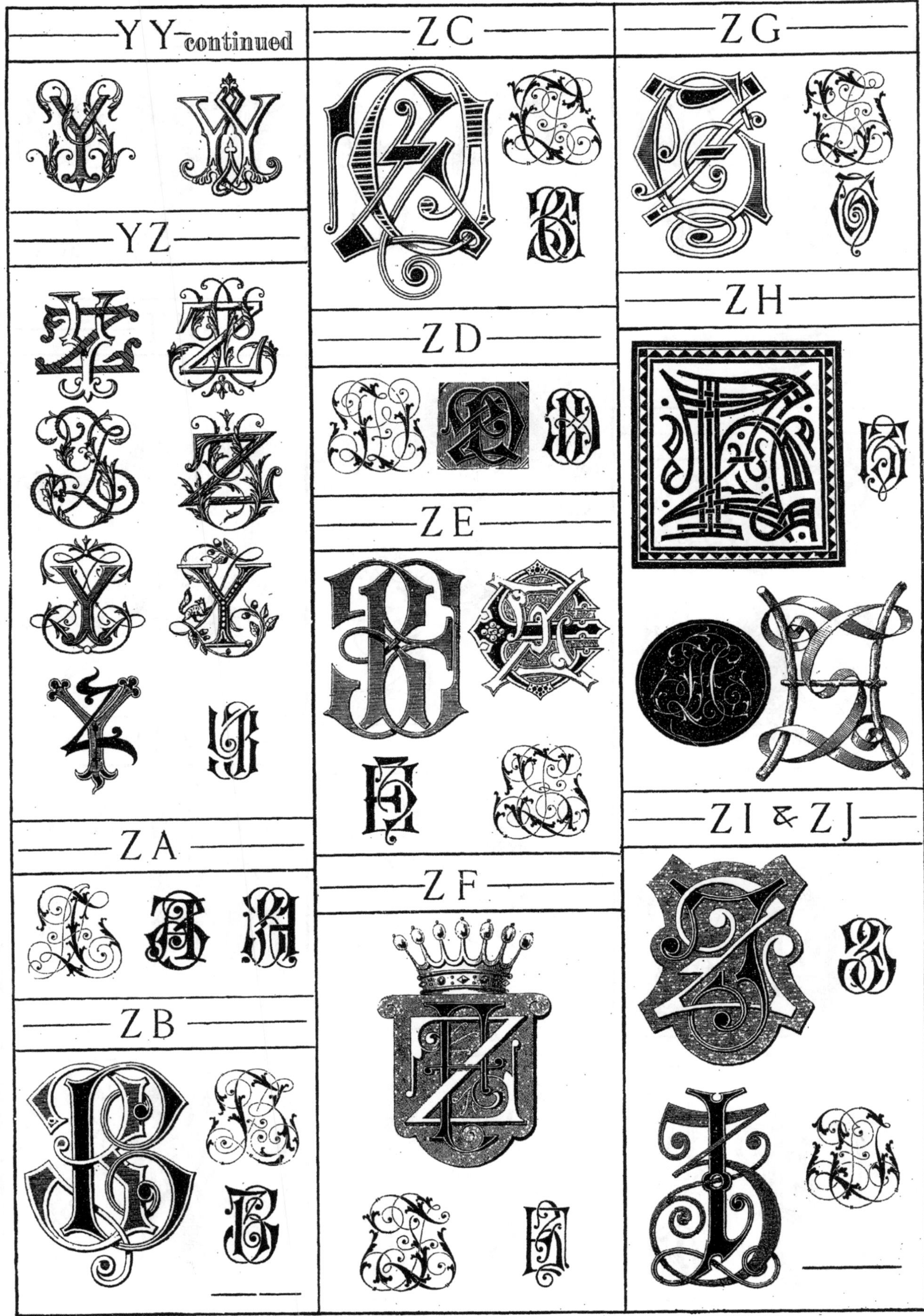
YY continued
YZ
ZA
ZB
ZC
ZD
ZE
ZF
ZG
ZH
ZI & ZJ

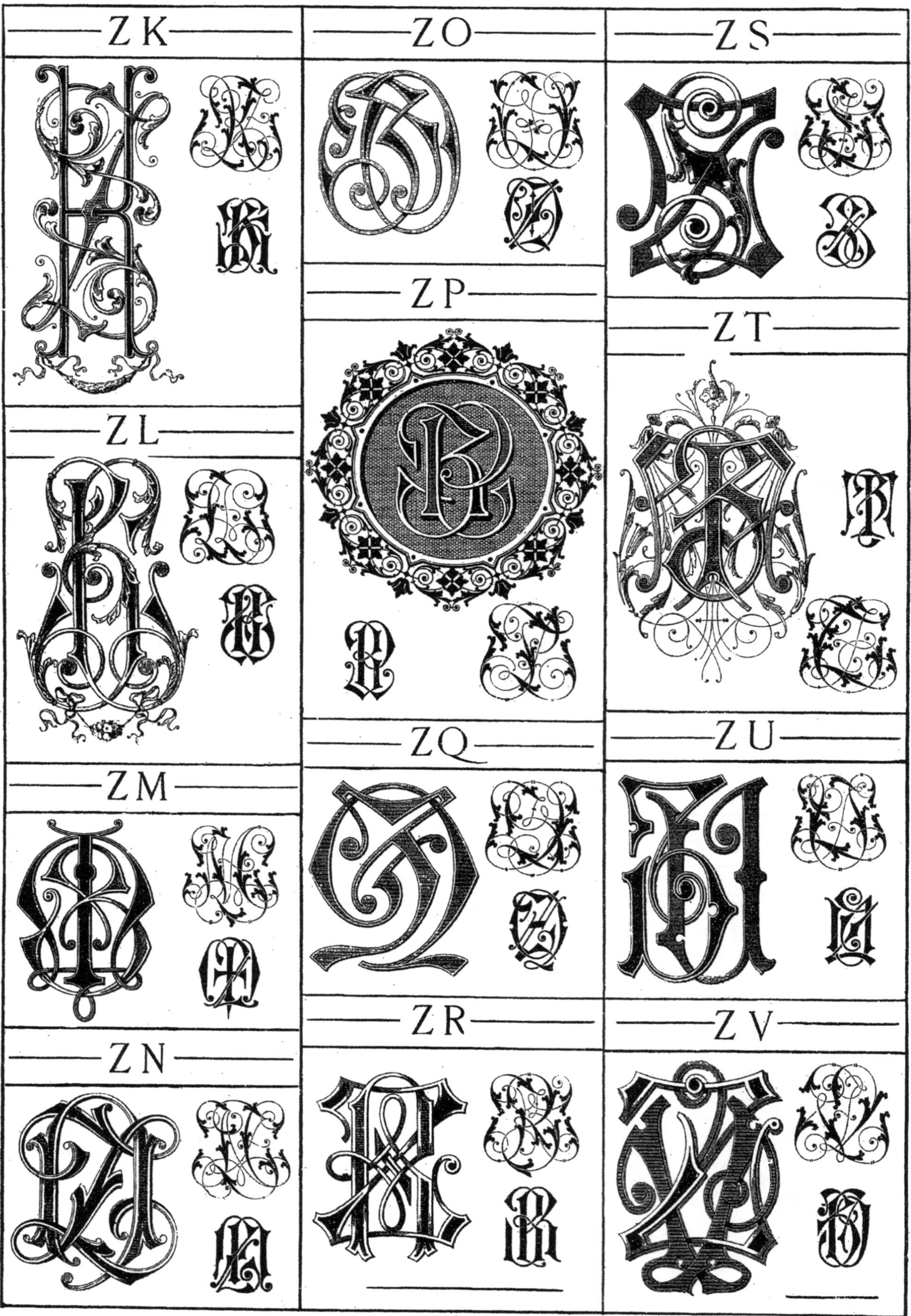
ZK
ZO
ZS
ZP
ZT
ZL
ZM
ZQ
ZU
ZN
ZR
ZV

ZW
AAB—ADC
ADS—AWM
AAB
ABC
ADSC
PER
ADVERCA
VIRTUS
AFL
AFL
ZX—ZY
ABC
AGF
AGT
AHD
ZZ
APE
ABC
ABCE
ABE
APS
ARN
ABL
ABM
ARR
ATI
ACSC
ACSC
1867
ACW
ADC
AWM

—BCD—CDA—
—CDE—CFH—
—CFH—DEC—
BCN
BCD
BCP
BCVA
BFC
BGC
BDC
BHS
BHS
BLS
BNJ
CAG
CABE
CAI
CCFC
CDA
CDE
CDE
CDEA
CDF
CEG
CFH
CFH
CFH
CFH
CFH
CFH
CFH
CFY
CGDLB
CIB
CLF
CPC
CSH
CTI
DAC
DCA
DEB
DECOA

—DEF—DOC—
—DPA—EBB—
—EBC—EDLR—
DEF
DEF
DGA
DGC
DIC
DIE
DISC
DLR
DLC
DOC
DPA
DRP
DSA
DWI
EAEB
EAEB
EAEB
EAEB
EAEB
EACB
EALH
EAP
EBA
EBA
EBB
EBC
ECK
ECM
ECMI
EDLR
— continued

—EDLR- continued
—EDLR—continued
—EEB—EGM—
EEB
EEC
EEC
EEC
EFG
EFG
EGM
EGM
EGM
EGM
EGM
EGM
— continued

—EHB—ERS—
—ESE—FFS—
—FGH—FRL—
EHB
EHB
EHB
EJB
EKB
EKB
ELPK
FMDC
EPA
EPA
EPS
EPSN
ERG
ERPF
ERB
ERL
ERS
ESE
ESL
ESL
EST
EWB
FBC
FCM
FDC
FDC
FEH
FEPK
FFC
FFS
FGH
FGH
FGH
FGH
FGH
FGH
FGH
FHG
FIC
FJC
FLM
FRL
FRL

—FVT—FWH—
—FWM–GHJ—
—GHL—HCS—
FVT
FWA
FWDLR
FWDLR
FWDLR
FWH
FWH
FWH
FWH
FWH
FWH
FWH
FWJH
FWH
FWM
FWM
GAL
GAM
GAL
GBF
GEN
GFS
GHC
GHC
GHJ
GHJ
GHL
GMJ
GQN
GPL
GPN
GRS
GTP
GTB
HAR
HAC
HAZN
HBL
HCS
HCS

—HCS—-HJK—
—HLA— IBG—
—JAK—JHC—
HCS
HFP
HFP
HFP
HHH
HEO
HHH
HJE
HJB
HJK
HJK
HLA
HLC
HON
HPB
HPB
HPB
HSS
HSG
HTS
HTS
HTS
HTS
HWH
IBG
JAK
JAK
JAP
JAP
JAP
JBC
IBG
JCE
IEFB
IDOB
JGZ
IFL
IHA
IHC

JHE JHS
JHS JKL
JLM JSR
JHES
JHM
IHS
IHS
IHS
IHS
IHS
IHSM
IHSM
IHSM
IHSM
IHSM
IHSM
IHSM
JJJ
II·N
IKL
IKL
IKL
TRIA JUNCTA
IN UNO
JLM
JMC
JMC
IMH
JMS
JPL
JPM
JR·N
JSK
JSM
JSM
JSN
JSR

—JTD— KLS—
—KMM—LTC—
—LYS—MEL—
ITDF
ITG
ITO
IVL
IWM
KEM
KEM
Junior United Service.
KLM
KLS
KPLA
KMM
LMA
LMN
LNS
LPK
LPI
LSD
LPK
LSM
CAVE
LTC
LYS
MAH
MAH
MAH
MAH
MAT
MDF
MEF
MEL
Amor a Deo Est
MEL

—MER—NCB—
—NLP—OOI—
—OPJ—PSN—
MER
MLG
MQA
MWL
M·W·F
NAS
NCB
NCB
NAS
NLP
NOH
NOP
NPL
NSM
OAS
OAZ
OCK
OFE
OOI
OPJ
OPQ
OYC
OSR
PCN
PDE
PLA
PLA
PLG
PQR
PSB
PSL
PSN

—PSP—RLD—
—RNP—SCI—
—SDW—SNI—
PSP
PYM
QWL
QWL
RAB
RCH
RCH
RFDM
REM
RHS
RLYC
RLD
RNP
RSAC
RSB
RTP
RTP
RTP
RST
RVH
RVH
SAL
SAR
SBA
SCH
SCIE
SDWC
SGN
SGO
SGO
SHS
SHS
SHI
SLP
SLP
SMI
SNA
SNA
SNI
SNO

—SOJ—TGE—
—TPC—TUV—
—TVN—WFM—
SOJ
SSC
STL
STU
SYPK
TAB
TAL
TBC
TBL
TCRI
TBS
TCWB
THS
TGEA
TPC
TRB
TRP
TRN
TRS
TSG
TSH
TSN
TSK
TUA
TUV
TVN
UNA
VMC
UVW
VTA
VWX
WAL
WAM
WAT
WFK
WFH
WFM

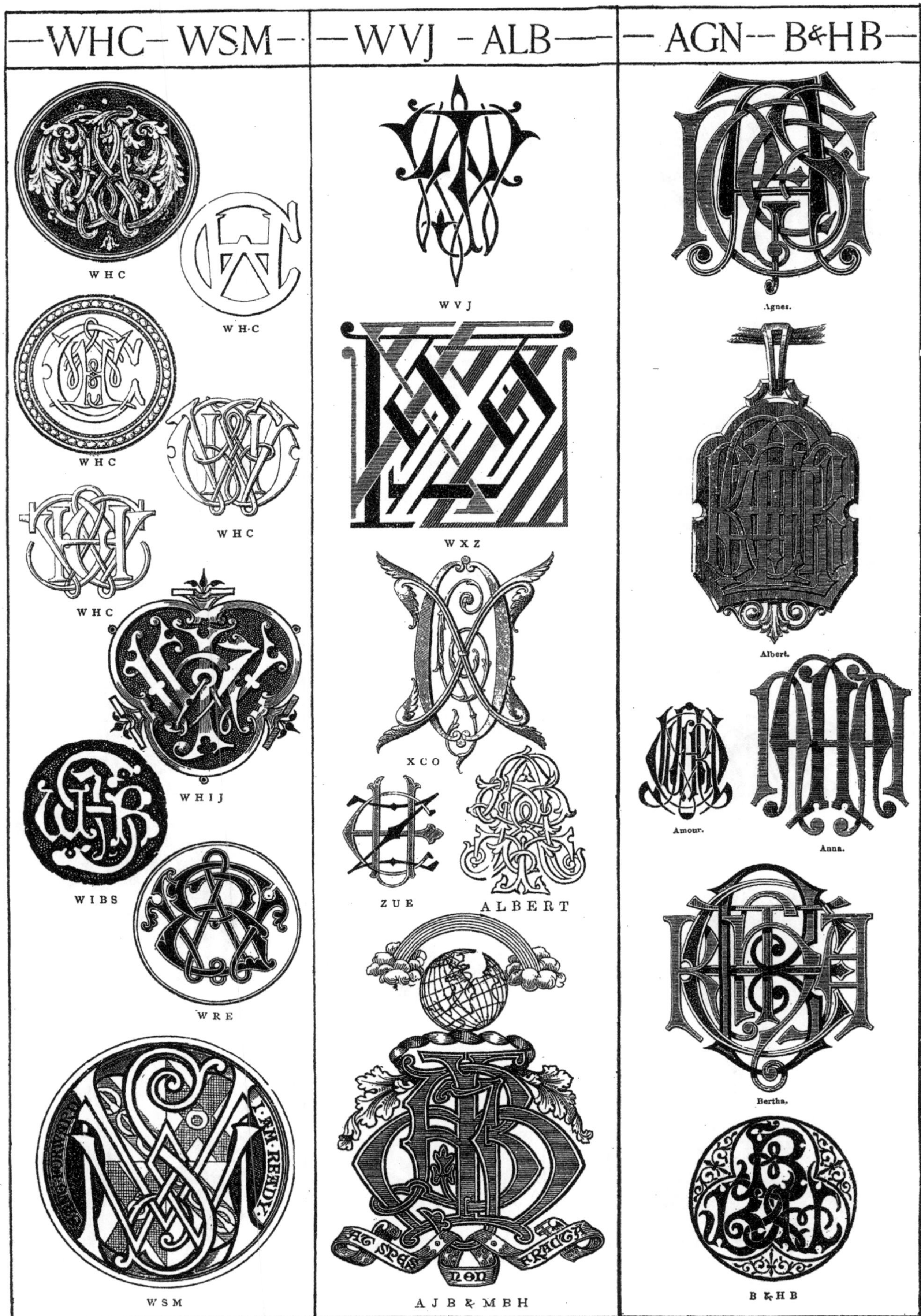
—WHC— WSM— —WVJ -ALB— —AGN— B&HB—
WHC
WH·C
WHC
WHC
WHC
WHIJ
WIBS
WRE
WSM
WVJ
WXZ
XCO
ZUE
ALBERT
AJB & MBH
Agnes.
Albert.
Amour.
Anna.
Bertha.
B & HB

—BRO—EDM—
—EDW—HEN—
—HEN—IOH—
BROOK
A. BURKE
CHARLOTTE
Clara.
Daniel.
De QUINEY.
Dorothea.
Edmond.
EDWARD
Emma.
Eugenie.
Felix.
Flora.
GARIBALDI
HENRY
HENRY
HODGES
HENRY
HODGES
HOPE
Hugo.
Ida.
IOHN

—LAU—LUT—
—LUT— MAR—
—MAR— O&G—
Laura.
Linda M.
LONDON
Lucretia G.
LUTHER
LUTHER
LUTHER
LUTHER
LUTHER
MABEL
MADGE
MARGARET
Maria.
MARIAN
Martha.
MARY
Martin.
MERCY
MILDRED
Mina.
MOLL
VISCOUNT NEWARK.
VISCOUNT NEWPORT.
NINA
Oscar.
O & G

—PAU—ROS— —RUT—THE— —THE—WOL—
Paul.
QUEEN.
Regina.
Ross.
ROSA
ROSE
ROSS.
RUTH.
St. A
St George.
Souvenir.
Thecla.
Theodore
Theresia.
U & I
Victor.
W B=S B
W A B=A B
I B=H B
A A B
Walter.
G. Wolf

ABCDEFGHIKLMNOPQRSTUVWXYZ

English Prince's Coronet
English Ducal Coronet.
Coronet of
Prince of Wales.
English Royal Crown I.
English Royal Crown II.
Earl's Coronet.
English Princess'
Coronet.
Royal Crown
of Prussia.
Coronet of an
Elector.
Coronet of the Heir-
Apparent of Germany.
New Imperial Crown of Germany.
Crown of the
German Empress.
Royal Crown
of Hungary.
Coronet of
Austrian Archduke I.
Imperial Crown of Austria.
Coronet of
Austrian Archduke II.
Austrian
Prince's Coronet.
Orleans
Prince's Coronet.
Bourbon
Royal Crown II.
Napoleonic Imperial Crown.
Bourbon
Royal Crown I.
Royal Crown of
Louis Philippe.
Cardinal's Hat.
Archbishop's Hat.
Bishop's Hat.
Abbe's Hat.
Archbishop's Mitre.
Papal Tiara.
Bishop's Mitre.

CPSIA information can be obtained
at www.ICGtesting.com
Printed in the USA
BVHW011515281218
536599BV00003B/147/P

9 780486 429793